I ALWAYS WANT
TO BE
WHERE I'M NOT

SUCCESSFUL LIVING
WITH ADD AND ADHD

WES CRENSHAW, PHD ABPP

Publisher's Cataloging-in-Publication
(Provided by Quality Books, Inc.)

Crenshaw, Wes.
    I always want to be where I'm not : successful living
with ADD and ADHD / Wes Crenshaw, PHD ABPP.
    pages cm
    LCCN 2014931317
    ISBN 978-0-9852833-0-8

    1. Attention-deficit disorder in adults.   I. Title.

RC394.A85C74 2014   616.85'89
                 QBI14-600020

Published in the United States of America by

✳FAMILY
PSYCHOLOGICAL PRESS

Also available on Kindle from Amazon.com

To the thousands of clients who've taught me more about ADD and ADHD than any textbook yet written. Since I cannot rent any of you out to teach others, this book will have to do. It better reflects your good work than mine.

The vignettes in this book are based on actual clinical cases seen over twenty-two years of practice. Identifying details have been disguised in such a way as to meet American Psychological Association Ethical Guideline 4.07 (www.apa.org) for publishing case examples. When I thought the veil might be thin enough for a client to recognize himself or herself, I asked for and received permission to publish the vignette with the understanding that it contained enough changes to protect confidentiality. The vignettes were selected to represent a broad sample of the many different kinds of cases we commonly see in clinical practice with clients having ADD and ADHD.

CONTENTS

Acknowledgements xiii

Foreword xv

Is This Book For Me? xvii

Chapter 1 On Being Where You Are 1

    Is This Chapter For Me? 4

    The Unrelenting Power of Boredom 4

    The Advantages of Wandering 5

    Principle 1: Be Where You Are Right Now 6

Chapter 2 Thinking and Acting 7

    Is This Chapter For Me? 9

    What ADD Is and What It Isn't 10

    All About Focus 11

    Who Cares? 12

    The Advantages of Spontaneity 15

    Principle 2: Think Before You Act 15

Chapter 3 A Right Path 20

    Is This Chapter For Me? 23

    All Kinds of Uncomfortable 23

    The Wisdom (Teeth) of Discomfort 25

    The Tantalizing Joys of Avoidance 25

    I'm Obliged 29

    Scratchy Noisy Stuff 30

    The Advantages of Having an Eye for Easy Paths 31

    Principle 3: Make the Right Choice, Not the Easiest One 31

Chapter 4 Decisions Big and Small 35

    Is This Chapter For Me? 37

    The Smallest Decisions 38

    Wishing and Wanting 38

    On Keeping On Keeping On 40

    Hope and Hopelessness 42

    The Advantages of Thinking Big 43

    Principle 4: The Most Important Decisions Are the Small Ones 44

Chapter 5 Follow Your Heart? 51

    Is This Chapter For Me? 54

    Two Styles of Decision Making 55

    Who Can Understand the Heart? 56

    The Advantages of Inspiration 57

    Principle 5: Never Blindly Follow Your Heart 58

Chapter 6 When You Don't Know How to Work Something 65

Is This Chapter For Me? 69

Bargaining in Good Faith With Your Destiny 70

Life's Instructions 70

The Advantages of Raw Exploration 73

Principle 6: If You Don't Know How to Work Something, Learn 74

Chapter 7 Going Down The Drain 77

Is This Chapter For Me? 80

If It's Not One Thing, It's Another 80

What Not to Do 81

The Advantages of Audacity 84

Principle 7: When Things Go Down the Drain, Don't Make Them Worse 84

Chapter 8 Responsibility 87

Is This Chapter For Me? 91

Free Will 101 92

Who's Really in Charge? 92

Responsibility: Take Care of Yourself So We Don't Have To 94

Responsibility: Face Up to Your Screw Ups 95

Psychological Integrity 96

Avoiding Avoidance...Again 99

The Advantages of Externalizing Blame 101

Principle 8: Take Personal Responsibility 101

Chapter 9 Radical Honesty 107

Is This Chapter For Me? 111

Attaining Character 112

Psychological Integrity 114

The Tricky Nature of Shame 114

The Advantages of Poor Character 117

Principle 9: Practice Radical Honesty 117

Chapter 10 The Joy of Organization 124

Is This Chapter For Me? 129

Lost in The Clutter 130

Time Management 132

What's In Your Head? 133

The Advantages of Disorganization 133

Principle 10: The Secret of Happiness is in How You Organize Your Life.... 134

Chapter 11 Love And Other Relationships 145

Is This Chapter For Me? 149

Where Do We Stand? 150

The Problem With Monogamy 150

Complimentary or Symmetrical?: ADD, Anxiety, and Love 154

Advantages and Disadvantages of Each Dyad 155

Principle 11: Love Intentionally 156

CONTENTS

Chapter 12 Testing and Diagnosis 169

    Is This Chapter For Me?..171

    The Big Conspiracy...172

    Principle 12: With ADD You Go From Where You Start...................174

Chapter 13 Medication Management 182

    Is This Chapter For Me?..187

    You're The Expert 187

    Finding The Right Prescriber...189

    Principle 13. Know What to Talk About When The Prescriber Arrives..........192

Epilogue Where Are They Now? 210

The Thirteen Principles...220

About The Author 221

ACKNOWLEDGEMENTS

I'd like to thank my friends from the Kansas City Writers Group who came together to form the ironically named ADD Focus Group: Dane Zeller (www.danezeller.com), Teresa Vratil (www.CrazieTown.com), Trudie Homan, Carol Babcok, Valorie Wells (www.hypnowells.com), and Gail Lerner-Connaghan. Their willingness to workshop this book, with only the promise of food and fellowship to sustain their effort, made a tremendous difference in how it turned out. A huge thank you to my line editor, Katie Guyot, who is entirely too obsessed with hyphens, Oxford commas, the banishment of semicolons, and subject-predicate construction, concepts that hold no meaning for me. Special thanks to Susan Pinsky (organizationallyours.com), who not only wrote a great Foreword, but spent many hours giving me good advice on how to make the book better. I am convinced her organizational skills exist at some profound sub-atomic level. I also appreciate my children Alex and Alyssa, who lent their wisdom on ADD to many pages of this book, and my wife of twenty-nine years…for everything.

FOREWORD

In this book, Dr. Wes Crenshaw, Board Certified Couples and Family Psychologist, uses his many years of experience treating the ADD and ADHD population to offer thirteen clear and wise principles for coping with this often frustrating condition. In entertaining and informative vignettes Dr. Crenshaw mines his clients' struggles and triumphs to illustrate the kinds of behaviors and challenges that hinder those with ADD and to show how, with the help of a mentor, medication, and the application of his thirteen principles, they can transform their lives.

Although this book is meant as a therapeutic self-help tool for an ADD client and his or her therapist or mentor, as it turns out, Dr. Crenshaw's thirteen principles—often punctuated with fun pop culture references—are good advice for all of us whether or not we have ADD. Just as Harry Potter's Professor Dumbledore exhorts the students of Hogwarts to "make the choice between what is right and what is easy[1]," Dr. Crenshaw teaches his clients that the hard road is often, ultimately, the more rewarding path. He counsels patience and perseverance while acknowledging that for those with ADD—who must expend so much more effort and discipline than the average person in order to complete a task—the rewards will be gruelingly hard won. Fortunately, Dr. Crenshaw's formulas and advice provide readers with a handy road map to keep them on track and on task while they calculate the wisest course. If the only guidance the reader takes away from this book is a profound understanding of Crenshaw's Formula *Hard Path* → *Easy Life, Easy Path* → *Hard Life*, his or her money will have been well spent.

As we are invited into the intimate and heartbreaking challenges of Dr. Crenshaw's therapy sessions, we see graphic examples of the severe debilita-

---

[1] Page 724, *Goblet of Fire*, American Edition, paperback.

tion many ADD clients suffer. They find it difficult to complete their educations, keep jobs, maintain relationships, or even manage their households. As we watch them founder, as we see so many of them lose heart and start to go under, Dr. Crenshaw is there with uncompromising support and wisdom, throwing out the lifesaver that can help tow them back to shore. Make no mistake; this often takes the form of very tough love, like a boot camp for people with ADD, and readers who've never experienced a directive therapy, may be taken aback. But when a client's entire life has been compromised by ADD and his or her future happiness is threatened because of it, Dr. Crenshaw's blunt take-no-prisoners guidance and thirteen principles could be the deciding factor between failure and success.

This same pragmatism is also to be found in his pithy and well-reasoned response to "deniers" who eschew medication. To those and others who perceive this as a disease of character rather than chemistry Dr. Crenshaw replies "ADD doesn't care whether you believe in it or not. It's no more faith-based than are diabetes or kidney stones." He solves the mystery of the uptick in both diagnosis and treatment of ADD as a result of the complicated lives we lead in a modern world that is so unforgiving of disorganization.

As a psychologist, Dr. Crenshaw focuses mostly on the mental and emotional aspects of ADD which he then very helpfully breaks down and restructures into the kind of practical advice that can help to save jobs and relationships. As a Professional Organizer specializing in an ADD clientele I was particularly impressed with Dr. Crenshaw's sound advice on organizational systems. Not only does he stress minimalism—a therapeutic necessity that I have been preaching to my clients and in my books for years—but he lays out some concrete steps on how to achieve it.

But mostly this book is a chart for the therapeutic journey that ADD sufferers must embark on if they are going to achieve the success in relationships, schooling, and jobs that we all desire. The thirteen principles and their practical solutions provide a game plan for tackling the challenges of this condition. Obviously a book this size cannot provide detailed advice on every challenge, but it can serve as a broad template which the client and mentor can then customize to meet individual needs. As such, it offers a clear and experienced guide for those who suffer from ADD on how to live with it and ultimately how to triumph over it.

-Susan C. Pinsky, author of *Organizing Solutions for People with ADHD*

IS THIS BOOK FOR ME?

Destiny is no matter of chance. It is a matter of choice. It is not a thing to be waited for, it is a thing to be achieved.

— William Jennings Bryan

I often tell new clients diagnosed with Attention Deficit Hyperactivity Disorder[2] that they cannot afford the time, attention, or money for me to beat around the proverbial bush. We just have too much work to do on the road to a better tomorrow. Few wonder what I'm talking about. Most are in pretty dire straits by the time they reach my comfy couch[3]. Some have put off getting help. Others have tried treatment before, but haven't gotten out of it quite what they were hoping for.

And then there are those who don't yet have a diagnosis. Many of those folks are coming to be evaluated for ADD. Others know something is wrong, but don't know what it is. They just don't feel very good at some facet of life— usually school, work, family, or love. Quite a few come at the direction of frustrated family members, spouses, or dating partners, perhaps even close to losing one of those relationships. Some of these clients I'll only see a few times, but for most, this first session will begin an important and lasting

---

[2] This is the official and rather baffling diagnostic label which yields the acronym ADHD from the Diagnostic and Statistical Manual (DSM), of which there is an inattentive type, a hyperactive type, and a combined type. However, for the rest of this book we're going to refer to this condition generically as ADD, because the vast majority of people who have it are not hyperactive. Moreover, most laypeople simply refer to this condition as ADD, and laypeople are the audience for this book.

[3] Don't worry, it's not a cliché shrink couch. Just an overstuffed living room couch.

relationship unlike any other. That's what therapy is all about—making a personal connection for change.

I don't want to waste your time, attention, or money either. I'm a no-nonsense guy when it comes to getting people the help they need and deserve. So, let me give you a little preview of what you're getting yourself into here. This book goes beyond the basics of ADD and into the nature of how it affects who you are, how you live your life, and how you get along with others.

Over twenty-two years working with thousands of teens and adults, I've come up with thirteen principles to help you think through who, how, and where you want to be, and chart a course to get there. While the research on ADD is vast and important, it's no substitute for getting to know people deeply and honestly and learning how they make it in life—and just as importantly, how they don't. So, I've included thirteen diverse vignettes in this book, all based on real cases. The stories range from simple and straightforward, to complicated and severe. Some are kind of fun, others heartbreaking.

It would be great if you identified with every person you read about and found every one of my thirteen principles incredibly helpful in all aspects of your life. But that's not likely, because I've included more information, examples, and advice than could possibly relate to any one person. To make this book relatable to the largest number of readers, I had to describe "people with ADD" as if you're all alike and have every single problem, impairment, and advantage outlined herein—even though I know that's silly.

Every ADD person has at least one "special power"—something you do really well that's hard for most people with the very same diagnosis. It could be reading, sports, relationships, math, or taking things apart and putting them back together correctly. So, there's no need to

Your job is to find what fits for you and leave the rest for someone else.

email me saying, "I have ADD and I'm not at all like you said I was on line 41 of page 39" or, "What's the deal with Principle 9? I don't have problems telling the truth!" If you're great at being responsible, you might not need what's in Chapter 8. If you've created your own system for organizing your life or you're already a technology whiz, Chapter 10 will seem elementary. In reading this book, your job is to find what fits for you and leave the rest for someone else.

To help you do that, I've included a section called "Is This Chapter for Me?" right after each vignette. Use the checklist in that section to decide whether or not the chapter addresses a problem you face. But before you skip a principle or discard an idea, *consult your people*[4]. It's their job to see things about you that you might be missing.

You'll notice that most of the vignettes feature clients aged fifteen to thirty. That's who I most often see in my private clinic in a university town, so that's my target age group for this book. However, early readers felt the principles applied equally to folks over thirty and to parents raising younger kids with ADD who want to get an early start on the critical transition from adolescence to adulthood. Readers who are getting a bit beyond their thirties, as I am, should be able to find plenty of examples from their own past or present lives to fully explore each principle.

When I wrote this book, I had three audiences in mind. Each will get something a little different from reading it:

People With ADD. Maybe you've been diagnosed or suspect you should be, and you really want to start solving your many riddles and living a more successful and productive life.

This book is for you. In fact, I'll usually be speaking directly to you, just as I would a client in my office. While a book is no substitute for therapy, this one is a pretty good primer on what a directive therapy[5] is like.

I should warn you right up front that most of my advice will be a lot easier to follow if you're taking a stimulant medication[6]. I'll explain why in Chapter 13. I know other books teach something like "Seven Steps to Curing ADD Without Meds" or "Balance Your Brain with Mental Exercise." You're free to read one of those instead, but a lot of books sell because they make change look really fun and simple, when we all know it's not.

This book is about doing what's hard so life turns out better and easier in the long run.

You may find that some of my advice fits you pretty well, but is hard to accept. Hang in there. A lot of good advice in life will get you riled up and a lot of bad advice will make you feel pretty great—until you realize it's bad advice. If you start to feel uncomfortable, remember that my goal isn't to judge you or make you feel bad about yourself. If it were, I'd have no clients at all and nobody

---

[4] In this book, "your people" are your family, friends, dating partner, classmates, coworkers, roommates, etc. Anyone who influences you, or who is influenced by you.

[5] Directive therapy involves any method of treatment in which the therapist gives specific advice or direction to the client, versus a "non-directive" therapy which is based more on listening empathically and is purported to be neutral and value free. If you're super interested in that topic, read my 2004 book *Treating Families and Children in The Child Protective System*.

[6] I do not knowingly own stock in, nor am I sponsored by, any pharmaceutical company. I do own a Prozac mug I got from a drug rep back in the early 1990s.

would refer their friends and neighbors to me. No one would listen to my radio or TV appearances or ask me to speak at their clubs or organizations. My goal is to give you new ways to think and act, based on what I've learned from the real experts: people with ADD who've found ways to succeed.

If you've played a team sport or watched one on TV, you know what it's like to have a tough coach. Think of me that way, just as my clients do. I will challenge you at times, but I'm on your side and I want you to win.

We do a lot of winning in my office.

People Who Love People With ADD. Perhaps your partner, child, roommate, or friend has ADD and you find yourself exasperated with that relationship. You wonder what's going on in his or her head, and you really want to understand the secret code so you can better love him or her. I know how you feel. I've raised ADD children myself and I understand how hard it can seem to get them on a right path and keep them there.

This book is also for you. Use it like an operator's manual for your ADD person, or a diary of how he or she experiences the world. Or read it as if you *were* your ADD person to build empathy and understanding for what it's like to be him or her. Use it to help your ADD person put all my advice to work, without becoming ensnared in chaos yourself.

ADD-Leaners. Maybe you've never been diagnosed, but you find yourself a little scattered or organizationally challenged. Perhaps you've never achieved as much as you thought you could, because you don't finish what you start. You might be creative, insightful, or highly sought-after in your field, but when it comes to details and follow-through, you struggle to convert ideas into results. Maybe your family or dating partners see you as fun and energetic, but uncommitted and difficult to pin down. Maybe you're restless, always trying to find yourself, but never quite sure how or why you got lost. You might be what I call an "ADD-leaner."

This book is for you, too. Leaners have some ADD symptoms, but not enough to drive you to treatment or medication. You might even wonder if you should go looking for a diagnosis. Maybe. Maybe not. That depends on how far you lean, how often you tip over, and how serious the consequences. This book can help you discover what it's really like to have full blown ADD and let you gauge your level of impairment to get a better idea of whether you need an evaluation or just a little life adjustment using my thirteen principles. Just remember, this book is primarily written for people with the real deal, so if you're just a leaner, you'll want to tone down the advice a little bit.

Now that you have a pretty good idea of where we're headed, you can decide if you want to take the journey with me in this book, as many others have in my office.

I hope you'll join our team and achieve your own unique destiny.

CHAPTER 1
ON BEING WHERE YOU ARE

No matter where you go—there you are.

— Confucius

"I've decided I don't want to be a social worker any more." Morgan sighed as she worked her way deeper into the overstuffed couch in my office. "I thought I did, but then I got into Dr. Wilson's class and there's so much reading and you know how I hate to read. Social work should be about helping people, but it's all just policy and crap."

I furrowed my brow. "This is your third change of majors."

"I know. But I'm only a junior. A lot of people take five years to finish. Don't they? Someone posted that on Twitter."

"Some people do," I said. "Especially if they spend too much time tweeting. In your case, I think we're looking at more like six, maybe seven, and that's only if you don't change up again."

"My parents are getting so sick of this conversation. We've had it twice already, unless you count freshman year. Would you count freshman year? Being a Animal Chiropractor was more like a dream or something because I didn't know you'd have to go to like, graduate school. So that wasn't a real major, was it? I'm not going to count it."

"I'm not sure the number really matters. It's the whole 'finishing something' that counts in the end. Your folks won't keep paying the bill if you aren't progressing toward graduation."

"They have to or I'll move home. Remember what happened after that whole incident in the residence hall? God, I should never have been arrested for stealing Sadie's care package. She was such a bitch and it was only worth, like $25. How is that even grounds for getting kicked out of the dorm? And then she called the cops! It was a prank. Geez. Anyway, after I moved home it was always 'clean your room' and 'help out with chores' and 'get up in the morning,' like I was fourteen again. Oh my God. I forgot to tell you what happened with my roommate's boyfriend. He totally—"

"Hold on." Impolite as it seemed, interrupting was a normal part of any session with Morgan. "Let's finish this conversation first. Which major caught your fancy this week?"

"Library Science." She giggled. "The library is so quiet and they have great WiFi. It's the perfect career for me."

"Except for not liking to read."

"I know, but I was really good at retail when I worked at Forever 21, and the library is pretty much the same thing, except for—"

"You only worked at Forever 21 for six months and then quit without giving notice."

"Well, I just got so bored. I thought I'd like it because I love shopping there, but it was like the same thing day after day."

"Right." I drummed my fingers on the dark oak end table. "Jobs aren't recreation, Morgan. They're not supposed to be super-interesting. You have to build up some tolerance to boredom. Same with your major."

"Anyhoo, I started two novels last week. I was trying to decide which to finish, but then I started browsing Amazon and I saw this really interesting one, so I'm going to try it out tonight. I *want* to like reading, Dr. Wes, but some authors just don't know how to grab your attention." A smile returned to her face. "Eventually, I'll be able to tell anyone who comes to the library how every single book starts."

I chuckled. "Or you could be a college advisor. You also know how English, Communications Studies, Social Work, and Animal Chiropractic start too. How any of them end? Not so much."

"Whatever!" Morgan glared comically at me over the glasses she'd recently retrieved from under the cushions of my couch after searching everywhere for them.

"Hmm. Kinda the same thing with the boy situation, isn't it?" I closed my eyes. "I see a pattern! Three books, three majors, three boyfriends."

"Wrong! That frat guy doesn't count. I mean we only hooked up for like, a week. Would you count him? I wouldn't."

I opened my eyes. "By that measure, I'm not sure any of them count." I eased my body forward and rested my elbows on my knees. "So, let's say you go into Library Science. What do you want me to do if, after a semester or two, we end up here again? What should I say to you?"

Morgan leaned forward to meet me, her face suddenly serious. "You have to stop me, Dr. Wes. You have to tell me 'no' and make me listen. Or give me electroshock therapy or something. I can't be a forever twenty-one student. Mom and Dad will give up on me. Or kill me." She mussed her brown hair with her fingertips as if frantically trying to stir up some lost inner wisdom. "If I just take my Adderall this semester like you're always telling me to—I know I can finish something. You have to believe in me. *Please*."

"I do." I nodded slowly. "But it's going to take more than that. You have to follow—"

"The thirteen principles. I know." She smirked and dug out her iPhone from her enormous Coach purse. "I have them all right here on my to-do list. Whenever I master one I put a little check by it[7]."

"That's great. But if you want anything in your life to really change, you can't just check them off and think you're finished. You have to keep them up here, too." I tapped the side of my head. "Every single day, sunup to sundown, in every aspect of your life."

"Can do!" She swiped the screen on her phone, tossed it on the couch, and then lifted her mighty purse to her chest, displaying it like a QVC sale item. "Look, I got this cool thing to clip my keys to the strap so I won't ever lose them again. So, at least for today, I've totally nailed Principle 10, or-gan-i-zation!" She tossed the purse next to the phone, then reached across the coffee table to give me an eager high-five. "Woo hoo!"

"You bring it, Morgan," I kidded back as our palms met. "But before you can check off a degree in Library Science, you'll have to learn to be where you are and deal with here and now."

"Good luck with that, Dr. Wes." She flopped back onto the couch and gave me a dismissive wave. "That's one place I *never* want to be."

---

[7] You can find that list at the end of this book and scan it straight into your phone.

Is This Chapter For Me?

Most likely. In fact, if you've been diagnosed with ADD or ADHD you probably don't need me to explain the title of this book or this chapter. You were born with a great fondness for Somewhere Else—that glorious place, person, thing, or idea that's anywhere but here. Ask yourself and your people if any of these apply:

❏ Do you tend to be restless, always pursuing something or someone different, certain that if you just wander a bit more, you'll eventually find exactly what you're looking for there?

❏ When you get to Somewhere Else, do you find the different someone or something is apparently somewhere else instead. So you go looking there?

❏ Once the new stuff, ideas, places, and people in Somewhere Else get old, does there emerge at the forefront of your mind the most dreadful of all words: Boring?

❏ Does "boring" seem to happen more often to you and more quickly than it does for everyone else?

If these proverbial shoes fit, this chapter is for you.

The Unrelenting Power of Boredom

Don't get me wrong. Everyone's curious about Somewhere Else. We write about it, dream about it, project ourselves into it. Whether it's Paris, a different English class, Forever 21, a new love, or Narnia, we all envision Somewhere Else as more interesting than where we are now.

And there's nothing wrong with a little restlessness. What would life be like if we just stayed here? Variety is not just the spice of life. It's a great teacher. That's why we send kids away to college or let them study abroad. It's why we take vacations and have 750 cable channels. It's why everyone should date different people before marrying.

Having ADD means having a unique relationship to Somewhere Else.

However, having ADD means having a unique relationship to Somewhere Else. At its psychological core, ADD creates a yearning for novelty that's not very practical in daily life. While everyone likes new things and experiences, people with ADD become upset when they can't frequently experience them. So no matter where you are or what you're doing, you'll usually want to be Somewhere Else doing something else.

We all understand how Morgan became disinterested in her majors, jobs, and boyfriends, because we've all been bored. Does that mean everyone has ADD?

Some folks say so, which is actually pretty demeaning if you think about it, like maybe you're just making excuses for something we all share and we just handle it better than you do. Nor does that really make sense. ADD is a disorder. If everyone had it, then nobody would. So, boredom itself is not how we tell the ADD people from everyone else.

It's your intolerance of boredom.

People with ADD have an excruciatingly difficult time dealing with stuff that's not interesting, which is troublesome because most stuff isn't. As but one example, nobody really likes editing. I wish I'd have just hammered out this book once and sent it off to press. But good writing is really good editing, again and again, for hours, trying to be sure we're saying what we want to say the way we want to say it.

Most people with ADD hate that.

Likewise, once you've mastered a math problem, you don't want to do fifty more just like it. If you've done one experiment in science, you don't want to do ten replications, even though that's the basis of the scientific method. Homework or work product is kind of like spit. Once it's out there you don't want it back again. Same with books, TV, and movies. After you've been down a certain path, you don't like going down it again.

The rest of us put up with boring stuff because we have to and because we can. For people with ADD, boredom seems like the death of a thousand cuts, so you keep on looking for something better, Somewhere Else.

The Advantages of Wandering

In each chapter, I'll offer one of my thirteen principles for successful living with ADD and a list of strategies for putting it into action. Before doing so, however, I'll point out some advantages people with ADD have over the rest of us. I'm not trying to be Dr. Feel Good by minimizing the difficulties you face. But there really are some positive aspects of ADD, especially for those who put them to good use.

Having a wandering spirit can have benefits. Because you crave novelty, people with ADD often adapt to change better than the rest of us, but only if you feel you have some control over it. Since you may have little anxiety in approaching new situations (more on that in Chapter 2), you often do so with greater creativity, hope, and adventure. You may be especially good at jobs that require frequent relocation or lots of travel, as long as you develop methods of organizing yourself to get where you need to be when you need to be there. You'll also like jobs that preclude routine and structure, like working in a hospital emergency room or doing exploratory science.

Principle 1: Be Where You Are Right Now

You are where you are right now and you have to make the most of it. That's the paradox of Somewhere Else. The more you daydream about it or wander around, bumping into things, trying to find it, the less time and energy you have to make something out of Here and Now. And if you can't deal effectively with Here and Now, you'll never be ready for Somewhere Else when the time comes to find and explore it. It is in the nature of life that things come in order, one building on the other.

Besides, Somewhere Else is not always better and it can often be worse than where you are right now. Be where you are and accept what it has to offer before you move on. Here's how to avoid leaping before you look and landing were you really don't want to be.

- **Don't** skip or drop out of formal education (high school, college, trade school, etc.) because it's full of too much silly crap. It probably is, but that's just one of those things we have to tolerate on the road to a better tomorrow. Yes, some people have pulled off good careers without a good education, but they are rare.

- **Don't** try and fix a boring relationship by dating or marrying a different person, because the new partner will become just as boring as the old one. Date different people to find out who you do and don't belong with, but remember that the point of a serious relationship is stability. Loving someone is something you do, not something you feel (more on that in Chapter 11).

- **Don't** hop from job to job, believing you're getting ahead, like a grasshopper seeking a patch of greener grass. These days, changing jobs is often necessary for advancement, but if you jump without a plan, you'll go *whoosh* right down the job slide instead of climbing the career ladder. Do your best at the job you're in and keep an eye out for better opportunities.

The goal of living Here and Now is not to prevent you from striving for Somewhere Else. It's to make every change an improvement, every step a step forward, and every new day better, rather than just different. That way, when you end up Somewhere Else, it will be the right place for you to be and you'll be more likely to tolerate its inevitable same-ness.

On that happy note, let's learn the most important tool for living a better life with ADD: Intentionality.

CHAPTER 2

THINKING AND ACTING

Before you act, listen. Before you react, think. Before you spend, earn. Before you criticize, wait. Before you pray, forgive. Before you quit, try.

— Ernest Hemingway

"Even before this incident with that girl in the janitor's closet, we were getting really concerned about Jason." Mrs. Turner glanced sideways at her son. "The teachers say he's smart—maybe even gifted—but he's immature and not working up to his potential. One even said he's lazy."

"Does that sound like you, Jason?" I asked.

"I dunno. Pretty much, I guess."

Mrs. Turner shook her head. "If he'd just apply himself he wouldn't be getting Cs and Ds. I think the work's too easy for him. Maybe he'd be more motivated in harder classes."

I chuckled and nodded toward Jason. "What do you think of that plan?"

"Sucks, man. Last thing I need is more homework."

Mrs. Turner let out a motherly sigh. "School doesn't matter to him. He only gets his work done if his dad and I make him. We have to sit right next to him to keep him going and it takes an hour to do something that should take fifteen minutes. Then he takes it to school and doesn't even turn it in. The other day, I went and cleaned out his locker and found six assignments his teachers had marked missing. He'd finished half of them."

"I guess they really were missing, huh?" I said. "So, how does your homework disappear into the black hole of your locker?"

"I dunno. I forget to turn them in, I guess."

"Why would he do the work and not turn it in?" Mrs. Turner said. "It doesn't make any sense."

I looked over the referral paperwork before turning back to Jason. "So how'd you end up in the janitor's closet with Taylor?"

The boy fidgeted in this chair. "I dunno. Just getting it on I guess."

"Is she cute?" I asked.

Jason tried, but he couldn't suppress a grin at the one question he wasn't expecting me to ask. "She's got really nice boobs." He raised both hands and made the universal sign of breast fondling.

"Jason!" Mrs. Turner's cheeks flushed. "That's no way to—he'll think—"

"He asked, Mom!" His grin opened into a full, broad smile, obviously pleased he'd made her squirm. "You said I had to be honest in here and Taylor's got the most amazing boobs in school."

"They must have been," I said. "Because they got you expelled for the semester."

His delight faded only a bit. "Who knew you could get kicked out for that? We were trying to keep it private. It wasn't like we were doing it in the hall."

"So, let me ask you something." I paused for emphasis. "What exactly were you thinking when you decided to take over the closet with Taylor? I mean, other than about her boobs?"

"I dunno. Not much, I guess. It seemed like a good idea at the time. Besides, I didn't think we'd get caught."

"Seriously?" Mrs. Turner's exasperation escalated. "When was the last time you got away with anything?"

"I snuck out last Saturday night—" His mouth instantly sagged and he sniffed a quick breath through his nose. "Oh shit."

"See?" Mrs. Turner folded her arms, triumphant. "That's what I'm talking about. He always gets caught, yet he keeps doing things he's not supposed to do, no matter how much we punish him."

"That must be frustrating, huh?" I said. "Getting away with things requires one to be detail-oriented. That's not your special power, is it?"

8

"Nope." He slumped in his seat. "I always end up that one guy who gets nailed. Even when other people mess up just the same as me. Like this one time, Toby Phillips was out in the parking lot after school and—"

"Wait!" I held up both palms. "Stop talking before you get yourself or Toby Phillips or anyone else into trouble." I thought a moment and then glanced back at Mrs. Turner. "Has Jason ever been tested for ADD?"

Her face went blank. "Uh, no. I mean, how could he have ADD? He'll play that video game online with his friends for hours, and when he watches TV you can't get him back to reality with a police whistle. He's totally focused."

I turned back to Jason. "Ever wonder if you have ADD?"

"Huh?" He blinked. "Sorry. I was, uh...when's this session over?"

"Hot date?" I asked.

"Sorta." He grinned and made the breast fondling gesture again.

"Jason! You're still grounded and as soon as we get home I'm nailing your bedroom window shut, recoding our security system, and calling Taylor's mother to ask her to keep that girl on a shorter leash."

Jason put his forehead against his palm and shook his head.

"So," I said cheerfully. "Since that idea's pretty much shot, why don't you hang around here and we'll talk about your brain and why it doesn't seem to want you to think before you act."

Is This Chapter For Me?

Probably. How you focus your attention, think, and act on your thoughts are key elements of ADD. So, if you have an accurate diagnosis, you're likely to find something of yourself in this chapter. Do you or your people think you:

❑ Can't prioritize your attention very well, so you focus on things you shouldn't and don't focus on things you should?

❑ Act or speak impulsively, before thinking things through?

❑ Don't care enough about things that other people seem to care a lot about (school, work, exercise, friends, finishing things, cleaning, obligations, etc.)?

❑ Do things that you don't really mean to do and then try to explain why you did them, even if you don't understand it yourself?

If you or your people checked off any of these items, you should probably read this chapter. If not, you might want to reconsider your diagnosis, or as I'll explain later, see if you might also have anxiety. Or maybe you've already gotten great treatment and conquered this problem. If so, consider this chapter a victory lap.

What ADD Is and What It Isn't

It only takes fifteen seconds on Google to dig up controversy about ADD. Some of it deserved. Most of it based on false beliefs, rumors, and denial. The arguments range from whether it even exists to all sorts of banter about alternative treatments. The real scientific debate centers on how ADD is diagnosed and treated, but there's even disagreement on its underlying neurology and what causes it.

There are two things I want you to know about the research while reading this book. First, ADD is a neurobiological disorder, not a moral problem. You're not lazy or bad, even if you feel you are or if others have told you this. ADD is about thinking and how, when you're doing it, your brain just isn't operating in the same way as other people's.

Having ADD isn't your fault, but dealing with it is your responsibility. This book is all about dealing.

The folks who study brains have pretty much proven this. Most believe there are four areas of the frontal region involved in ADD—the lateral prefrontal cortex, dorsal anterior cingulate cortex, caudate, and putamen. Those parts of the brain are thought to control the ability to focus. They've also found that frontal cortex and temporal lobe development is delayed by about three years in grade school kids with ADD, who, as a result, tend to seem less mature than their peers. So, having ADD isn't your fault, but dealing with it is your responsibility.

This book is about dealing.

That brings us to what the research says about treatment. The American Psychological Association, American Psychiatric Association, American Medical Association, and American Academy of Pediatrics all agree. The best approach for ADD is a combination of medication and behavioral therapy designed to help change how you organize and live your life. Medicine without therapy is like putting gas in your car and then driving around and around the block. If you don't have a destination or a map, you won't end up anywhere. The advice in this book can put your metaphorical gas to good use.

Not everyone agrees with the vast body of research. If you Google "Best Treatments for ADD," you'll find plenty of sites selling homeopathic remedies, brain exercises, and supposedly proprietary biofeedback techniques. Some charge thousands of dollars and many look and sound quite professional. Yet none are covered by health insurance. Why? Because there's no research backing them up. In fact, most sites include a disclaimer that their program isn't intended to treat any mental health or psychological condition, along with a claim that ADD isn't really a mental health or psychological condition, so come on down and we'll treat it.

Spend your money how you see fit, but remember that science is science and marketing is marketing.

That said, I have met people diagnosed with ADD who got better by eliminating certain foods from their diet or avoiding gluten. You're free to try that, but if diet corrects your inattentive symptoms, the problem wasn't ADD to begin with. In Chapter 12 I'll discuss other factors that can mimic ADD, like sleep deprivation and substance abuse.

All About Focus

There's an old joke that goes like this: "Some people call it ADD. I call it multitasking." People who don't have ADD find this one pretty funny. ADD-leaners chuckle with pride at the supposed gift of being psychologically everywhere all at the same time. People who really have ADD just scratch their heads and think, "Huh?"

That's because this joke doesn't make any sense.

ADD is exactly the opposite of multitasking. It's a problem of taking in all the information going on around you and in your head, and trying to sort out and make sense of it when your brain isn't wired that way. *Attention deficit* means the inability to focus on what you want to focus on because your mind wants to focus on something else.

Speaking of focus, we use that word a lot, but have you thought about what it really means? Focus is the ability to select only the most important aspects of what's going on and ignore other, less important things. This lets you control what you think about and what you do in response. If you want to read a book, you put your mind to that task. If you want to exercise, you tell your brain to make it happen, even if your body hurts or you find exercise boring. If you want to do both at the same time, you direct your mind and body to work in sync, so you and your e-reader don't fall off the treadmill.

Focusing this way is hard for people with ADD—especially if a complex task is involved. People who don't have ADD, like Mrs. Turner, can't imagine how anyone would struggle with something so basic. Focus just comes naturally, doesn't it? Not if you have all those lateral prefrontal cortex, dorsal anterior cingulate cortex, caudate, and putamen issues going on.

This lack of appreciation for the neurological difficulties of focus puts the ADD people at odds with the non-ADD people, just as we saw with Jason and his mom. That's what makes others see you as difficult to deal with and what makes you see them the very same way. It's what makes you feel judged.

Driving is a good way to illustrate focus because most of us over fifteen have done it and know what it's like. To be focused in driving does *not* mean staring down at the highway right in front of your bumper. Mrs. Turner sees Jason engrossed in a video game or TV show and believes he's "highly focused." But being fixated on a screen has no more to do with focus than watching the white lines disappearing under your car as you rear-end the guy stopped in front of you.

Instead, a focused driver consumes a whole world of information. He takes a quick look around his car as it sits in the driveway to be sure he's not going to run over anyone or anything. He gets in, puts on a seatbelt and backs into the street. There's a car parked on the left and one a block away proceeding slowly toward him. There's a child playing with a ball in the yard across the street. Then his phone chimes in. He ignores it because he doesn't want to hit the child if she runs into the street, smack the parked car, or block the approaching car from passing. The driver chooses what he pays attention to by weighing all these variables and basing his decisions upon what he learns.

It's exactly that way for everything else in life—school, job, friends, romance, reading, exercise, even leisure time. We consciously and unconsciously set priorities for our attention, which shift as the environment around us changes. What we prioritize moment-to-moment as our subject of focus, guides our response. Sometimes we have a long time to respond, like with getting married, going to college, or buying a house. For most things, however, we have to respond quickly.

Who Cares?

Another way to think about focus is in terms of how much people care and what they care about. Research shows that anxiety has a curvilinear relationship to productivity. You'll do best when you have just the right amount of anxiety, so you care enough to put forth good effort. Too much anxiety and you'll care so much that you get stressed and can't function efficiently. Too little and you won't try hard enough.

I find that most people exist on a continuum between ADD and anxiety. People with ADD don't care enough. Anxious people care too much. Of course, most people fall well short of either diagnosis, so just as some folks are ADD-leaners, others are anxious-leaners. How far you lean toward anxiety or inattention determines whether it's just an interesting part of your personality or an actual problem requiring diagnosis and treatment. Let's look further at how ADD and anxious people differ, in order to understand where I'm headed with this whole caring thing.

ADD People. Nothing causes more trouble for people with ADD than not caring enough. I'm not saying that you don't care morally—like you don't worry about the environment or you ignore the rights and welfare of others. Maybe you do, maybe you don't. As I'm using it here, "caring" means taking seriously all the important but largely boring details you encounter in life, rather than ignoring or avoiding them.

Believe me, I'm not alone in this observation. The loved ones of ADD people often make the same observation, and rarely with my gentle nuance. They toss out words like "lazy," "thoughtless," and "lackadaisical" in response to your lack of intent, incomplete projects, lost assignments, blown-off commitments, and relationship failings. In fact, I learned this whole "caring" theory of focus from talking to the frustrated loved ones of people with ADD.

Think about the word "carefree" for a moment. It's the fun term we use to describe people with ADD and their decisions. We even envy your untroubled spirit and freedom from worry. Then, when those ill-considered decisions go wrong, we fire off a different word.

"Careless."

People may have used this word to describe you on occasion, just as I would use it to describe Jason. Or maybe you've been labeled with one of its synonyms: impulsive, irresponsible, reckless, haphazard, rash, hasty, etc. Nothing seems important to you, except whatever you're interested in at the moment, and that will soon fade.

ADD-leaners also seem carefree, but they usually care enough to get business done. They're the creative free spirits we all know and enjoy. They're fun at parties, interesting, and spontaneous. They have fresh ideas, keep several projects going at a time, finish their most interesting work, pursue their strongest ideas, and foster their best relationships. They easily drop plans, relationships, or obligations that aren't working, and get over problems and regrets more quickly than anxious folks. They plan what they're going to do, though not as easily or as thoroughly as anxious people.

When they break, ADD-leaners become overwhelmed and disorganized in thought and behavior. They feel an urge to cut and run to Somewhere Else, even when they know better. Such breaks usually come when life throws too much complex input their way, or, paradoxically, when they get stuck in something really difficult or boring that they can't get out of.

Anxious People. Talk about caring too much. Anxious folks take in more information than they can use. They're so focused that they notice every detail of themselves and their environment. They often can't get their minds off what *might* happen, no matter how unlikely, so they over-plan everything. Regardless of how skilled or talented they may be, anxious people feel inadequate to meet other people's demands, not because they actually fall short, but because they fear they will. They need things to be orderly and predictable to feel safe and to give themselves a sense of peace. In extreme cases this gets to the point of obsessions and compulsions.

Anxious-leaners are far less intense. They're seen as conscientious, thoughtful, intentional, and precise. Employers and parents love them because they strive to please. They win favor from teachers, friends, and dating partners, who find them attentive, authentic, and considerate.

When they do break—perhaps in response to a traumatic incident, divorce, a loved one's death, or other serious loss—an anxious-leaner's primary workaround is to just concentrate and try harder. That sounds like a great plan and it really can work. However, as we'll discuss in Chapter 7, when things are going to pieces, it pays to step back and calmly consider a new or different approach. That can be hard for anxious people who are naturally attracted to structure and predictability.

It would be really nice if this whole caring business were as black and white as I just made it sound. It is for most people—they lean either anxious or ADD. But about 25% of people with ADD also have a diagnosable anxiety disorder.

Let's take a look at how caring works for them.

Anxious-ADD People. Anxiety tends to counteract ADD, forcing these folks to care more than they otherwise would and to be more organized than their ADD-only peers.

"So," you might murmur as you ponder the nature of your brain. "Anxiety sounds pretty helpful for people with ADD. Sign me up."

Be careful what you wish for.

On one hand, anxious-ADD-leaners and those with moderate impairment often get farther in school, at work, and in life than their ADD-only peers. It's an imperfect analogy, but anxiety gives them a kind of built-in stimulant. They may neglect what they're supposed to focus on, but then they get upset about neglecting it and get back on task. It may be at the last minute, but the work gets done and it often gets done well. Unlike dear Jason, who didn't have a teaspoon's worth of anxiety, the anxious-ADD people are too conscientious to ignore what needs to be done, no matter how badly they want to.

On the other hand, anxious-ADD people often feel really tortured—always at the mercy of their brains, dragging them back and forth from not caring to caring too much, to feeling overwhelmed. They have an especially hard time feeling at peace if their anxiety is bad enough to be diagnosed. They become overwhelmed, give up, then berate themselves for giving up. They second-guess themselves constantly and lack confidence in their abilities and decisions, even when others see them as competent. They often say, "I hate myself," or at least, "I hate my brain," and are especially prone to depression.

I wrote this book for folks who fall neatly into the ADD side of the continuum. However, if you tone down my thirteen principles a bit, many can help anxious-ADD people make the most of their anxiety. If you're considering medication, however, be sure to read Chapter 13. Trying to prescribe for two opposite problems gets complicated in a hurry.

The Advantages of Spontaneity

People with ADD can shine in situations where raw spontaneity gives them an edge over the "think before you act" people. Many musicians, comedians, and artists cite ADD as part of what makes them successful. Impulsivity and creativity are handy in trades like that, where looking at the world differently is the whole point. Unbridled energy is often at the core of great art.

By definition, being carefree reduces the stress you feel in daily life. It can be a relief to not worry about failure, how others see you, or what you stand to lose and just forge ahead with whatever you're doing. Caring less can also be an asset when managing conflict, because it's easier to walk away from a bad relationship than continue on like a zombie just because you worry too much about how it will end. ADD people often recover from traumatic losses more easily and quickly than the rest of us. That ability to move on can be jarring for anxious friends and family members, but it does spare you long periods of readjustment.

Principle 2: Think Before You Act

Thinking through what you mean to do before doing it is one of the many things I suggest that fall into the category of "easier said than done." However, if you don't do it day in and day out, decision by decision, you'll remain at the whim of your latest impulse. To get you started, I've broken the whole process down into several interrelated sections. I was tempted to call them steps, but they don't really go in order. You have to do them all at the same time and make them work together.

Practice Mindfulness. Mindfulness is defined as "a state of active, open attention on the present."[8] It allows you to observe your thoughts and feelings almost as though you are your own therapist, without judgment or ridicule.

---

[8] www.psychologytoday.com/basics/mindfulness

Mindfulness sets you down here and now and opens you to your own inner wisdom.

That might sound like a line from a romantic comedy where a girl drags her boyfriend to a mountain retreat to see a clichéd guru, at which point hijinks ensue. It's not. It's how you, a person whose mind seems always to be operating on its own, can dig a little deeper and make better decisions. It lets you tune in to what's important and tune out the background noise.

One of my favorite mindfulness tricks is to take a moment and ask myself, "What am I about to do right now?" I often do this as I'm sitting in the front seat of my car, getting ready to go somewhere. I go through the list of places I need to go and what I need to do there. If the list starts to get complicated, I dictate it into my phone. I do the same thing before I see a client, look over the notes and think about where we might want to go today. After working with me for awhile, many clients text or bring in their own lists to go over in therapy.

You don't have to do a formal practice of mindfulness meditation, though you might want to give it a try. Just learn the basic principles so you're more able to do the next important step.

The right decision is always the mindful one. That's what it means to be intentional.

Intentional Living. The problem of ADD is not that you have trouble making choices; it's that you have trouble making the right ones at the right times. I like to think of life as being made up of many "equations" we each have to solve to get by. This one is pretty simple and straightforward. Tattoo it on your wrist so it will be there for you when you need it.[9]

Poor focus = Poor decisions = Poor outcome.

"And what," you might rightly ask, "Constitutes a poor decision? How do you know what the right choice is for me in my situation?"

I don't, actually. But you do. The right decision is always the mindful one. That's what it means to be intentional—doing what you mean to do; using your "wise mind"[10] to choose a path and then follow it.

---

[9] I'm sort of kidding here, but if you're going to tattoo things on your wrist anyhow, the little equations I have in this book would be worth considering.

[10] Dialectical Behavioral Therapy (DBT) is really the gold standard for using mindfulness in psychological practice. I particularly like the interactive *DBT Workbook* (McKay, Wood, and Brantley, 2007). While it includes a lot of material that doesn't apply directly to ADD, quite a bit does. In DBT, everything is about the "wise mind."

Jason's mind didn't do much of anything intentionally because he couldn't think things through to their end consequence. He did his homework, which he found rather painful, only to leave it in his locker. He hooked up with Taylor before considering how things might turn out if they were caught. He blurted out funny but inappropriate comments in front of his mother, then accidently outed himself for a recent sneak and a planned liaison after our session.

Jason would have had a much easier time—and probably gotten away with more teen adventures—had he put a little more thought into his actions. And the same holds true for you. Don't worry, you'll still have your carefree moments. We all need them. But serious decisions require intentionality, and carelessness is rarely helpful when making them.

Get a Mentor. Without a doubt, the best tool for intentional living is a mentor. It can be a therapist—that's largely my role in treating ADD—but it doesn't have to be. It could be a respected teacher, parent, or organized friend. It's rarely good to have your spouse or boy/girlfriend serve as your primary mentor. Those relationships are so emotionally close that a conflict of interest is guaranteed. But neither should a romantic partner work against you. Here are the qualifications of a good mentor, as you might post them on a job notice if you could actually advertise for this on Craigslist or SimplyHired:

WANTED: ATTENTION DEFICIT MENTOR WHO:

- Leans to the anxious side, but doesn't fall over. Attends to detail, but isn't so impaired by anxiety as to get overwhelmed in the face of difficulty. Is seen by others as wise, intentional, calm, responsible, conscientious, and planful.

- Has my best interests at heart and nothing else.[11]

- Is good at seeing what's around the corner and is willing to warn me, even if it makes me mad.

- Is preferably older than me or at least more mature.

- Is successful in areas of life that cause me trouble, like school, work, life planning, organization, relationships, etc.

- Is tolerant of the difficulties ADD causes me.

- Can help me organize without doing everything for me.

---

[11] It's worth noting that therapists *have* to practice this way because we are your servants. All other mentors need to be screened for benevolence.

- Is willing to share honest opinions without being overbearing, judging me, or talking down to me.

- Can have ADD too, but must really understand it and have mastered Dr. Wes's list of life principles or a list very much like it.

Once "hired," your mentor's job is to sit down with you, discuss whatever significant action you're about to take, help you make a list of and weigh the pros and cons, predict the outcome, and advise you on the wisdom of moving forward. Your mentor should point out variables and outcomes you haven't considered yet and challenge your thinking about how to proceed.

Of course a mentor can't be there for every decision. There are dozens of small ones you make daily, some with great consequence. But a mentor can help you with something that's even more important than making a decision—learning and practicing *how* they are made. That way, you'll make decisions wisely even when he or she isn't around.

Slow Down. The best thing about waiting to talk to your mentor before making a big decision is that it forces you to take a break from your natural impulsivity. Where ADD is concerned, a slow decision is usually a better one. I ask clients to text me *before* making a critical choice and give me a chance to weigh in. My quick response often prevents a more complicated intervention.

Texting, emailing, and tweeting are great opportunities to say things you'll have to take back later. To slow yourself down on these media, make a draft copy of what you want to say. Don't even format it in the medium of choice, because you might be tempted to hit "send" before you've thought things through. Just type your thoughts into a word processor or note app and then leave the message alone until at least the next day. Nine out of ten times you'll decide you don't want to send it. On the tenth time you'll have made the choice intentionally and not on impulse. Harry Truman used this technique. Since he didn't have a note app, he just put his emotional writings in a box and locked them away.

Cognitive Override. This is a fancy term for using what you know to consciously guide your brain toward the wise choice. This whole book is basically a formula for doing just that, making decisions about your life based on what others have found helpful in managing theirs. As you incorporate all that information and see what works for you and what doesn't, you'll feel energized to take the next step and then the next.[12]

---

[12] www.apa.org/monitor/julaug02/exercise.aspx

Let's close this chapter with the old good news/bad news situation. First the bad news: the latest research suggests that ADD doesn't go away with age. It's a life-long issue that impacts nearly every aspect of your life. You'll always be struggling from moment to moment to care enough about what's important, ignore what's not, recognize the difference, and think through good decisions.

Here's the good news. If you follow the principles in this book, there's a good chance you can pull yourself out of the land of the impaired people and into the land of the ADD-leaners.

And why is that such a cool place to be? Because you'll end up with all the advantages of having ADD and very few of the impairments. You'll still be you, only better. I know you can do this, because I've seen hundreds of others do it many times. I believe in you.

CHAPTER 3

A RIGHT PATH

If the time should come when you have to make a choice between what is right and what is easy, remember what happened
to a boy who was good, and kind, and brave, because he strayed
across the path of Lord Voldemort. Remember Cedric Diggory.

— J.K. Rowling, *Harry Potter and the Goblet of Fire*

"So, David..." I stared at the long email his parents had sent after
scheduling his first appointment. "I'm not sure where to begin. Your
life is kind of, well...a mess."

"Tell me about it." He nodded a mop of brownish blond hair toward the
computer stationed on my lap. "I'm sure my parents gave you their version."

"They did. So now you can give me yours. How, at twenty-four, did you end
up living in their basement with no job, no education, and no girlfriend?"

"You got me. I guess I just didn't try hard enough."

"It says here that you have a monthly Adderall scrip, but you don't actually
take it—"

"I do sometimes."

"Dare I ask where the rest of it goes?"

"No."

"Let me guess." I shook my head slowly. "You're selling a medication to
college students that would do you a lot of good because you're actually
diagnosed with ADD, so they can supposedly do better, even though they're
not diagnosed with ADD. Am I close?"

"Yeah, but I mostly sell to high schoolers. Those kids have more disposable income. This is all confidential, right?"

"Right. Except, isn't that sort of—I don't know—insane?"

"Not from a profit standpoint. Besides, I hate how Adderall makes me feel. I'd rather just be chill." He lifted his hand and let it glide smoothly in front of him.

"So chill, in fact, that you ended up homeless."

David shifted on the couch. "Adderall's not the reason why I'm…between residences, so to speak."

"Okay. How do you see it?"

"People are always so serious. Especially girls. They always want to put a label on the relationship or make you have, like a…what's the word?"

"Obligation?"

"Exactly. Especially when you live with them. I just don't want anyone to expect anything from me." He made the same hand-gliding chill-out gesture.

"David." I gave him my well-practiced wise look. "Have you ever read *Harry Potter*?"

"Uh, no. But I saw the movies." He laughed. "And I rode that ride in Florida. Man, I was totally ready to hurl when I stepped off that thing. It was all going every which way." He waved both hands in front of his face and wagged his head. "It was cray, man."

"Why don't you download Dumbledore's image from that movie and set it as your smartphone background, or maybe get a ringtone of him saying, 'We must all face the choice between what is right and what is easy.'" I intoned a bad impression of Michael Gambon as Dumbledore. "'Cuz basically that's where you've gone wrong, David. You prefer the easy path to the right one."

"Hey. That's what Yoda tells Luke Skywalker in *The Empire Strikes Back*." He raised an imaginary light saber and made the noises: "Woove, woove, woove. I've seen that one a bunch of times."

"Okay, download this instead." I switched to Yoda's voice. "'If you choose the quick and easy path as Vader did, you will become an agent of evil.' Imagine hearing that every time somebody calls."

The joy quickly ebbed from David's face. "I'm not an agent of evil, Dr. Wes. But that's pretty much what my parents think."

"Because they're frustrated with all your lying, not to mention stealing money from their account. It makes them want to kick you out on your butt."

"I know. Same reason my girl gave me the boot."

"Whoa. You stole money from her, too?" I didn't hide the alarm in my voice. David needed to feel the severity of breeching core social contracts.

He nodded. "Don't tell my parents. Then they'll think I'm totally hopeless." He hung his head. "I get what you're saying about the easy and hard paths, but how do you know which is which? It never seems that obvious to me until it's too late."

I channeled Yoda again. "Know it you will, because always hard and uncomfortable it will be. Force you to work harder than you like, it will. And longer. Your guiding light discomfort will be."

For a moment David looked puzzled. Maybe it was my made-up Yoda-speak, or maybe he understood the words but couldn't quite grasp their depth. When it finally hit him, his eyes widened. "Wait. You're saying I have to be *uncomfortable* to be right?"

"Pretty much."

"Are you effing[13] crazy?" he asked.

"Not that I'm aware of."

"Seriously? Who the eff wants to be uncomfortable?" Anger rose in his voice, a precursor to one of the tantrums his parents had mentioned in their email.

"Nobody I know," I said. "We do what's hard not because we like it, but because it gets us to where we need to go. Then, in the long run, life really *is* easier and better."

"Well I can't do that, man." He stood, pulled on his jacket, and headed for the door. "Not for you or my parents or a girl or anybody. Not even for Yoda. I don't like stuff that sucks."

"I can see that. Unfortunately, you're proving my point with every step you take toward that door. Things get even a little hard and you cut and run."

David paused, his hand resting on the doorknob. "Isn't there any other way, man? Like you could give me some tools or something. That's what Mom said you'd do. Give me tools for coping. She didn't say anything about—"

"Yeah, David. I have plenty of tools. Except learning them is the easy part. Using them is what's hard. The first tool is to seek the wisdom of discomfort and let it guide you."

---

13 Dear Friends of The F-word: I decided to keep this book PG-13. You can read my novels if you want to hear how young adults really talk. In this one they say "effing."

"Oh yeah?" He opened the door, stepped through, and headed down the hall. "Who said that?"

"I did."

Is This Chapter For Me?

Probably so, but maybe not. People with both ADD and anxiety often force themselves down the right path whether they want to go there or not. ADD people with little anxiety often struggle mightily as they pursue one easy path after another and end up on a much harder road later on. A few even end up like David, alienated from family and friends. But even if things aren't *that* bad in your particular situation, ask yourself and your people if you:

- ❏ Seem to find yourself in the middle of one messed-up situation after another with friends, school, work. or family.
- ❏ Tend to take the easy path, even when you know for certain, or someone you really trust has told you, that it's the wrong one.
- ❏ Have a harder time than other people seem to have handling difficult or uncomfortable problems or situations.
- ❏ Avoid, deflect, or procrastinate doing difficult things.
- ❏ Often disqualify yourself by saying you're incapable of doing something others seem able to do.
- ❏ Lie to get out of doing something hard.
- ❏ Avoid making or keeping obligations to others.

As difficult as it may be to face, if any of these strikes a chord, this chapter will give you a lot to think about.

All Kinds of Uncomfortable

Confession time. I'm one of the last twenty-three people who hasn't read *Harry Potter* and I only saw the first movie, but I have ridden that ride at Universal Studios in Florida six or seven times now, without hurling. I know who Dumbledore is, though I had to look up how to spell his name.

Though not as dramatically as Harry Potter or Luke Skywalker, we each choose easy or right paths every day. Unfortunately, a big part of having ADD is being neurologically prone to select the easy path. That can end up somewhere between irritating and disastrous, just as it did for David. Yet, when we drill down into most bad plans, we find that even as they're pouring out of your head and into the world, you can list about ten things likely to go wrong with them. David knew his girlfriend was eventually going to catch him stealing, but he just decided to cross that bridge when he came to it—or in this case, when she threw him off of it.

So, what does "easy" really mean in the context of making choices? It means free of stress or anxiety; requiring little work or effort; familiar and unchallenging. Summed to one word, it means "comfortable."

David was right about one thing before he stormed out of my office—nobody likes to be uncomfortable, so the easy path is powerful and seductive for us all. That's why it shows up again and again in literature. It's relatable.

Just as with boredom, discomfort isn't really the problem for people with ADD. It's your *intolerance* of discomfort. For people with ADD, comfort is like a giant psychological magnet, drawing you in and distracting you from harder, more productive choices.

Why is this so? Poor focus yields a whole series of secondary problems. At the top of the list is inability to sustain mental effort. That's why many (but not all) people with ADD have trouble with math. One needs more sustained mental effort to solve a complex algebra problem than just about any other task. Putting up with discomfort requires the same effort. You have to mentally power through a lot of "stuff that sucks," as David so aptly put it.

"Wait," you say. "You told us in Chapter 1 that people with ADD are drawn to novelty because we like to try lots of new things. How does it make sense that we'd also be drawn to the familiar?"

For many people with ADD, chaos seems comfortable and order feels awkward.

Good call. For you, feeling comfortable doesn't mean staying in one place, literally or figuratively, or avoiding new things. Quite the opposite. You're more likely than the rest of us to fling yourself into all sorts of new adventures, or misadventures. But that's not necessarily the kind of "goal-directed energy" that moves you somewhere for some purpose.

We have a different name for ADD energy. We call it "chaos."

For many people with ADD, chaos actually seems comfortable and order feels awkward. Chaos is easy, order is hard. Since a right path is nearly always an orderly one, you need to be on a daily search for the discomfort of order.

Wait. Don't storm out of my book just yet. Let's look at some examples. I bet they'll seem familiar.

The Wisdom (Teeth) of Discomfort

While writing up David's story, I went Googling for quotes on "The Wisdom of Discomfort." Surely someone greater than I had uttered a few words with which I might open this chapter.

Nope. Instead, I got a hundred listings for what to do if your wisdom teeth hurt. Not quite what I was looking for. But then, just as I started entering a different string into the search field, I realized how this pain in the mouth illustrates my point.

I actually have all my wisdom teeth. They fit nicely inside my oversized mouth. Most folks aren't so fortunate. They need to have them removed, which usually hurts, particularly if they get "dry socket." That's when the blood clot in the hole where the tooth used to be dislodges or dissolves too soon, leaving the bone and nerve exposed to air, food, fluid, and anything else that goes in your mouth, leading to infection.

Yikes. Just reading this is uncomfortable, isn't it?

Why would someone go through all that? Aren't wisdom teeth fine where they belong, and their removal is a plot by dental surgeons to drum up business? Why not just wait and see what happens to them?

Because doing nothing is worse.

Most people's wisdom teeth come in at an angle or are impacted, leaving them prone to decay. The older you are, the more difficult and painful they are to remove. So, in your late teens, if your dentist doesn't like what she's seeing back there, she sends you to an oral surgeon *before* those teeth cause problems.

The Tantalizing Joys of Avoidance

When left to your own devices, people with ADD prefer to avoid dealing with sucky stuff like wisdom teeth, conflict, awkward social situations, tests, driving, money shortages, class, work, dishes, laundry, the truth, studying, and so on. It's sort of the opposite of impulsivity. Instead of jumping too quickly, you try not to jump at all. Here are a few of the most common tricks ADD people play on themselves to avoid doing what needs to be done:

"I Can't." When something requires sustained attention, obligation or discomfort, people with ADD tend to self-handicap. When invited to do something hard, the first answer will be, "I've never done it that way before," or, "I don't know how." You may not say it out loud, but "I can't" will be floating around in the back of your mind, limiting you to what's easy.

To be fair, determining your true ability is a tricky business. By definition, ADD causes impairment, meaning it creates challenges you may find nearly insurmountable, especially if you lack the energy of anxiety. But whenever you're considering what you can and can't do, remember what I said in Chapter 2—*having* ADD isn't your fault. *Not dealing* with it is.

So if you find yourself coming up with "I can't" more often than you should, fight back by compiling a list of what you *can* do and add to it every day. You might want to put "get treatment" at the top, followed by "find a mentor." Most people can do those two things, and they'll add immeasurably to your progress.

Distraction. People with ADD often focus on things that aren't important in order to avoid focusing on things that are. I realize you may have a hard time deciding which is which. But here I'm talking about obvious distractions, like working on something you enjoy (a hobby, a video game, Facebook) when you should be working on homework or a remodeling project or spending time with your children.

Some distractions are tricky, because they're important but not well prioritized when compared to other things. If you really like math, you might work the problems in the next chapter instead of doing your boring American Literature project that's due the next day. Everyone should put effort into his or her job, but when you stay late just to avoid arguing with your partner, that's a problem. Or, conversely, you find any excuse to stay home from work to take care of your family, when really you're just shirking a job you don't like.

Of course, today's super-distracters are the Internet and smartphones. While the web brings an enormous amount of information into our lives, that information is only as good as what we do with it. Smartphones allow everyone to stay connected, which can be a networking goldmine or a distraction minefield.

Procrastination. For people with ADD, putting off until tomorrow what ought to be done today is an art form. Cramming for an exam, writing desperately at 4:00 a.m. a paper that's due at 8:00 a.m. the next day, turning in shoddy work on deadline, not paying bills on time—they're all forms of procrastination. It's why your partner or parent complains that you put off loading the dishwasher until the counter is stacked six-deep in dishes.

Why is procrastination so seductive to people with ADD? Because it's easy. It feels better. It relieves you of the worry and discomfort of taking action, at least until disaster is imminent and you can't procrastinate any longer. Hopefully, at that moment, a surge of anxious energy comes over you and you push yourself on to the finish line while everyone else is asleep and not distracting you. Or, if you're not so good at procrastination, you realize the hopelessness of your situation and collapse in a heap.

Lying. David was an expert at this one. It's a common reason ADD teens and young adults get sent to therapy or kicked out of their homes. If you keep it up for any length of time, your people will begin to consider you a "pathological liar," callously violating the core fabric of our social contract. And they don't like it very much.

> *Lying isn't compulsive or pathological in the sense that you do it for no reason or can't control yourself.*

If you have ADD, lying probably isn't compulsive or pathological in the sense that you do it for no reason or can't control yourself. It serves a purpose—avoiding the uncomfortable problems you've created for yourself and your people while wandering down the easy path. It's always more comfortable to lie than to face the truth head-on.

Until you get caught.

In David's case, when caught stealing from his parents and his girlfriend, he lied to cover up his behavior. He wasn't a sociopath. He didn't have criminal intent. He just took a shortcut.

Shortcuts. Being broke was uncomfortable for David, particularly since he wasn't good with money. Holding consistent employment was also uncomfortable. Given his problems with obligation, he found his bosses expected more of him than he wanted to give, like showing up on time and being productive. His parents had money they weren't using, so he took it. As their child he felt entitled. So rather than solve the problem of poverty as we all must, David took the shortcut of stealing.

His girlfriend also had a little extra cash. He thought of that as a loan. After being caught several times, she kicked him out. His friends didn't want him couch surfing, because he never helped with food or bills. That left him sitting in my office, on the brink of homelessness.

It happens more often than you might think.

Shortcuts avoid necessary steps or concerns that you find tedious or uncomfortable. They could include anything from not putting things away to selling drugs to cheating on taxes to using sex as a way to advance your career or manipulate a dating partner.

School frustration can seduce people with ADD to use shortcuts. For instance, a student finds the correct answer to a math problem, only to lose points for not showing the step-by-step method for getting there. That's how math, and a lot of other things, work. The secrets are in the process, not the outcome. ADD people hate that. Another example is copying someone else's work instead of doing it yourself. I'm sure you can think of many others.

Perfectionism. Where avoidance is concerned, this one's a "sleeper," because it masquerades as something quite noble—striving for flawlessness, setting high performance standards, and being self-critical and concerned about the criticism of others.

"Wait," you might say. "That sounds like something anxious people struggle with." And it is. But for them, perfectionism is like an obsession, something they feel they must do to prove their own worth and manage their insecurity.

For people with ADD, perfectionism can become a way of avoiding finishing something. It's really a specialized version of "I can't," as in, "I just can't finish this project because I know it won't be good enough," or, "I was halfway through and I realized this is never going to be how I want it to be. I just can't turn it in like this." Another that drives partners and roommates crazy is, "I can't make dinner. My cooking never comes out the way it looks on Martha Stewart." This might sound like someone conscientiously trying to do a good job, but if you dig a little deeper you find avoidance.

All of us have to turn in imperfect work. I probably could have found a hundred ways to make this book better, but if I kept doing that long enough, you'd never read it. So I have to settle for good enough. And where unattainable perfection is concerned, "good enough" is your best friend.

That doesn't mean you can't keep improving your work. For example, modern publishing allows permanent revision, so this book never really has to be finished. You can send me your tips and stories and maybe they'll appear in future versions of this book. Likewise, many teachers allow you to revise a project and employers are always excited to see you improve something. But you still have to meet deadlines for each revision.

Good Intentions. Here's another one that sounds like a good thing, when it really isn't. It's easy to say that you want to do this or that. Doing it, is an entirely different matter. In the next chapter we'll talk about striving for something rather than just wishing for it. Expressing good intentions without follow-through is just another way to avoid actually confronting a problem and doing something about it. For example, anyone can buy a bookshelf full of books. But reading them takes time, focus, and commitment.

Pretending. Another popular method of avoidance is acting as if a problem doesn't exist. Ignoring stuff that sucks saves you the trouble of procrastination, like a kid plugging her ears because she doesn't want to hear what her parents are telling her to do. Your people really hate this one, because it requires a crazy level of denial. Rather than saying, "I'll load the dishwasher later," you just disappear or throw the dishes away. No, I'm not kidding. An ADD teenager was tossing the dishes rather than putting them in the dishwasher. Nobody could figure out where they were going.

A far more common example is laundry. As teens move toward adulthood they usually get concerned about how they look and smell. Many teens with ADD do care about this, but quite a few don't put enough interest into it to get it done. So, when given the task of doing their own laundry, they pretend it's not dirty and keep wearing it day after day. And yes, I've seen ADD teens throw clothes away rather than wash them. That's even harder to detect than dishes, particularly for kids who like to shop.

Computer-savvy students have hacked parent email addresses to filter out the negative grade reports the school is sending. That works great until graduation, or the lack thereof, at which point student hackers realize they've pretended themselves into failure.

Pretending is especially serious in dating relationships. One partner will argue that the relationship is going down the drain, while the ADD partner will suggest they watch their favorite DVD that evening or go out to dinner. It's also how affairs get started. One partner pretends that the solution to a stagnant relationship is to be with someone else and jumps straight into an imaginary love affair, instead of fixing the current relationship or ending it. In fact, without pretending, one couldn't really cheat on a partner.

Deflection. This involves brushing off a conflict or critique rather than dealing with it. David used the nuclear bomb of deflection. He left my office. But there are more subtle methods, including changing the subject, dodging responsibility by blaming someone else, attacking the person who's confronting you, or arguing passionately just to confuse the situation. And then there's stonewalling (refusing to communicate). John Gottman[14] sees this as one of the greatest threats to couples and a high predictor of divorce. In fact, all of these deflection strategies are guaranteed to fail—unless your goal is to piss people off. In that case, they work pretty well.

Speaking of which, let's move on to the most fundamental and uncomfortable part of human relationships for people with ADD. Obligation.

I'm Obliged

Obligation is any agreement you make with others and your commitment to see it through. Obligation can be explicit—"We are an exclusive couple, you can't date anyone else;" or, "You must report to work at 9:00 a.m., five days a week." It can also be implied—"If you live with me, you don't steal my stuff;" or, "Cheating on a test destroys the grading curve for the rest of the class."

You may really get what David meant when he said, "I don't want anyone to expect anything from me." You've probably felt overwhelmed by the expecta-

---

[14] www.gottmanblog.com/2013/05/the-four-horsemen-stonewalling.html

tions of others. Did it seem like an unmanageable burden? Did you wonder how others fulfill their commitments every day? Was it easier to "just say no" than get yourself into something you couldn't handle? Or did you get hooked and then bail out? You're not alone. There are three reasons why obligation is scary for ADD people:

- By definition, being obliged means owing something to someone in return for something they give you. Fulfilling an obligation is much harder than making it, especially if the agreement wasn't well thought-out.

- You can't escape an obligation without incurring negative consequences. That may feel constricting, like a straight-jacket, even if you freely committed to it.

- Obligation requires consistency, or what I'll call in Chapter 8 "psychological integrity." What you agreed to on Monday may not feel so great on Friday, yet the obligation remains.

I have a tough message for you: obligations lie at the very core of our coexistence on this planet. People who cannot make and keep them will ultimately become the outcasts of their families and our society. They will fail at romance, marriage, and childrearing. They'll have patchy job histories, poor academics, and career stagnation. This in turn leads to loneliness, depression and hopelessness. Some folks even become self-harmful or adopt a sociopathic personality style.

Take a deep breath, dear reader. *None of this is inevitable.*

You can avoid the way of Lord Voldemort and Darth Vader by choosing a right path even when it's hard, acting intentionally, facing things head-on, and making and keeping obligations or renegotiating them honestly.

No, it's not easy. That's what makes it the right path.

Scratchy Noisy Stuff

Before I let you get too comfortable, there's a last annoyance many ADD people have—sensory discomfort. This includes scratchy tags, noises, certain textures on clothes or bed sheets, and ways of being touched. I met a client recently who shaves her forearms because she can't stand the feel of the hairs rubbing against her sleeves. Another is sensitive to chewing and keyboard clicks. In Chapter 10 Kylie describes her aversion to underwear.[15]

---

[15] This is not unique to ADD. For example, people with mild autism often struggle with tactile discomforts too.

Avoiding physically uncomfortable things isn't usually a big deal, as long as others understand you're not trying to be difficult with your idiosyncrasies. The exception is when avoiding them gets you in trouble or prevents you from accomplishing something, like going to class or work. For example, I'm sure the right to go commando is in our Constitution somewhere, except that doing so often violates a dress code or causes hygiene problems. Kylie actually got fired after two verbal warnings about going braless. "But I'm only a 32C!" was not considered a good excuse. She wouldn't wear anything to bed and refused to sleep under the sheets. Her roommates' boyfriends found this quite intriguing.

Her roommates did not. They kicked her out.

The Advantages of Having an Eye for Easy Paths

Despite my warnings on the dark side of easy paths, people with ADD can bring unique strengths to this table. Because you hate difficult or laborious things, you may strive to make your workflow faster, more efficient, and less boring. Just be certain your workarounds actually improve rather than degrade performance or work product. As I'll discuss in Chapter 10, making the right path easier can be pretty helpful when used wisely, and ADD people are wired to be good at finding ways to do that.

Perfectionistic ADD people are especially good at finding flaws in just about anything, and often lack the filters that make others hesitant to speak up. If you hone this natural talent and learn to use it diplomatically, you may become an asset to your employer by improving efficiency there, too. ADD people are good at the KISS principle (Keep It Simple, Stupid), and what boss wouldn't like to make things easier for employees so they get more work done?

Because people with ADD are quicker to move on to the next thing, you may suggest shutting down an idea that's not working, and moving on to something more productive. Just tread lightly. Systems, no matter how inefficient, are difficult to change, and even good ideas can create resentments and conflict. Others don't like to see their pet projects go down in flames, so tact is everything.

Principle 3: Make the Right Choice, Not the Easiest One

Choosing a right path over the easy one is an hourly chore, twenty-four hours a day, 365 days a year. All the while, comfortable avoidance calls out like a siren on the rocky shores, luring you in. Here are my tips for tolerating discomfort and seeking its wise guidance toward better choices.

Cognitively Override The Comfortable Choice. The key to choosing what's hard is to use everything you know about what's easy. Every time you're tempted to follow an easy path, remember this equation and how avoiding it has messed up your life before.

Hard Path → Easy Life.

Easy Path → Hard Life.

No doubt you have your own "easy" path disaster stories. Remember them and let them override your unhelpful comfort at the moment of truth—whenever you're tempted to toss your clothes on your roommate's bed, your keys where you won't find them, or your relationship under the bus.

Be Noticing. Observe the subtle behaviors your people appreciate, even if (and especially when) those behaviors annoy you. Whenever possible, push back your annoyance and do what they like. You'll end up with better, longer-lasting relationships. This is especially true of dating partners, but it also applies to family, friends, coworkers, and teachers.

Gary Chapman's *Five Languages of Love* offers a straightforward tool for becoming more noticing.[16] Chapman believes people feel most loved when we communicate through their preferred love language—gifts, words of affirmation, acts of service, quality time, or physical touch. To become more noticing, figure out your loved ones' language and interface with them around it. His books and website can help you figure that out.

Create Order. In a moment of serendipity, the day I entered the hyperlink for Dr. Chapman's work, he'd posted the following question from a reader on his blog: "I am a very orderly person and my husband is not. I am very frustrated having to always clean up after him. Suggestions?"

Sound familiar? It's probably a core issue in how you and your people deal with each other. In fact, every conversation with your mentor should involve how to push back chaos and replace it with order. That will never look like an anxious person's order, but it must be enough to get you organized. For example, when considering whether to put that dish in the dishwasher or toss it into the sink, think of how the easy choice turned out in the past. Dishes piling up on every level surface. Ants marching two by two. Your people yelling at you. The cat knocking the whole precarious stack onto the floor, breaking another glass. An hour spent sweeping up all the tiny shards.

Or how about this one. It's early in the morning and your alarm clock beckons you to a new day. The easy path here is called "snooze." In your sleepy, befuddled state, meditate on how it will turn out if you stay in bed. Let yourself experience the anxiety of being out of work or on academic probation. Remember what it was like when you bombed your last class or got

---

[16] www.5lovelanguages.com

written up by the boss. Tell yourself to get into the shower and see how it goes. Imagine actually surviving the morning. Once you're underway, you'll look back and wonder why you even hesitated.

If you still can't seem to beat your addiction to "snooze," check out my super alarm clock tips and other organizational ideas in Chapter 10.

Nothing alienates you from your people faster than blown obligations.

Treat Obligations with Respect. Nothing alienates you from your people faster than blown obligations. Let's take your romantic partner as an example. Everyone has to date different people before settling on a life partner. Don't be in a rush to make a romantic commitment, but once you do, stay true to your partner unless you clearly break off the relationship.

When an illicit romance knocks, think of your partner. Could you gain back his or her trust after cheating? Would it end the relationship? If you've already given up on that person, consider how others, especially future partners, will view you. Think of the names you'll be called behind your back because you cheated. Same for a job. Don't simply no-show one day and leave. Give your boss two weeks notice. This creates good karma.

Manage Procrastination. You'll never be rid of it, but you can learn to procrastinate more efficiently by using deadline anxiety to get things done. Create artificial deadlines with enough time in advance of the real deadline that you can procrastinate to the revised date and still be protected if anything goes wrong—and believe me, anything will. This works particularly well in high school and college or trade school, but it's applicable to any task that has a due date.

The best thing about this strategy is that it's self-rewarding. A few times relaxing while your friends freak out in the days leading up to their deadlines and you'll be convinced. You'll also get new material for future cognitive overrides.

Manage Perfectionism. Force yourself to take a chance and turn things in when they're "good enough." For example, if you're remodeling your home, don't let minor errors in drywall or paint cause you to give up. Override that urge and finish the job. You'll always notice little imperfections, because you know exactly where they are, but nobody else will. The same is true for homework and work product. Perfectionistic clients are always shocked when papers they thought weren't that great came back with a decent grade. Likewise, showing up for a test usually lands a better grade than giving up, and if that isn't true, re-read the paragraph on "snooze." There's a good chance you were doing too much of it during the semester.

If you resist relationships because you think you're not perfect enough or you'll never find anyone else perfect enough to be with, spend time meditating on radical acceptance—the idea that we must come to a peace about things that cannot be changed. Perfection is, by definition, unattainable, and its pursuit wastes both time and energy.

Let's say you have accepted living Here and Now, resolved to think before you act, and responded to Yoda's plea to follow the difficult and uncomfortable path. There will be no dark side for you. You're home free, right?

Not quite. Choosing wisely where you want to go is only half the battle. You also have to know how to make the decisions that will get you there. And they're not even the big, hairy ones you think they are.

CHAPTER 4

DECISIONS BIG AND SMALL

Sometimes it's the smallest decisions that can pretty much change your life forever.

— Felicity Porter in *Felicity*[17]

"I just want things to happen. I don't want to have to *make* them happen." Janessa smiled her perfect, toothy grin. "Is that too much to ask?"

It was easy to like Janessa. Everybody did. Almost eighteen, she was one of those ADD people whose energy fills a room. She was smart enough to pull Bs and Cs in one of the best public high schools in the state, but keeping her on medication had been tough and her grades directly correlated with her med compliance. She liked the main effects of Vyvanse, but the stimulant made her so serious that she no longer felt like cheering for her high school team.

This posed a problem, given that she was a cheerleader.

After some trial and error with her prescriber, we all agreed Janessa could take her full dosage three days a week, half a dose on cheer days, and nothing on Saturdays. She had to take a full dose on Sunday to finish leftover homework before 4:00 p.m. This strategy worked pretty well, but even on meds she had a hard time finishing anything.

Janessa's face squinched up into a pout as she described her college application. "It's just too much. I have to take the ACT, fill out that stupid FAFSA and then do like, volunteering, and write all sorts of essays. And then there are cheer try-outs for every school I've applied to. Senior year is supposed to be fun, but it's all just work, and that sucks."

---

[17] Screenplay by J.J. Abrams

"Well, Janessa." My voice was firm and direct as I spoke to a girl who'd been coached all her life. "I've got three words for you."

"Are they, 'You're totally screwed?'" She batted her eyelashes, comically.

"Nope. 'University of Kentucky.' You're this close to a full ride." I made a tiny space between my thumb and forefinger.

"I know." She sighed so deeply I couldn't believe she had that much lung capacity. "But getting it together is just so hard."

"Right. Big goals take patience—"

"And persistence and yada yada. I know. But we're talking about me, here. Follow-through isn't exactly my strong suit."

"How can that be? You run and jump and put so much effort into competitive cheer, but when it comes to something like this you're a click away from surrender. It's paperwork, girl. Not a forced march through Death Valley."

"I'm four-foot-eleven, Dr. Wes. I'm a flyer. Hot boys throw me in the air. All I have to do is be fearless, which we both know I am, and I have to make spirit fingers." She stretched and wiggled her fingers and mocked a cheer smile. "It's no thing."

"Oh, bull," I said. "I've seen you compete, Janessa. You're fierce out on the mat. I couldn't do it."

"You're fifty. Besides, I'm one of those girls who does like, nine crunches and gets perfect abs. These college applications are different. They're so hard I want to just give up and go to junior college."

"You certainly have that option."

"Seriously? What idiot would go to JUCO when she could get a scholarship to Kentucky?" She held up her hand, palm toward me. "Wait. Don't answer."

"I *am* going to answer." I leaned in toward her. "This is all about making decisions—"

"I told you, I already decided. I want to go to Kentucky so bad."

"Who cares, Janessa? Just deciding to go isn't going to get those papers filled out. Nor will it get you up every day and off to class or practice. Choosing to go to Kentucky isn't just one big decision. It's fifty little ones and hundreds more after you get there."

"I want to make those decisions. I mean, I'm trying."

"No, Janessa. Nobody's interested in what you *want*, or what you're *trying* to do. When you're at a meet, does your coach say, 'Hey, try and give me a good performance today, if you want to?'"

"No."

"So, tell me what you're *going to do*. Tell me you're going to choose to get online and register for the ACT today, and tomorrow you're going to choose to fill out the FAFSA, and next week you're going to write those essays and teach gymnastics to underprivileged kids. Make those choices or else those choices will make you. Then you really will be screwed."

A sweet smirk creased her lips. "Harsh much?"

"Sorry if it comes off that way."

"Don't be. You have to do what you have to do. And I have to do what I have to do."

"Which is?"

"A lot of boring crap that I hate." She sighed again. "Otherwise I'm at JUCO…which also means I'd be stuck with you for the next four years."

"We can't have that. I'm planning on you firing me in August."

Janessa popped off the couch as if dismounting the uneven bars, lifted both arms, and made spirit fingers. "Don't worry. You won't miss me too much next year. I'll be on ESPN!"

"I'll be watching."

Is This Chapter For Me?

Probably. People with ADD often do pretty well when making big decisions, like whether to go to college or get married. They have a harder time making the little ones. Do you or your people find that you:

- ❏ Generate big dreams, ideas, or goals, but fail to follow through on the behavioral details (like getting out of bed or going to work) that get them done?

- ❏ Have trouble choosing healthy goals and aspirations over problematic ones?

- ❏ Get overwhelmed imagining the many steps needed to reach a goal, and give up before you finish?

❏ Easily slip into hopelessness about your future or your ability to succeed there?

❏ Don't make decisions in an orderly, predictable way?

The problem of making small decisions can play out in numerous ways and you may not struggle with every item on this checklist. Or it might sound like a point-by-point description of your very existence. But if even one item applies to you, read on. At the heart of daily life, the only thing that guides us to success is the next choice we make. The better you get at making that choice, the further you'll get in life.

The Smallest Decisions

Fifteen years after its release, *Felicity* is still great TV. While it's weird to watch late teens talk on phones with cords, it's still a smart college primer. The small decision Felicity mentions in the opening quote involved nothing more than asking classmate Ben to sign her yearbook at high school graduation. Before that, the closest she'd ever gotten to Ben was holding a pint of his blood during a plasma drive. Yet, instead of just signing her book, Ben plops down on the football field and starts writing about how he's watched her through four years of high school, wondering what this quiet, thoughtful girl was really like, and that he's always admired her.

He signs off, "Love Ben."

"And suddenly," Felicity narrates, "I knew what everyone else was feeling."

In response, she does the obvious—at least in TV land. She goes home, dumps her scholarship-funded admission to Stanford and follows Ben to New York University, as her slack-jawed parents watch her being sucked through a vortex into an alternative dimension. The four-year series emerges from that single moment, documenting Felicity's many humorous, agonizing missteps.

Wishing and Wanting

Have you ever sat down and thought about what it means to *want?* Probably not, yet almost every choice we make comes from wanting something or someone. Wanting is the desire to attain something that brings survival, meaning, pleasure, or substance to life. It's both the trigger for setting a goal and the motivation for attaining it. You can want something small, like a cute guy to sign your yearbook, or big, like moving to New York to date him.

Janessa wanted something really big, to cheer for the University of Kentucky, one of the top squads in the nation. She also knew that while college cheer might fund a good education, it rarely leads to a career, and when it does it won't last long. So, she decided to major in exercise science and go into physical therapy because she liked working with trainers in high school. All in all, Janessa had a good plan, exactly the opposite of David in Chapter 3.

What could possibly go wrong?

This: I've come to understand that people with ADD don't want in the same way as the rest of us do. Once we have the spark of a great idea, we consider the costs and benefits and decide if it's doable and worth pursuing.

People with ADD don't want in the same way as the rest of us do.

If it is, we develop a step-by-step plan, and then move forward one step at a time. We don't always reach our goals, but we learn a lot about reaching them, even when we fall short. We see failure as an annoying teacher, not a feared enemy. For ADD people, wanting is more like a wish made upon a star, a statement of how you'd like things to be, without much consideration of how to make it happen.

I'm not a Buddhist, but I think they have much to say about wanting. Buddhists see *craving* (what I call "wishing") as the cause of suffering, something to be eliminated on the path to Nirvana. In contrast, Buddhists see the desire for wholesome things as liberating and enhancing to our lives. They encourage us to direct our desire toward attaining skillful qualities and to abandon unhelpful ones. This kind of wanting is the spark within each of us that opens our eyes to a problem to be solved or a goal to be achieved, and energizes a solution.

I've come to see "wholesome wanting" as meeting three criteria:

- **Realism.** You are reasonably likely to reach the goal of your desire by following a step-by-step plan.

- **Substance.** If you reach your goal, it's likely to produce something of meaning, value, and necessity, however you define those terms.

- **Ethics.** The goal and the process for reaching it treats you, your people, and your society honestly and respectfully. More on that in Chapter 9.

Anybody can *want* to go to college, but not everyone *solves the problem* of going to college, much less graduating. It's like that in marriage too, or in any marital-style relationship. You can't just say "I do" on your wedding day or declare your exclusivity in dating and be done. You have to get up every day and choose to be in your relationship. It's a problem to be solved one day to the next. Some days that's a wonderful problem. Other days, not so much.

The same goes for having children. For most people, making babies is much easier than getting married. And it's fun. It hardly requires a choice. But children are not bundles of joy and parenting requires constant problem solving, decision making, and permanent obligation. You can't break up with your kids or drop out of their lives when you get tired of them. Actually, you can choose to do that, but would it be responsible and ethical?

I'm not saying you shouldn't have kids. I know many ADD people who are great parents. It's from them that I've learned a lot about how different it is to want children and to raise them. I'm just suggesting you delay starting a family until you've mastered most of these principles in your own life. Then you'll be ready to master them with your kids.

On Keeping On Keeping On

Whether we're talking about school, work, marriage, parenting, or learning to ride a donkey, two words describe what it takes to succeed: persistence and patience.

Persistence means sticking with it until you reach your goal, even when that gets uncomfortable and hard. Sometimes you'll change your plan. Occasionally, you'll change the goal. But you'll keep striving for a right path, solving all the little problems as they arise, even when you want to give up.

Patience is more complicated than you think. It doesn't just mean waiting without complaint. It means delaying an immediate reward in order to get something better or taking time to think through your options.

Persistence and patience are the Holy Grail of intentional living—what people with ADD most envy in the non-ADD crowd. Or, as Janessa put it, "Follow-through isn't exactly my strong suit." This isn't a new idea. In the fourth century BC, Plato argued in *The Republic* that individual desires must be postponed in the name of higher ideals.

In 1972, Stanford researchers offered a marshmallow to a group of preschoolers, then told them they'd get a second one later, if they could resist eating the first. The scientists recorded how long each child resisted and then followed the subjects for many years thereafter. Guess what? The longer the child held out that day, waiting for that ridiculous second marshmallow, the more successful he or she was later in life[18]. While this wasn't a study of ADD people, or at least the researchers didn't intend it to be, it illustrates why patience is magic. It also shows how persistent people overcome discomfort. Some children covered their eyes with their hands or turned around so that

---

[18] Mischel, Walter; Ebbe B. Ebbesen, Antonette Raskoff Zeiss (1972). "Cognitive and attentional mechanisms in delay of gratification.". *Journal of Personality and Social Psychology* 21 (2): 204–218. Available at psycnet.apa.org/journals/psp/21/2/204/

they couldn't see the marshmallow. Others start kicking the desk, tugging on their hair, or stroking the marshmallow "like a tiny stuffed animal."

If patience and persistence are uncomfortable for everyone, they can be excruciating for people with ADD. For example, in middle and high school many kids with ADD start skipping class in seventh or eighth grade because they see school as difficult, boring, and pointless. Many describe it as intolerably painful. Some have social problems because they don't read social cues. Others feel stupid and ineffective because they can't learn the way others do. So they "eat their marshmallow," so to speak, and run.

Sometimes well-meaning teachers and parents contribute to their pain by telling ADD kids they're lazy, irresponsible, or not trying. In twenty-two years I've never known anyone who felt motivated after hearing something like this, though I've known a few who succeeded just to prove others wrong.

The easy path for many kids with more severe ADD is to drop out. Others stay but zone out, get stoned, cheat, or do as little as possible to get through each assignment. A bunch of those kids—maybe you were one of them— imagine the problem to be the way school is organized or taught. Who can blame them? Educational systems are designed for a fairly narrow group of students, and those with ADD aren't usually a great fit. Likewise, schools may demonize tracking programs that could help these teens to find their own unique paths, focusing instead on the arguable value of Advanced Calculus and Physics.

All this dropping out doesn't end in high school. Forty-six percent of U.S. college freshman won't finish in six years,[19] and many never will. Some run out of money or choose a different path, but most just don't get up each day and make the choice to be in school.

For teens who don't finish a diploma and more education, the transition to adulthood is tough. From my chair, nothing is sadder than a high school dropout who goes straight to work at seventeen. I'm not talking about working a couple of years before college or technical school. That can work great, especially for kids with ADD. I'm talking about a late teen with no plan. A GED or alternative school diploma isn't competitive in today's workforce. Long gone are the days when factory work was abundant, and today's manufacturing jobs often require technical skill. Working construction is great when you're twenty-one. As you pass forty, your body won't hold up and any injury can leave you without a way to make a living.

---

[19] www.huffingtonpost.com/2013/01/24/college-dropout-crisis-american-dream-20_n_2538311.html

So, think hard before leaving high school, and if you're hell-bent on dropping out, make a plan for alternative education in one of the "gold-collar" careers I describe later in this chapter. If school isn't your thing, one of them might fit you perfectly and keep you from living out your twenties in your parents' basement.

Hope and Hopelessness

Why is it hard for people with ADD to want in a patient and persistent manner? What stops you from achieving what you first set out to do?

Hope.

Successful wanting depends a lot on how hopeful we are. From a psychological perspective, hope means having the will and the way to get what you want. The late C.R. Snyder[20], a favorite professor of mine, studied hope at the University of Kansas. Shane Lopez, PhD, also one of Snyder's students, published an excellent book on the same subject.[21] They propose that hope is comprised of three things, all of which are relevant to your journey with ADD.

- **Goals.** We imagine objects, experiences, or outcomes ranging from complete impossibilities to sure things. These become the targets of our wanting.

- **Willpower.** How we think about our goals and the mental energy we have to achieve them. Do we believe our goals are attainable? Will getting what we want be useful? Do we have the patience and persistence to get there? If so, we have willpower.

- **Waypower.** It's great to believe in yourself, but if you have no plan or your plan is flawed, you're back to wishing and not wanting. Waypower is the mental plan that guides us to our goals.

Though Snyder wasn't studying ADD people, his thoughts align nicely with what I've learned in treating them. In Chapter 3, David lacked waypower. He had no plan. In this chapter, Janessa had an awesome plan but lacked willpower, noting rather poetically, "I just want things to happen. I don't want to have to *make* them happen."

Perhaps you don't set realistic goals or you lack the mental energy to reach them. Maybe you get overwhelmed imagining the many steps needed to succeed and give up before you begin. Or maybe you start toward a goal, only

---

[20] Snyder, C.R. (2003) Psychology of Hope: You Can Get Here from There

[21] Lopez, Shane (2013) Making Hope Happen: Create The Future You Want for Yourself and Others.

to wander off on something totally different. After a series of such failures, you may decide it's too difficult to strive for something better.

We call that feeling hopeless.

You may use this word to express your deep sadness at your lack of progress in life, or your bitterness at not being understood in that struggle. "Hopeless" may also be used by others as a way to label and disconnect from you, as in, "That guy is hopeless, don't even try."

Kind of depressing, isn't it? Over the years, I've seen many undiagnosed ADD people treated for depression by a family doctor, without improvement. Some got more depressed because medications for depression also lower anxiety and with it the energy to care enough to succeed.

In contrast, thousands of times over twenty-two years my clients have found the right stimulant medication for ADD and began to recognize the possibility of accomplishment. Some describe it as if clouds had cleared from their minds. Others could finally imagine a goal and how to get there. Most said it helped them persist until they completed a project or reached a goal.

I recently had a nice young student with a 1.8 cumulative college GPA score a 3.9 in her junior fall semester after going on medication. She decided to stay an extra year in college to pull up her grades and apply to graduate school. "This is the first time in my life that I really love learning," she said. "I finally think I can do something with my life." That was an awesome day in my office. You too can have a day like that, or many of them.

The Advantages of Thinking Big

Sometimes, focusing on all the steps it takes to get to a goal actually gets in the way of big thinking. People with ADD can be great at imagination and goal-setting, even if you struggle to attain what you want. Maybe you're an "idea person," someone who prefers to delegate the details of how to actually accomplish an ambition. Smart employers can use you to brainstorm a project, then move you on to the next big thing while the anxious-leaners bring your vision to fruition. If you get that far in you own career, this arrangement could be ideal.

Some people with ADD, like Janessa, benefit from a carefree, impetuous decisional style. Maybe you're a trial-and-error person, confident in choosing new things or following a different path, even if you haven't thought it all through. Your spontaneity may inspire others toward a spirit of adventure, and your ability to "just let go" can offer balance to those who are more cautious or serious than necessary.

Principle 4: The Most Important Decisions Are the Small Ones

It is in the nature of life that there are about a hundred ways to fail at most things and about three or four ways to succeed. Here are my tips for doing less failing and more succeeding:

Consider Life a Series of Problems in Search of Solutions. Making good choices is harder than I make it sound, but it's not nearly as hard as you think it is. And it's a whole lot easier than making bad ones. So, add the following equations to your tattoo list, or at least insert them into the notes on your phone:

Good Decisions = Liberation and A Better Life

Bad Decisions = Your Mom's Basement

Persistence + Patience = Success

While we're pretending to do math, let's try a word problem. Think of your goal as Y and what you'll need to do to reach it as X. At the end of each day, solve for X by asking yourself what you've done to reach goal Y. Occasionally, your X will be big, but it will usually be one small step or two. If you find that X equals nothing that day, get up tomorrow and make it count. If you can't even come up with a good Y, then you're spending too much time wishing. Find a mentor, fast, and…

Set a Goal. Brainstorm ideas and let your mentor make suggestions and offer feedback and critique. This may be hard on your ego, because only a few of your ideas will add up. But it will be a lot easier for others to spot those than it will be for you. Your mentor won't always be available, particularly for lesser goals, so ask yourself, "Would he or she approve of this goal or decision?" Once you've spent enough time with a mentor, you can predict this easily. You can also ask yourself, "Would I advise my best friend to set this goal or make this choice?"

Determine If Your Goal Is Attainable. Janessa wouldn't have had a shot at a University of Kentucky scholarship if her competitive cheer wasn't really strong. A lot of young people with ADD start off with fun goals like becoming a video game designer or winning *The Voice*. That happens, but not very often. It's more likely you'll be struck by lightning. Instead, set an achievable goal and focus on that, while striving for higher aspirations in your spare time. I want to publish a bestselling novel, but I won't quit my day job to pursue it. It's the rare author who makes that kind of money and keeps making it.

Do A Cost-Benefit Analysis. List all the reasons to try something on the left side of a page and all the reasons not to on the right side. In thinking about going to Kentucky, Janessa had about fifteen pros and cons. She rated "far from home" -4 and "making new friends" a +3. She gave "chance to be on

ESPN" a +10 and "working sunup to sundown" a -8, and so on. When she added everything up, Kentucky scored a +5 and JUCO a -6.

After you get good at this, you'll find the numbers rarely lie.

Make Every Choice An Authentic One. Real choice requires at least two valid options, both of which deserve serious consideration. For example, staying married really means that you are choosing marriage over divorce. You have to see divorce as an authentic choice in order to decide to remain married. The same is true of college or trade school. You shouldn't go simply because you don't know what else to do or your parents say you should. That's not a real choice. It's an edict.

On the other hand, people with ADD often overcomplicate decisions by imagining they have more choices than they do. This can emerge from your creative, out-of-the-box thinking. More often it comes from the inability to sort things down to their core components. Believe it or not, most decisions can be reduced down to a series of binary, yes/no choices. There is no "maybe." That's the decision-making equivalent of "try" and "want."

Here's an example of how Janessa thought through her college decision:

- "Am I ready to go to college?" Yes.

- "Am I ready to live at an out-of-state college?" Yes.

- "Is Kentucky where I want to spend four years of college?" Yes.

- "Would I be more satisfied at JUCO without the stress of maintaining my cheer scholarship and GPA in exercise science?" No.

- "Will I register for the ACT?" Yes.

- "Will I complete the application materials?" Yes.

Some decisions are better made using a "pairwise comparison" model, in which you put two options up against each other and choose the better one. Here's how Janessa could put that model to work:

- "State school versus JUCO?" State school.

- "Big NCAA school or small four-year college?" NCAA all the way!

- "Kentucky versus USC?" Kentucky.

Sometimes you have a long list of options. Create a "card sort." Write down every possibility (e.g., the colleges on your top-ten list or the five cars you're considering buying) on index cards. Then pair each card with another, compare, and choose the winner. Then move the winning card forward in the deck until your choices are in perfect rank order.

If there are several variables to measure—cost, distance, excitement, impact on career, time away from home—make each of these a category and sort according to that variable. For Janessa, Kentucky on a full-ride scholarship would put that college at the top of her cost list. But cheering all the time might put "career impact" several cards down in that category because she'd be less focused on her education.

No matter how you do it, organize your decisions toward authentic, binary choice. Otherwise, you'll find yourself submerged under a pile of pseudo-options and, more often than not, avoiding the real choices you do have.

Know Your Limits. Once motivated, people with ADD may impulsively bite off more than they can chew, from how many events they put in their daily planner to the size and number of projects they start at work or school. That just sets you up to fail. A lot of this is neurological, but it also comes from parents telling kids, "You can do anything you set your mind to." That sounds inspirational, but it's nonsense. Not everyone is good at math or science or English. But everyone is good at something.

Find a career expert to assess your talents and aptitudes or check out the many websites that offer self-help aptitude testing[22]. They sometimes come up with whacky suggestions—Katie my honor student line editor, took an aptitude test in high school and learned she was perfectly suited to window washing. So, just use them for brainstorming career options, not as a well-washed window to your inner soul. Only after you know your limits can you...

Stretch Your Limits. Maximize what you're able to achieve by pushing a *little* farther than you think you can. In Chapter 7, we'll meet Melissa, an ADD client who got a nursing degree. It took her seven years and three tries at her board exam, but she pushed herself beyond anyone's expectations—not by wishing or dreaming, but by solving for X every day.

If college isn't your thing, there are many alternative forms of education that lead to what are being called "gold-collar" jobs because they're paying off better than many of the careers four-year colleges offer. Even if you drop out of high school, you can get a diploma or GED through an adult education center. Then you can attend JUCO or a trade school for cosmetology, electrical wiring, heating and air conditioning (HVAC), welding, information technology, car repair, truck driving, computer repair, or entry-level nursing. These are high-demand careers in and of themselves, but you can also use them as platforms to finance further education.

---

[22] www.quintessentialcareers.com

Pace Yourself. You'll have to make many authentic choices on the way to reaching any goal. But if you try and think them all through at once, you'll get overwhelmed. When solving for X, pace yourself by choosing achievable short-term objectives:

- "I will get up today and go to class and reward myself with an Americano with half and half for my effort."

- "I will say one nice thing to my dating partner today to make him or her feel good."

- "I'm going to arrive early three out of five days so the boss sees that I'm dedicated."

- "I will talk with my mentor about something hard today, rather than let him set the agenda."

Big goals with small objectives always win.

Another way to manage your pace is to take breaks from the march to your goal. These can be small, like taking ten minutes off after fifty minutes of studying. Or they can be large, like taking a gap year from college when you're just not feeling it. The secret is to either do something that's time-limited (e.g., take a shower, eat a snack, join AmeriCorps) or to set a timer so you don't get distracted. It's rarely wise to start a video game or TV show during your break, as that ten minutes can easily stretch to an hour or more. If you're going to take time off from school, be careful that you don't get into a well-paying, dead-end career you'll grow to hate after you've missed your chance to easily re-enter college or trade school.

Taking breaks may slow your progress, but in most cases it's better to be the tortoise than the hare. Used correctly, a break makes it more likely you'll persist once you return to your goal, refreshed and ready to succeed.

Banish "Try" and "Want." Master Yoda famously advised an indecisive Luke Skywalker, "Do or do not. There is no try."[23] Put that on your tattoo list. As I discussed with Janessa, "try" and "want" are verbal dodges. Here are some examples of how to change your words and therefore your thinking to become more goal-directed and intentional:

- "I'll try and get to class (or work) on time this week" becomes, "I'm going to set two alarms, each ten minutes earlier than usual, so I won't sleep in and can get to class early."

---

[23] Star Wars: Episode V: The Empire Strikes Back (1980)

- "I want to start talking to Jesse this week, but I don't know what to say" becomes, "I'll figure out what Jesse likes this week. Then, when we start talking, I'll know what to say."

- "I want to try and turn in some job applications this week" becomes, "I'll fill out a minimum of one application per day for the next week and preferably two."

Eliminating two little words may seem like a Jedi mind trick, but words are magic. They create their own stories by how we use them. For people with ADD, stories that start with "try" and "want" usually end with "didn't."

Never Make Life-Altering Decisions While Altered. Substance abuse does not promote good choices. Quite the opposite, in fact. I realize people like to party, but those with ADD have more trouble with impulsivity to begin with. Adding a little booze, weed, or narcotics won't improve your judgment.

Because partying and dating overlap, altered decision making is especially serious when it comes to sex. You've heard that (un)funny quip about "beer goggles" letting drunk people overestimate a potential partner's attractiveness? Even less funny is the way alcohol fuels impaired-consent sexual encounters and overt acts of rape. And then there's the problem of drunk driving, which kills 10,000 people a year in the U.S.[24] and injures tens of thousands more. As we discussed, driving is a perfect metaphor for what it means to focus and make decisions from moment to moment. You can't do it well if you're drunk, let alone ADD and drunk.

Unfortunately, this awesome bit of advice asks you to make the decision to avoid making a decision while your decision-making is impaired. So, take a wingman or woman on any party excursion, one who will stay sober or, at the very least, keep a one- or two-drink maximum early in the evening. I realize this seems old-school in an age of teen and young-adult binge drinking, but if a trusted friend keeps you out of decision-making trouble (or jail), things will go much better in the long run. Next weekend, you can return the favor.

Document Your Success. Everyone needs a reward in order to stay encouraged, especially people with ADD. So, when you do something well, celebrate. You might take a picture of your achieved goal with your smartphone and look at it whenever you're feeling hopeless. Many of my clients love checklists for the same reasons. List your objectives, large or small, and check them off one by one until you hit your goal. Then keep the list and bask in its glory, a reminder that you really can finish something.

---

[24] National Highway Traffic Safety Administration FARS data, 2013

Build A House (or A Life). Let's walk through a successful goal, plan, and execution from my own life to illustrate many of these tips. One day I decided to build an addition on my home. I wanted a two-car garage so I could convert the existing garage into a shop. I decided to add space on the master bedroom and a large room for my model railroad. All this came out to a 1400-square-foot structure. That's the size of a small house. Here's how I did it:

- **Ability Assessment.** I'd built a garage on an earlier house and was pretty good with a framing hammer. I owned almost every saw made. But I'd never attempted to build anything with two stories. After watching the pros build a couple of houses, I was pretty sure I could do it. However, I did not want to do the concrete. That's aggravating for anyone but a pro, and you get exactly one chance to make it right. I knew my limits and concrete was at the top of that list.

- **Goal-Setting.** I worked with an architect to develop a blueprint that was manageable with my skills. That formed a visual image of my goal.

- **Small Objectives.** I never stopped to consider how gigantic this project really was, so I never became overwhelmed by the big bite I'd taken. I just took the project one decision at a time and solved for X every day. I avoided setting a long-term deadline and thus took unnecessary pressure off myself. I got up every morning and asked myself, "What do I need to do to make my day?"[25] When I reached that objective, I took a shower, quit on a happy note and went to the office. Even if I had time left over, I stopped working while I was ahead, lest I get myself into something sticky that would worry me the rest of the day.

- **Break.** I framed my addition, roofed it, and finished the exterior. Then I had kids, quit my job, opened a business, and wrote my first book. I couldn't afford the time or money to finish the interior. After a six-year break, it took me two years to wire the building and finish the drywall up to code. The whole project took about twice as long as I'd expected, but it came out even better than I'd imagined.

- **Reward.** When I finished, I stood back and looked at what I'd done. My jaw dropped. Several people asked, "How did you build that all by yourself?" One said, "Man, I knew you were building a

---

[25] "Making your day" is a term used in the film industry. If you "make your day," it means you're staying on your filming schedule.

garage, but I didn't know it was so grandiose." At our last meeting, my building inspector, an electrical engineer, declared, "Wow, I couldn't have done this."

You can apply this same formula to any large goal you want to achieve, as well as the many small ones you're likely to encounter each day.

As we close this chapter, it's worth noting that you can't *not* make a decision. *Not* making a decision is making a decision. Yet four or five times a week I'm coaching an ADD client on this topic, only to get the response, "Oh, let's just wait and see what happens." That might sound like a thoughtful, reflective approach, but it's really just another form of procrastination and avoidance.

Now that you understand the first four principles, let's dig deeper into the many obstacles that trip up ADD people in making them work. We'll start with the biggest stumbling block of all.

Your heart.

CHAPTER 5

FOLLOW YOUR HEART?

The heart is deceitful above all things and beyond cure. Who can understand it?

— Jeremiah 17:9[26]

"Just let me try and get this straight, Sienna." Her plan spun around my brain like a spiral staircase going nowhere. "You're moving to Portland to live in a tent city?"

"Yep. The city sponsors it. You can look it up online." She nodded toward my laptop, her long dreadlocks bouncing with the energy of her latest inspiration. "It's safe there and we each have, like a task that we perform for the community."

It only took a moment on Google to find it. The photos reminded me of the government-sponsored camps Steinbeck described in *Grapes of Wrath*, except in high-definition color. I looked up from the screen and shook my head. "This is for homeless people."

"Well, yeah."

"Except you're not homeless. Or in Portland. You live here, with a girlfriend who's rather nice, if you want my opinion."

"Not as nice as you seem to think. Sophie is always getting on me."

"Right. Because you're basically a twenty-two-year-old kept woman. Sophie feels used. What does Sophie think about this whole—"

---

26 New International Version

"I have a friend who hitchhiked to Portland. She says it's really nice."

"I'm sure this tent city is lovely." I gave her my zany, one-eyebrow-up-one-down look. I'd practiced it in the mirror for just such occasions. "But what exactly are you going to do once you get there? I mean with your life."

"Hey dude, it was *your* idea for me to drop out of college." Her blue eyes sparkled as a tight little smile creased her lips. "My mom is still mad at you for that one."

"It was my idea for you to take *a break* until you were serious about school. You had a 130 IQ and a 1.6 GPA. You were about to sign another $10,000 in student loans. What did your mom think of those numbers?"

"She thought I should have buckled down." Sienna mimicked a stern voice I knew her mother didn't have.

"Great. When you're ready to do that, college will be waiting, along with a lot of dollars that weren't spent to fail. Back on topic. Your parents have been really fair. They gave Sophie six months' worth of your expenses to tide her over. But everyone just wants to know your next move."

"I told you. Hitchhike to Portland this spring when it's warmer."

"And do what?" I pounded out the words, somewhere between doubtful and chagrined. "I hear lots of running away and not much doing."

"It's always do do do with you, isn't it?" She twisted one dread around the other. "I just want to *be* there. Feel truly alive for once. Seek my bliss."

"That's a poem, Sienna."

"I knew you'd be all sour about it." She puckered her mouth like she'd eaten a lemon. "I want to be like Alexander Supertramp in that book *Into the Wild.*"

"Dead in an abandoned bus in Alaska?"

"You are not listening to me." Sienna exaggerated her articulation as if I was hard of hearing. "It is in Portland. There is no bus. I will not be dead."

"You haven't actually read *Into the Wild*, have you?"

"I have, thank you." She stuck out her tongue and then giggled. "But the ending isn't the point of the book. It's about the freedom he felt and every-thing he experienced. He lived his life to the fullest and then he wrote about it—"

"In a journal, which, you may recall, they found in the abandoned bus next to his body. Then people other than that guy made a million billion dollars off of it. Talk about ADD. Actually, Alexander would have died a lot sooner if not for the kindness of strangers who gave him whatever he didn't stop to realize he needed. And in return, he disregarded any obligation he formed with them, or with his family. He just cast aside everyone who cared for him."

"It was his journey." Her voice carried the gravitas of a National Geographic narrator. "He had to follow his heart or else he'd end up just another cog in someone else's machine."

"Look, Sienna, all young people go on a journey and make mistakes along the way, but this Portland thing isn't like that at all. It's just avoidance. You're not running toward anything, just away."

"Why are you so against me doing what makes me happy?"

"Living in a homeless shelter makes you happy? Really?"

"Well…" Her expression changed, no longer sunny. She bowed her head and dropped her hands to her lap. "You just don't understand. It's like torture."

"What is?"

"Living in your world."

"Which is what to you?" I softened my voice to match hers.

"It's like you, or I mean, all adults. You have to get up every single day and go to the same job and do the same thing all the time and when I think about even putting in an application for what amounts to job hell, I just can't do it. It hurts so much to even think about it." She touched her fingers to her temples, as if pushing back a migraine.

"So, you'll follow your heart to a tent city to avoid doing what's hard?" I kept my tone neutral. "You think that will be easier than living like we do, with obligations and expectations?"

"It can't be any worse."

"I understand."

"Do you?" She gazed up. "Are you being serious?

"Yes. Except this really is how people become homeless. It may seem like an adventurous way to avoid things that are hard for you, but this tent city isn't a commune. It's a shelter for people who've hit hard times or can't do for themselves. You can do for yourself. Nothing can shelter you from the world, Sienna. You live here and now, not Woodstock in 1969."

"Hippies had it so good." Her voice yearned. "They just smoked and made love, and shared what they had, and listened to The Mamas and The Papas."

"And grew up and became lawyers and stockbrokers and are now retiring in Boca Raton. This isn't a revival of *Hair*, and 'follow your heart' is about the worst idea ever."

"You're saying that nobody can just go with their gut? Seriously?" She stared at me with a mix of shock and scorn. "God, not even you are that practical...or boring."

"I am exactly that practical, and boring is in the eye of the beholder. Actually, some people can go with their instincts. You're just not one of them."

"Thanks." The sadness crept back into her voice, and instantly I missed her stubborn feistiness. "My gut only leads to Portland, huh?"

I nodded. "So you say."

"There's just nothing else I want to do. It sucks so much to be this way."

"Don't abandon hope yet, Sienna. I'm sure we can find things you do like to do that actually draw a paycheck. Probably not a normal 9-to-5 job, but lots of people with ADD find their niche."

"And you're totally sure that a tent city doesn't count as a niche?" She mocked a hopeful, wide-eyed look.

"Only if you're a Girl Scout."

Is This Chapter For Me?

Maybe. For people with ADD, following your heart is often a matter of degree. Some people get away with it and others don't, depending on where and how far one journeys before his or her brain kicks in. As always, people who are also anxious limit themselves more than non-anxious ADD people, so they can trust their hearts a bit more. In determining how much your heart is getting you into trouble, ask yourself and your people the following questions:

- ❏ Do you act on emotion and later regret it?
- ❏ Do you make choices (like falling in love or spending money) simply because they feel good?
- ❏ Do you feel your way into something and then think your way out, or vice versa?
- ❏ Do you find yourself more confused than others seem to be about how you feel, or do others find your feelings confusing?

- ❏ Are you very emotional in some situations and kind of cold in others, making it hard (even for you) to know which way you'll lean at any given moment?
- ❏ Do most of the reliable people in your life tell you that your dreams are unrealistic?

If any of these apply, this chapter is for you. I've met many people with ADD for whom this was only a minor problem. For quite a few others, heart-following leads to a lifelong obstacle course of stumbling blocks.

Two Styles of Decision Making

There are two styles of problem solving and decision making that appear in nearly every theory of personality. The first is based on emotion, the second on thought. They're pretty evenly distributed across the general population, and people can usually tell you which style they prefer.

There's nothing good or bad about having one style or the other. It's just who you are. People pick up these styles early in life and get better at using them as they grow up. There's no gender difference. Men and women may express an emotion-based style differently, but women are not more prone to emotion, nor men to logic.

You may have taken the Myers-Briggs Type Sorter (MBTS) or similar test for school or business. If not, you should. It's a fun way to know more about your personality and way more accurate than a horoscope. The MBTS drops you neatly into one of sixteen categories with initials like INTJ or ESFP. It's one of the best-known personality models and, sure enough, it includes feeling/thinking among its four domains. That's what F and T stand for.

Emotion-based decision makers use instinct to feel their way toward a solution, then apply well-honed skills at trial and error to test out their ideas. The advice to "follow your heart" makes sense to them and they know how to use it. Thought-based folks use reason and prediction to consider all sides of a situation before deciding how to proceed. They think anything to do with the heart sounds like frou-frou.

"I know where you're headed," you say, a look of triumph in your eyes. "People with ADD are emotion-based because they aren't as intentional as non-ADD people. Sienna yearned to follow her heart, even if it took her over a cliff. Alexander Supertramp didn't seem to give much thought to anything. Right?"

Nice guess, but no. I find people with ADD tend to be "ambitent," a wonderful but obscure psychological term drawn from The Rorschach Inkblot Test. It means a person has a mixture of both emotion- and a thought-based coping styles. Read all about ambitence in the work of the late John Exner, PhD and colleagues, the world's foremost experts on the Rorschach.

As personalities go, ambitence sounds like the ultimate level of cool—equally balanced between two valuable problem solving styles, able to flex back and forth. It's not. To make solid, efficient decisions, people need to favor one primary style. While it's normal to switch back and forth occasionally as the need arises, that's not what happens with ambitent people. They vacillate between styles in an unpredictable and inefficient manner. They think their way into situations and feel their way out, and then, on a different occasion, feel their way in and think their way out. That confuses them and their people with a hodgepodge of disconnected choices and ideas. Who knows what they'll do next?

This connection between ADD and ambitence is mostly a Dr. Wes-ism, based on clinical experience rather than research. There's a very small body of dissertation data to support this connection, but nothing conclusive[27]. I've explained these two styles to hundreds of people in therapy and asked them which they think they are. I didn't define or even mention ambitence. Non-ADD people could usually identify their primary style, and their people usually agreed. Most ADD people either felt like a mix-up of both, or couldn't decide which one fit them better. In fact, many felt like I'd plugged a USB drive into their heads and downloaded the secret of how they made decisions, or how they didn't make them. Their friends or romantic partners rarely differed.

Who Can Understand the Heart?

Like Sienna, ADD people love catchy advice like "follow your heart," "chase your bliss," or "pursue your dreams." That sounds so stirring and looks great on a poster. But it doesn't encourage you to want in the wholesome, intentional way the Buddhists propose or in the hopeful way Snyder and Lopez describe. It sort of suggests having the *will* to reach a goal, but it doesn't include any *way*. For people with ADD, "follow

> *Your brain may be imperfect but it's the only tool you have to make good decisions.*

your heart" just validates a restless, impulsive approach to life that won't take you anywhere. So, to be really successful, you'll have to pretend to be a thought-based decision maker in every choice you make.

"Wait a second," you say. "You just spent fifty-six pages telling me that I have a neurological disorder. Now you're asking me to listen to my brain? You haven't looked inside there lately, have you?"

---

[27] If you're a doctoral student, email me. I'd like to see this get closer examination because I think it's critical to understanding how ADD people make or don't make decisions.

That's my story, and I'm sticking to it. Your brain may be imperfect and even unreliable at times, but it's the only tool you have to make good decisions. So the goal in treating ADD is to improve how your brain makes choices while giving your heart, and its many whims, its place. Which brings us quite nicely to…

The Advantages of Inspiration

Let's return to Sienna's story to illustrate what joys the heart may truly bring. She did not hitchhike to Portland, which was fortunate, because a year later, her hitchhiking buddy had a scary incident on the road. Sienna instead enrolled in a government-subsidized art training program where she learned to make artisan jewelry. She saved money from her stipend and travelled to Africa to work in an orphanage for six months. Neither of these choices seemed logical. Jewelry makers rarely earn enough money to cover living expenses and Africa cost her $4,000. It would have been more profitable to go back to college and major in engineering.

But guess what? I applauded Sienna for both endeavors, because while each started from a heartfelt impulse, both ended up as well-planned, productive experiences. She took a real journey of growth, learning, and service that gave her a new perspective on life and how to live it. It's also worth noting that she was in her early twenties at the time. Had she a spouse, children, or a career, I would have offered different advice.

So that's what your heart is good for: inspiration, ideas, flashes of brilliance. Or insanity.

It all depends on whether what your heart is telling you to do *makes any sense* to your brain. Listen to your heart, then train your brain to evaluate if its inspiration constitutes a wholesome want or a random impulse. That's what we call "executive function"—the deliberate control you exert over what you think, feel, and do.

Like Sienna, many folks with ADD live nonconventional lives that stretch their limits. I wouldn't include a tent city or abandoned bus on anyone's bucket list, but a trip to Africa, a summer in AmeriCorps or the Peace Corps, or a year backpacking in Europe could offer a lifetime's worth of inspiration. Most of us are not so bold. We go down a narrow path and perhaps, later in life, regret it. We envy the ADD people their passion.

Some people with ADD are tremendously successful precisely because they channel flashes of inspiration into successful enterprises. Sir Richard Branson, the guy behind Virgin Records, Virgin Airlines, and every other Virgin offshoot, is a good example. Some make tons of money in the entertainment industry off their heartfelt exuberance. Examples include Zooey Deschanel, Bill Cosby, Jim Carrey, Howie Mandel, and Justin Timberlake. All have ADD.

Political guru James Carville does, too. He dreamed of making a president out of Bill Clinton before anyone imagined that George Bush, Sr. could lose the 1992 election. Carville takes a lot of heat for his inability to keep his mouth shut when an impulse strikes, but that same spirit gave him the edge when he needed it. And his opponents fear him for it.

Principle 5: Never Blindly Follow Your Heart

If you have ADD, you'll have a thousand heartfelt inspirations a day. Okay, I'm exaggerating. Let's just say a bunch. Enjoy them. But know they can be quite deceptive and even dangerous if left unchecked by your mind. Nobody, including the stars and entrepreneurs cited above, got anywhere because they were inspired. Thomas Edison said this best: "Genius is one percent inspiration, ninety-nine percent perspiration."[28] Here are some pointers to guide you as you perspire:

Stop and Think. While people with ADD often procrastinate making a decision, you're even more likely to jump on your latest impulse. Be certain any pressure you feel to make a move is not simply the product of impatience or a way to satisfy a craving. Once again, the only way to know is to slow down the decisional process.

Take Seriously the Advice of Your Mentor. Bounce all your heartfelt inspirations off someone who is *not* impacted by the decision you're about to make. A good mentor will test your inspirations with questions. This will be painful sometimes, as it was for Sienna. No one likes to have his or her dream stomped on—no matter how unwise it may be. But the whole point of mentors is to challenge your thinking. Find one that understands the wily ways of the heart and you'll actually see a lot more of your dreams come true.

If instead your people find they can't influence your decisions, they may get impatient and let you fall on your face. A key tension in the *Star Wars* movies is whether Luke is even capable of being trained as a Jedi. At a key point in *The Empire Strikes Back*, Yoda is pretty much fed up with Luke's impetuousness.

"This one a long time have I watched," Yoda complains to Obiwan Kenobi's ghost. "All his life has he looked away to the future, to the horizon. Never his mind on where he was. Hmm? What he was doing. Hmph. Adventure. Heh. Excitement. Heh. A Jedi craves not these things." Yoda then turns back to Luke and adds a stinging insult. He says, "You are reckless."

---

[28] Quoted in *Harper's Monthly* (September 1932)

Sound familiar? Yoda implores Luke to be where he is, focused and intention-al, to pay attention to here and now, to think with his head and push back the distractions of his heart. Luke's heart is what we call in fiction writing his "fatal flaw." The first time you see *The Empire Strikes Back*, you genuinely don't know whether he can overcome it.

Here's a less intergalactic example. I had a rare[29] ADD couple come in to see me. In their early twenties, they were about to leave for California and wanted pointers on living together. Asked what they were planning to do there, the girl said, "I want to become a singer." I asked if she had done a lot of musical performance or theater in high school.

"No," she said, "but I took some singing and dancing lessons as a child. I just know I'm going to make it. I can feel it." She touched her heart.

I bit my tongue and asked the boyfriend for his plan. "I'm going to buy a brewery," he said. "I've been working at a microbrewery pub for the last couple of months and I think that's my calling."

I asked if they were independently wealthy. The couple excitedly shared how they'd managed to save just over $2,000. Neither had a job in LA, a city with a 10% unemployment rate at the time.

At that point, I gave up, just as had both sets of their parents. Perhaps Yoda could have used the force to point out their heartfelt folly, but no one in this galaxy could penetrate this couple's flawed planning. So, they got in their Kia and drove to LA to join thousands of aspiring singers and brewers already living there.

If you're known for having ill-considered schemes and not taking "no" for an answer, your people may just let you "learn it the hard way."

If you're known for having ill-considered schemes and not taking "no" for an answer, your people may just let you "learn things the hard way." Any time you hear those words, take heed. Your people aren't challenging you to succeed. They're letting you fail.

Sleep On It. As clichés go, this is a darn good one. Cosmic as it may sound, sleep is where business gets done in your unconscious mind. All of us, and especially people with ADD, miss small clues in the environment. Those actually come back in our dreams as we reprocess the day (cue eerie *Twilight Zone* music). You don't need a psychoanalyst for dream interpretation. You don't even have to remember them. Just let your mind and body do what they know how to do. Calmly consider your choices as you go to sleep, then see

---

[29] Rare because, as I'll discuss in Chapter 11, most people with ADD tend to couple with anxious people. This story illustrates why.

what you think in the morning. It may take several days, but sleep can help you sort out the smart stuff from the crap. This holds true for learning, too. Research tells us that going to sleep after studying improves retention. It's like hitting the save button on what you've learned.[30] Try it, you'll like it.

Meditate. Mindfulness meditation teaches specific techniques to relax and focus your awareness so you can listen to your own wisdom. It won't fix your neurology, but it can help you consider your inspirations more fully. In Chapter 2, I mentioned Dialectical Behavioral Therapy (DBT). It's a well-researched method for working with extremely difficult clients who can't regulate their emotions, and it includes meditation. In 2009, I saw DBT's founder, psychologist Marsha Linehan, speak at a national conference. She quipped to the thousands of therapists in attendance, "If you knew me, you'd know I'm about the least mindful or meditative person around. But I started doing this because it works. If I can do it, anyone can." So, whether you're the "mindful type" or not, give meditation a try.

Beware The Shiny Things. Everyone with ADD has heard the old shiny things analogy. It's a funny way of describing how novel stimuli distract the eye and heart. It could be a cute guy or girl, a sporty car, nice furniture, a cool gadget, a celebrity, or any other object of desire. Shiny things create that love-at-first-sight feeling, whether or not they bring anything wholesome to your life. Some shiny things live up to their promise, but many are gussied-up junk. In most things (cliché alert), beauty is only skin-deep. Evaluate everything you take into your life on substance as well as style, and before committing to anything…

Gather Real Data. When making any choice—dating partners, a car or appliance, a college, or anything else—rely on unbiased data. That's easy when shopping for a car or fridge. Pick up *Consumer Reports*. Talk about anxious leaners, the CR people wouldn't know their hearts if they were sitting on the shelf in front of them. Their reports are all hard, cold science. Use online reviews for products that aren't covered in CR, but be very careful. Many online reviews aren't really unbiased. They're posted by affiliates or agents of the product, or the result of free goods given to a known reviewer. Still, I've bought some really good stuff (shoes, gadgets, the yard light on my house, etc.) after carefully studying online reviews.

It's easy to find this kind of information on colleges and trade schools. Numerous reviews are published. Use them to pick the schools that not only get good ratings, but also have the best "special services" departments. If you Google "disability services" and the name of your prospective college, you'll

---

[30] www.npr.org/2013/09/08/220065467/memory-pinball-and-other-reasons-you-need-a-nap

find what you need. Like anything else, some schools will excel at helping ADD people get through and others won't.

Once you get there and start enrolling in classes, do careful research to select instructors who are organized, available, and offer clear testing and instruction. People with ADD need this style of teaching. Never select the easiest professors if they're teaching in your major. If I need to tell you why, go back and re-read Chapter 3 on right and easy paths. Some students swear by RateMyProfessor.com to do this kind of research and others swear at it. If you use a site like this, be sure to actually read the reviews both positive and negative, and not just the numerical rating, which may be easily skewed by a small number of negative respondents out for revenge.

When researching careers, Google "US Department of Labor" plus whatever career you're considering. You'll instantly get a tremendous amount of information including salary, necessary education, and employment statistics.

Dating may not seem to be a great place to use a hard-nosed approach, but it is. In fact, I use research and shopping metaphors a lot when guiding people in finding good relationships. More on that in Chapter 11.

Develop a Hobby. Hobbies are great places to follow your heart without impacting the main part of your life. Just be careful how many and how extravagant you make your diversions. For people with ADD, hobbies can take over your life, particularly expensive ones like car restoration or model building. But it's usually better to confine your whims to well-regulated play than to let them invade your larger life plan.

Nowhere is the problem of heart-following greater than when it comes to spending money.

Practice Intentional Finance. Nowhere is the problem of heart-following greater than when it comes to spending money. Think of finance as one more solution to a problem, one requiring intentionality, not heartfelt wandering. That can be challenging for people with ADD, who tend to follow their bliss right over a fiscal cliff. That's gotten even worse in an era of online shopping and easy credit. Back in the day, you had time to think things through as you drove to a store, looked for parking, and then pushed your cart up and down the aisles. You checked out several stores or departments. You clipped coupons, watched for sales, and counted the bills in your wallet to see what you could afford.

Today, it takes about ten seconds between your latest shopping impulse and "Buy it Now" or "One Click," and easy credit has become a comfortable way to avoid the consequences. Fortunately, Amazon.com and its competitors take stuff back when you click unwisely. Unfortunately, people with ADD don't like sending stuff back. Here are my tips for financial success. They work pretty well whether you have ADD or not.

- **Assess Wants and Needs.** Know the difference between what you need and what you just want. TV financial guru Suze Orman did an interesting video on this for Oprah's website.[31]

- **Always Shop From a List.** If an item isn't on your list, think hard about whether it's important. If you left toilet paper off your list, toss a case in your cart. TP is a need. But if you forgot to add a new DVD or video game, then leave it be. You might decide to buy it, but if you haven't read the reviews, checked your budget, and done some price shopping, you're acting on impulse.

- **Use Cash and Carry.** Unless your special power is money management, using credit cards is usually dangerous for people with ADD. I understand credit makes the world go around, but that's only true when your credit is good. If you want to build good credit, use a card with a very low credit limit for a few purchases a month, and pay it off at the end of every billing cycle. If you can't do that every single month, cut up the card.

- **Avoid Payday Loans.** Far worse than credit cards are payday loans, weekly payment car dealers, and pawn shops. All of these charge insane interest and they prey upon impulsive people who don't plan their finances well, offering short-term satisfaction and long-term ruin. I understand desperation, but there are few situations so desperate as to justify the use of these services.

- **Avoid Paper Checks.** If you have a checking account, don't even order checks, unless you balance your checkbook perfectly after every purchase and keep a cushion of at least $200. For ADD people, paper checks are like gold...for the bank. They charge you $20 to $35 for every bounced check, *each time it runs through*. The law allows the merchant to hit you hard, too. So that $4.25 latte you over-drafted to purchase could end up costing you $50 or $60. If you don't pony up the cash, they close the account and it goes on your credit history.

- **Be Careful with Debit Cards.** If you do have a checking account, a debit card might be safer than a paper check for moving money. That's because if you keep track of your account on the

---

31 www.oprah.com/money/Money-Management-What-Are-Your-Wants-and-Needs-Suze-Orman-Video

automated teller, these things are essentially self-balancing. When you run out of money the debit card will show "declined" at the point of sale. Embarrassing, but cheap. However, fraud protection is a serious problem when using debit cards. You're pretty much putting access to your bank account out for the world to see. If a credit card number is stolen (it's happened to most of us), you're protected from fraudulent charges as long as you report it immediately so they can lock the card down. Debit cards offer no such protection. If someone gets your number, they can drain your account and you may not get the money back. Debit cards also make it super easy for you to drain your own account, so you could easily come up short when something serious like rent, car payment, or utilities is due.

- **Buy Cash Cards.** I like these best. Most discount and grocery stores now offer cash cards you can purchase, load and reload. They run the same way as debit cards at the point of sale, but the only cash you're exposing to fraud is what's on the card. There's a fee to buy and load them, but they greatly limit your risk exposure from both bad purchase choices and hackers. If you only load what you're going to need for daily purchases, you'll have enough for your necessities, which you can pay for with online checking.

- **Surrender Your Money, Or Else.** If you're really bad with finances and you're headed toward the road to ruin, turn over your money to someone else. It could be your parent, or, later in life, a responsible partner. With wealthier clients, we advise parents to set up a restrictive trust fund with an advisor who serves as a financial mentor. Just be sure you can trust your helper implicitly. Because many ADD people don't always read situations correctly, you can miss the dishonesty of others, to the point of being gullible. So, never use your heart to select a financial mentor.

Mind Over Heart. Here's a little story to close out this chapter that illustrates the tips I've just shared. While it's literally about shopping, it's figuratively about making any intentional choice.

Like most children his age, my ten-year-old son, Alex, is an ultimate consumer. He watches lots of TV shows that amount to little more than half-hour commercials. So, when we travel together, he wants to buy everything he sees. Last year, his full shopping ferocity was released on the Mall of America.

By day three Alex had already found about thirty-five items he "just had to have." He compared this LEGO kit to that one, then Build-A-Bear, then The Disney Store, and so on. He decided on a new soccer ball, a gift for Mom, a souvenir shot glass (uh…no), and enough other wants to make Suze Orman cringe. Even the convenience store was fair game for his wish list.

Examining each new item, Alex was extremely, positively, absolutely certain beyond any doubt that this new shiny item was exactly what his heart told him to buy. And shortly thereafter, each was displaced by a different, even more necessary item, until, at the end of his epic shopping quest, one item won out: *LEGO: Legends of Chima.*

What he chose isn't important. It's how he made the decision.

Having done this before, I've learned it's best for Alex to ponder what he wants over the course of the trip. I used to suggest he make a paper list or take a picture with my iPhone, but he needs no props. Alex is like a human barcode scanner, recording, sorting, and prioritizing everything he sees at Mall of America. His purchase has to fit into his predetermined budget or he can get several less expensive items. The only other rule is that he can't buy anything *until the last day.*

Alex's heart burst with inspiration several times an hour at MOA. But with this system, he considered his inspirations carefully and made an authentic choice. At times his face looked a bit tortured as he compared items, weighing their pros and cons, then putting one back before moving on to the next.

I don't know the private logic that pushed *Legends of Chima* up that list and Build-A-Bear down. I only know that, in the end, his decision was an intentional one, and months later he still tells me it was the right one.

All these rules for heart/mind interactions may seem hard to follow, easy to ignore, and maybe, as Sienna suggested, too practical and a little boring. But the consequences of following your heart without data, experience, and reason are substantial. You can end up in a bad marriage, financial ruin, the wrong college, an unproductive career, or all other manner of general mayhem. You might even buy the wrong toy from Mall of America.

If instead you master the balance between heart and mind in every decision you make, I'll bet you succeed far more often than you fail.

CHAPTER 6

WHEN YOU DON'T KNOW HOW TO

WORK SOMETHING

One might be led to suspect that there were all sorts of things
going on in the Universe which he or she did not thoroughly
understand.

— Kurt Vonnegut, *Slaughterhouse-Five*

"I need you to tell me what to do." Heath clutched at his knees and rocked back and forth, closer to panic than I'd ever seen him before. "Everyone's so mad at me for hooking up with Ashley."

"No doubt." I shook my head, baffled. "It really is a mess."

"I'll end up with no friends and I might as well go back to Oklahoma." Tears welled up in his eyes. "Even as we speak, the other guys are talking about what to do with me. It won't be good."

I considered Heath among my ADD stars. I'd even told his story (disguised and released) in my newspaper column as an illustration of how successful treatment makes all the difference. He'd come to see me after his first semester of pre-med, wondering why college seemed so much harder for him than everyone else.

Bright and academically savvy, he'd graduated at the top of his class in a small high school outside of Tulsa. But by the end of his freshman fall semester, the rigor of a major state university was kicking his butt. The problem wasn't really his grades. It was the effort it took to get them. He'd done nothing but study and attend tutoring that fall, even though he was only taking general education courses. He ultimately pulled a 3.8 GPA in class and a 0.0 in having fun. He went home for winter break, worn out and worried. For a while, he considered dropping out or changing majors, but he returned in January to give pre-med one last try.

When he first came in, Heath didn't seem much like the other ADD people I've described so far in this book. I wondered if he just hadn't been challenged enough in high school, or didn't yet have the study skills required for college. That happens a lot when smart, small-town kids step out into the vastness of college. However, it didn't take long for me to suggest testing. Sure enough, his self-report scores and those from his mom and a brother, who was already in med-school, all matched. The numbers didn't top the chart—he scored higher on the ADD scales than 70% of young men in his age group—but that put him over the clinical threshold. Hypothesis confirmed.

You may think it's an easy and straight line from diagnosis to medication management. It's not. As I'll discuss in Chapter 13, it takes time and partnership to tune in the right prescription and dosage for any given person. It took four months with Heath. Fortunately, his prescriber understood the importance of teamwork and Heath hung in there until we got it right.

Ritalin-type[32] products initially worked for Heath, but they made him drowsy, a known side effect for people with ADD that actually supports the diagnosis. Adderall[33] worked better, but even the extended release (XR) pills washed out of his system too early in the day[34]. That left him easily annoyed by and annoying to his fraternity brothers at about 5:30 p.m. every day. Vyvanse, a more refined system of delivering amphetamines, proved to be the ticket. It lasted long enough to get his studying done by 8:00 p.m., made him less irritable, and didn't impact his sleep.

Within a month, Heath's academic career took off. His freshman spring and sophomore fall semesters weren't effortless, but he retained difficult material in advanced science and math classes and his test grades reached the pre-med range. For the first time he could fully express the intelligence everyone knew he had. Moreover, completing his studies early in the evening allowed him to have a modest social life. That in turn generated all sorts of new college adventures and more than a few mishaps.

---

[32] Ritalin is the brand name for methylphenidate, a core ingredient in about half the medications commonly used for ADD. I use the brand name because it's the more familiar term.

[33] Adderall is the more familiar brand name for mixed amphetamine salts.

[34] As we'll discuss later, medication for ADD doesn't stick around in your body very long. The effect is usually gone by the evening.

I was surprised when Heath listed a fraternity house on his initial paperwork. He didn't seem like the Greek type. For a good-looking guy, he hadn't dated much in high school. He'd been shy and awkward around girls because he didn't exactly understand how they worked. For many people with ADD, relationships are like our driving example—too many variables and too little attention to keep them all organized. So, he stuck to his books and his dog and didn't really hang out much with friends.

Heath's parents encouraged him to pledge a fraternity to open up his social life. That had proven a mixed blessing. Most teen boys have a lot of practice with girls by the time they hit college. Heath had none. If you've never lived inside a major university's Greek system, it's difficult to understand the complex rules of social interplay and dating. I'd done my best, but a therapist or mentor can't ride around on your shoulder and whisper in your ear. That left Heath open to all sorts of new intrigues that we could only unravel and process every other week in session.

Then, over his junior year Spring Break, Heath violated Cardinal Rules One and Two. He got caught having sex on the beach with Ashley, a girl Jay, his roommate, had hooked up with during the fall semester. That was exactly one night after Heath kissed Ashley's best friend, Tori. Tori liked Heath, but Heath didn't really like her back.

Disaster ensued.

"So let me try and get this straight." I needed a diagram to keep track of it all, but Heath was in no shape to draw me one. "Tori and Ashley are roommates in their sorority. We know Tori likes you, but you told her you're not interested, except then you made out with her one night at Padre."

"Right." Heath continued to rock. "But that didn't mean anything. It was just making out. I didn't know I'd be able to get with Ashley the next night."

"Except Tori didn't see it that way. She thought she had a shot with you. And then the next night you had sex with Ashley, at which point Jay and Tori caught you on the beach."

"Well, actually we were back at the motel by then. I mean, it's dumb to have sex on a beach. The sand sort of—you know."

"I can only imagine." I chuckled.

Heath didn't. This was the most serious moment of his college career so far. It could mean the functional end of his fraternity life. Since he hadn't made any outside friends since pledging, he wasn't exaggerating when he said he'd end up alone.

"I gotta ask." I leaned against the arm of my chair and rested my chin in my palm. "What's up with you and Ashley? I don't remember this being a romance."

"It wasn't. We've just been really good friends. I could tell her anything. You know how hard that is for me. I never thought Jay would be so mad. I didn't know this until Ashley told me after we did it, but I guess she was Jay's first."

"First, ever?"

"Ever." Heath's brow furrowed. "She got his virginity and he's pretty religious and after that he was kind of in love with her, but she didn't feel the same way and now he hates me and everyone is on his side. They told me I'm no kind of brother to them. It's like I'm banished."

"I don't want to be too hard on you, but..." I liked Heath and understood how delicate this was, but this situation was totally foreseeable. "Was hooking up with Ashley worth it?"

"It's not like that." His voice grew urgent. "I've been waiting for Ashley to notice me like that forever. I tried to be friends so she'd see I'm a nice guy, but I didn't think it was working. So, the first chance I had to be with her, I took it."

"Could you have mentioned this before?" I tapped my pen impatiently on the arm of my chair. "We've been discussing girls for months and how to get with them in an ethical way. Ashley's always been friend-zoned. I even questioned you about her as a prospect."

"I guess I didn't want to get anyone's hopes up. Especially mine. Sorry."

"And how does Ashley feel about all this?"

"Totally conflicted. She's catching hell from Tori. I asked her straight up, 'Do you want to be with me or not? This relationship is going to cost us and we have to be sure.' She said she understood and wanted to be with me. We just don't want to hurt our friends." He momentarily paused his rocking. "So, how do I make everything right with everyone?"

I sighed. "We're kind of past that point, Heath. The best we can do is figure out the least detrimental exit."

"This is like a bad romantic comedy, isn't it?"

"That's what happens when you get yourself into something you don't know how to operate."

"What do you mean?"

"Everything comes with instructions." I reached over to my desk and laid the huge Adobe Photoshop manual on the coffee table between us. "Photoshop is a powerful program. You can fool around with it and kind of get it to work by trial and error, but whether you learn it from this book or online or with YouTube, it won't do what it was designed to do until you learn its strange ways. That's how life works, too."

"And plumbing." Heath ran his palm over the cover of the manual and managed a faint smile. "I tried to replace the float in the toilet in our floor's bathroom last month. Totally flooded it. Then I read where it says you have to turn off the valve under the tank before you disconnect the line. Who knew?"

"Let me give you some good advice. When it comes to girls and fraternities and plumbing and just about everything else, if you don't know how to work it, leave it alone until you do."

"But, you've been all over me to expand my horizons and start dating, and obviously I have no idea about any of that."

"True enough." I nodded. "There's always going to be some trial and error involved. But you have to study how things work before you take something apart, or, in the case of Ashley and you, put it together. Otherwise you'll get more errors than you can stand. See what I mean?"

"I do." Heath shook his head and let out a sigh.

"It might be wise to put off big decisions like this until we can discuss your next move and how it affects those around you. It doesn't mean you wouldn't get to be with Ashley, but there are ways of doing that without blowing up your friend group."

"I thought about texting you that night, but Ashley was looking really good and I guess—I couldn't keep my head straight, you know?"

"So, you didn't shut off the valve before proceeding."

He grinned for the first time that day. "Well said, sir."

Is This Chapter For Me?

For some people with ADD, glossing over life's instructions causes serious problems and terrible consequences. Others are so good at finding their own way, that they can just look at a thing or situation and intuit how it works. That's their special power. But before you decide you're one of those lucky ADD people, see what you and your people think of this checklist:

- ❏ Do you find that you just don't seem to "get" other people or why they do the things they do?

- ❏ Do you skip over textbooks, instructions, and how-to guides, preferring to figure things out on your own, even when that usually turns out badly?

- ❏ Do you often plead, "I didn't know I was supposed to [fill in the blank]," even when that irritates others?

- ❏ Do you miss critical details ("turn off the valve," "don't kiss two girls who are roommates, etc.") that everyone else just seems to naturally understand?

If ignoring or misunderstanding instructions has caused you these kinds of problems, read on.

Bargaining in Good Faith With Your Destiny

I met Kurt Vonnegut once. He had a wonderful way of wrapping up profound thoughts in familiar images. For example, in *Slapstick*, he proposed that comedy duo Laurel and Hardy were funny because they weren't very good at life, yet they were always ready to bargain in good faith with their destinies. He said, "they did their best with every test."

I actually considered subtitling this book *How to Bargain in Good Faith with Your Destiny*, because that's really what it's about—facing life's tests and doing your best. But then, you'd have had to read all the way to page 70 to have any idea what I was talking about. Besides, that Google and Amazon search string returned a lot of books on labor law.

Heath didn't really bargain in good faith with his destiny. He just hurled himself into random chaos because that's what his heart told him to do. While that makes for awesome comedic art, in real life it's not that fun going from one screwball adventure to the next, just because you don't understand how things work.

Life's Instructions

There's a groovy old saying: "Life doesn't come with instructions, you just have to live it and learn from it." Nobody knows the original source for this quote, because nobody would admit to saying something this dumb. I suspect the Internet just made it up.

You do learn from experience, of course. When you solve one problem, you apply what you've learned to the next one that comes along. We call this "generalizing" knowledge. If Heath learns to fix the toilet, he can generalize that to fixing the sink. If he learns something from the Ashley/Jay/Tori drama, he'll be more intentional and diplomatic the next time he pursues love, friendship, and social success.

But that doesn't mean we're condemned to endless trial and error, like pratfall comedians tumbling down the stairs of life. You see, life *does* come with instructions, developed over thousands of years of human existence, handed down from

Life does come with instructions, developed over thousands of years of human existence.

generation to generation and refined in each passing. That's why we have parents, schools, mentors, teachers, and therapists—to advance human knowledge. It's why we have law, philosophy, art, and language. Sacred stories were actually told, and later written down, to guide early civilizations in problem solving, well before everyday people had access to scientific, legal, and philosophical literature. People were expected, even commanded, to learn these stories, in the hope they might help everyone bargain in good faith with their destinies.

Learning and following life's instructions can be harder for people with ADD. Like Heath, you prefer solving problems quickly. So, you may gloss over instructions or fail to observe how things work before diving in. You favor trial and error because that's always more interesting than following the rules, particularly if you expect failure is likely anyway. However, for the vast majority of life's problems, understanding how something works is far better than testing the hell out of it until you eventually figure it out.

"But what about Thomas Edison?" you might aptly point out. "Doesn't he represent the triumph of trial and error?" Edison did in fact run 10,000 trials and had about 9,999 errors before creating a commercially successful light bulb. When asked how he persisted in the face of such failure, he famously noted, "If I find 10,000 ways something won't work, I haven't failed. I am not discouraged, because every wrong attempt discarded is often a step forward."

True enough. Except there are a couple problems with this analogy as it applies to your life, which is why Edison appears here and not in the "Advantages" section. First of all, Edison *was* following instructions. His own. He meticulously designed his inventions based on the design and theory of others, then modified them as he progressed. That's the scientific method. Remember his quote in Chapter 4 about perspiration and inspiration? There was nothing random about how he approached inventing.

Second, if you study Edison's career, you'll find that things turned out badly, precisely because he stopped following life's instruction manual. In fact, he completely blew the highest ambition of electrification—mass production. His first commercial power plant produced direct current (DC). There was already plenty of evidence that the better current was AC (alternating current), but

Edison couldn't accept that because it wasn't his idea. Nikola Tesla was a big fan of AC and no fan of Edison. The two fought a "current war" over which standard would prevail.

Instead of really studying and accepting the superiority of AC, Edison launched a propaganda campaign to ban it, including (I kid you not) electrocuting a zoo elephant to prove the danger of alternating current. This did not work out very well. Especially for the elephant.

AC was simply a better method for distributing electricity, which Edison was too bull-headed to see. Nearly bankrupted by the battle, he eventually lost control of his own company to financier J.P. Morgan and DC lost the war. Circus animals everywhere let out a collective sigh of relief.

Things went even worse for Tesla. Despite being a brilliant inventor, and the star of the AC team, he never found commercial success. He died alone and impoverished, while the Westinghouse Company made millions off his technology with a relatively small investment.

So, whenever you feel like giving up on instructions and giving yourself over to the fascinating world of experimentation, think of Edison and Tesla, not as brilliant inventors who pushed the limits of knowledge, but as two guys who probably should have spent more time learning how the world really works.

Ignorance is No Excuse. That whole "life doesn't come with instructions" adage is usually just an excuse for why someone did something unproductive, unwise, or downright bad. The poor fool didn't have any instructions, so oops, he or she blew it. Such is life. YOLO![35]

People with ADD often complain, "I didn't know we were supposed to do it that way" or, "If I'd have known it was going to turn out like this, I wouldn't have [insert bad idea]." Except your people have no patience for what you don't know because they expect you to learn. That's why Heath's Greek friends weren't very forgiving. He should have seen the Ashley/Jay/Tori situation coming.

Remember my singer/brew-master couple in Chapter 6? It's not a matter of whether they'll have to undream their dream. It's only a question of when, and how much it will mess up the rest of their young lives. It might just be a fun adventure they tell their kids about or the edge of a very steep precipice. Either way, failure is foreseeable.

"And how do you know how things will turn out for these two?" you ask.

---

[35]For those not on Twitter, this is an acronym for "You Only Live Once."

Because I've read the instructions. I've met people who've tried to make it in the music business and I know how much work, time, dedication, money, connection, and luck it takes. I've seen the statistics on how few people make it. I've owned several businesses. I grew up in an agricultural state and I've seen people lose all their money and their land on weak investments. I watch *Shark Tank*. Most people with ADD know that knowledge like this exists all around them, just waiting to be learned. Many don't spend the time and effort to find it, or like my young couple, they'd rather just follow their hearts and not be bothered with tidbits of reality.

The Advantages of Raw Exploration

We all love books and movies in which unconventional heroes succeed because they play by their own quirky rules. So, Hollywood churns out films in which following instruction hampers progress and out-of-the-box thinking wins the day. If you'll keep in mind that such stories are fun because they dramatize the exception rather than the rule, I'll admit that people with ADD really can excel in real-life situations that favor innovation over structure.

Because you see things differently than the rest of us, people with ADD can often imagine what lies beyond the rules, or find ways to rewrite instructions in ways others would never consider. That's especially handy in abstract or unstructured pursuits, or when experience and experimentation are more suited to the task. You're good at wondering, "What could I make this thing do?" or, "How could this world be different?" ADD people can also come through in situations that don't come with any instructions at all, because they're so strange or unexpected.

In World War II our GIs were great at taking something intended to do one thing, tossing the instructions, and making it do something no one had imagined. They adapted tactics from the Army Field Manual to an infinite variety of new battlefield situations. The movie *Saving Private Ryan* offers several great examples. Just remember that the D-Day invasion wasn't General Eisenhower's random inspiration. It was one of the most carefully planned military campaigns in history. Creativity often depends on working inside a larger plan that sets the stage for later innovation. You must have a structure from which to deviate. You have to have rules in order to know how and when to break them.

People with ADD can be just as innovative in relationships. In fact, what often attracts a partner is your tendency to march to a different beat; to do the unexpected. Or as one young woman put it, "I fell in love with him because I just never knew what was coming next. It was exciting."

Of course she told me that while in couples therapy.

Principle 6: If You Don't Know How to Work Something, Learn

I get more complaints about this principle than any other, because free-thinking clients like Sienna misconstrue it as an endorsement of conformity to dogma or social expectation, which it is not. It only suggests that you know what you're doing before you start doing it; that you understand someone before trying to influence him or her; that you know how something works before you tinker with it. In fact, non-conformity is itself worth studying. It has a rich history and literature. Why not understand it before joining up just because it sounds all rebellious and cool? So, in the spirit of understanding, not conforming, I'll offer my best instructions for following instructions.

Take Your Medication. At no time are stimulants more helpful than when plodding through instructions or taking in all the little details of a new social situation, dating relationship, class, or job. This is why medication management is usually a life-long process, especially for people whose ADD is severe. You're never not learning, so every day is a day of instruction. Because it helps you pay attention, medicine makes all the difference in noticing and interpreting all those little details.

Be Observant. Assume there are instructions for everything. Some are obvious and straightforward. Others you have to go out and find. Most instructions aren't written down. They occur naturally, moment to moment, like our driving example. These "environmental instructions" come from the social and contextual clues all around us. They connect us to our world and teach us how to respond to it. As but one example, the nicest thing you can hear from a dating partner or spouse is, "I feel like we're really connecting." That means you're noticing and following their spoken and unspoken instructions on how to love them. Less romantic are context clues like where someone is standing, or where cars should be parked along a street, or who talks to whom at a party or work. These details teach us how to get through the day efficiently and effectively.

Use Your Ears. Some people with ADD are auditory learners. You encode material you hear more easily than what you read. Audiobooks for self-help, sexuality, relationships, etc. are sometimes a bit more expensive, but they're usually free at the library. My computer has a pleasant voice[36] and I often let it read things to me that aren't otherwise available in an audio format.

You may even find it helpful to use the "podcast" in your head by talking yourself through a decision you're considering. Lots of ADD people do that. Just don't forget that we can hear you, so be careful what you say if others are around.

---

[36] I use a Mac and a program called GhostReader for this. I like "Heather's" voice.

When you're in your observation mode in a new setting, talk very little and listen a lot. One of Heath's special powers was his ability to sit quietly. Once he learned to decode what he was hearing, he did well socially.

Not All Instructions Are Created Equal. As with anything else, you have to vet instructions to be sure they're worth following. For example, self-help books, like this one, are a popular way people seek wisdom. Today, the publishing industry is all over the place and e-books and Publish on Demand (POD) make it possible for anyone to sell instructions for anything. Some are better than others and the differences are rarely obvious. Use your expert shopping skills (Chapter 5) to check your sources carefully.

As with anything else, you have to vet instructions to be sure they're worth following.

In the first pages of this book, I told you why I'm an expert in treating ADD. I've done it for many years and I've learned from thousands of people who have it. I'm successful and I don't offer easy solutions. I also take lots of continuing education to stay current in my field. That formula *should* apply to most expert instruction-givers. Instead, a lot of people hold themselves out as experts on this or that, when they're not. There are even expert books to teach you how to write a book as if you were an expert. No experience required.

Likewise, in any new social, school, or work environment, figure out who has wisdom and who just wants you to think they do. Some advice-givers are really gossips and rumor-mongers who want to get your information to make themselves more powerful. They offer up "good advice" on how the system works to get you to trust them. Don't. Shake everyone's hand, but don't align with anyone until you understand who's honest, who's helpful, who's connected, and who's toxic. No matter how functional an environment looks, there's always a crazy vortex lurking somewhere.

Pictures Are Worth Ten Thousand Words. Some people with ADD are visual learners. They like to see a diagram, map, photo, or drawing of what they're doing, whether it's setting up a tent or kissing your beloved (yes, they have great diagrams for that). YouTube and similar online video streams are the ultimate in pictorial instruction. I rarely use the thick Photoshop manual I tossed at Heath. If I want rounded edges on my website pictures, I Google that search string and several good video tutorials show up. I know enough to pick the ones that really work. They let me pause, click, revise, rewind, and fast-forward. It's amazing.

I often show the video clips cited in this book, and many others, on a big LCD TV over the fireplace in my office. This lets me illustrate the thirteen principles in an entertaining way using music videos, stories, films, and TV shows to help people with ADD retain core concepts. We also project client calendars, test profiles, sleep charts, and course schedules as visual organizers.

"How" Is Usually More Important Than "Why." *Why* something is necessary or important is interesting to ponder, but it often distracts people with ADD from how to actually get it done. For example, if your partner says, "I really wish you'd do this or that," go ahead and do it, rather than trying to figure out why your partner wants you to do it[37].

If a math professor demands you show your work instead of just solving the problem, assume he or she has taught this class a time or two before and might have a method to such madness. If your boss wants you to follow a certain policy or procedure, asking why probably won't win you Employee of the Month. Figuring out how to make the policy or procedure work well, just might.

The Most Important Instructions of All. Ethics are our shared rules of social and behavioral conduct. They tell us what is right and wrong. I've dedicated a section of Chapter 9 to that topic, so for now just understand three things about these crucial instructions:

- Most ethical instructions require reason, interpretation, and intention to correctly apply.

- You can't apply ethics if you don't understand how they work.

- There are some ethical absolutes that require no interpretation. Most of these have to do with harming people.

You'll find many benefits to learning how things work, operating within that framework, and only then going beyond or modifying it. However, at no time in your life will you appreciate the value of instruction more than when things start falling apart.

That brings us to a chapter on how to manage crises. Please return your tray table to its upright and locked position and assume crash positions. Your seat cushion cannot be used as a flotation device, but if you put it to work in your life, this next chapter can.

---

37 I am assuming that what your partner is asking you to do is reasonable and appropriate.

CHAPTER 7

GOING DOWN THE DRAIN

Things turn out best for people who make the best of the way
things turn out.

— John Wooden, UCLA Basketball Coach 1948-1975

"I'm giving up." In our ten years working together, Melissa had uttered those three words at least two dozen times, yet there was something different in her voice that morning. Something serious. "I'm *not* taking the nursing board exam again and you can't make me."

"No, I can't. But giving up isn't a reasonable option." My tone came out sterner than I'd intended. I tried to walk it back. "I just mean you've come so far. You graduated from college. That was amazing—"

"It's only amazing because I'm stupid." Tears streamed down her cheeks. "It took me seven years and I had like, a 2.3 GPA. I barely passed math after five tries and only because they felt sorry for me. Five tries, Dr. Wes!" Melissa blew her nose into a tissue and let out a bitter chuckle. "You told me I was stupid when I was fifteen and guess what? You were right."

"I absolutely *never* said that." The session was slipping into despair. For Melissa, ADD was the single most depressing subject we ever discussed, followed immediately thereafter by her IQ testing in high school. She hated her brain, even as she'd learned how to coax it to its maximum potential.

"You *did*. I was there." She patted her chest, then put her face in her hands and sobbed. "You said my IQ was 'low-average.'"

I left my armchair and moved into the one next to the couch, then reached across the end table and touched her arm. "Can you look at me?"

"No."

"Please, Melissa."

After a few moments she huffed and raised her gaze. Her perfectly applied makeup ran like a muddy river down her chin.

I handed her another tissue. "I thought we agreed you'd always wear waterproof mascara to therapy."

"Stop." A smile escaped her lips. "I feel worse than I look, so watch it."

"I know." I paused to gather my words. "Listen, Melissa. Whenever I'm trying to encourage someone who feels hopeless about their own ADD, I tell them about this girl I knew and how hard it was for her to drag herself from one class to the next, keeping her meds straight, forcing herself to study when her brain said 'no.' Taking a year off, then coming back to finish. I tell them one of the happiest days of my life was standing in that huge auditorium, watching that girl walk off the stage with a college diploma. I tell them, 'No matter how bad it got, that girl found a way to succeed.'"

"I remember seeing you in the stands that day. It meant a lot that you came." She returned her gaze to the floor. "My family was so proud of me...the first one of us to graduate college. Now, they just think I'm a—" She choked on the words.

"No," I said firmly. "No one thinks you're a quitter."

"I was actually going to say, 'loser.'"

"You're not that either. Actually, you're my hero. I seriously admire you more than just about anyone." I patted her arm again and then leaned back in the chair. "You'll never be the smartest girl in the class, but you're always the one whose still fighting, after a lot of the others have given up."

"I'm all fought out, Wes." She shook her head. "Do you know how it feels to be sitting in there, taking that stupid effing test and to think I'm like this close to being a nurse and those other girls are just whizzing through it 'cuz they know all the answers and half of them are probably hung-over. And me? I studied for hours and I'm always like six points away."

"Which feels like a thousand points."

"Exactly."

"Except it's not. It's just six. You can make up that difference."

"I can't. I just feel so hopeless."

"Melissa, I'm your biggest fan, so don't take this wrong, but I honestly don't care how you feel right now."

"And you're not the nice man I thought you were." She smirked, pulled another tissue and wiped her eyes. "I already know where you're headed with this. You're going to say, 'There's no try in victory,' or some crap like that. 'It only matters what you do, uncomfortable or not.' Except, what I *do* sucks."

"Actually, I was about to say that when things are going down the drain, don't make them worse."

"Oh my God." Melissa fell over sideways on the couch. "Are you even listening? I failed it *three* times. How could things get worse?"

"You tell me."

"Ehhhhh!" She pulled the remaining pillow over her face, so I could barely hear what she was saying. "It would be worse…to have a BSN, never pass the effing test and end up working as a CNA in a nursing home forever, or at least until my back gives out from lifting old people. Then I'd end up on disability and someone would be lifting *me*. Is that what you want me to say?"

"Pretty much. Listen. This whole test thing? It's what we call a temporary setback. I've had them, you'll have more of them. Your task right now is pretty simple—do not go down the drain."

"Simple for *you*. You're smart." She sat up again and glared at me. "How many more times do you expect me to go through this?"

"Same as the rest of us. Until you get those last six points."

Melissa sat in silence for at least a minute. I'd pushed her exactly as far as I could. Now, she had to choose.

"Fine. Whatever." She shook her head in resignation, then glared at me. "You know how you say 'we're partners,' how we're 'walking together down the right paths of my life blah blah blah?'"

"I do."

"I'd like you a lot better if you'd just leave me in the ditch."

"Not a chance."

"I hate you." The reluctant grin returned.

"And you're not the nice girl I thought you were."

Is This Chapter For Me?

Maybe. Maybe not. As I'll discuss later, some people with ADD actually do great when faced with a clear and obvious crisis. But other disasters just aren't that obvious. They sneak up on you when you're not paying attention. So it's worth considering this chapter, even if you have ADD and you're the star doctor or nurse in a busy emergency room. Here's a checklist of crisis management problems ADD people often face. See if you or your people think they sound familiar:

- ❏ You respond impulsively to crises, which usually makes them worse or last longer.

- ❏ When faced with a crisis, you try to avoid dealing, even when you see things going down the drain.

- ❏ You feel attracted to chaos, so you let yourself get embroiled in too much drama or perhaps even cause crises among friends, dating partners, or family.

- ❏ You get overwhelmed and collapse in a heap in the middle of a crisis that others seem to handle pretty well.

- ❏ You seem to get into the same kind of crises again and again, without learning much in the process.

Two wrongs never make a right. Nor do three. Thirty-six most definitely do not. When your world is coming unglued, it takes calm, careful observation and planning to get things back in order. If those adjectives don't describe you at the moment of crisis, this chapter is for you. It can help you manage disasters large and small, even when your brain doesn't really want to.

If It's Not One Thing, It's Another

Saturday Night Live has been on the air since I was thirteen. In its early years, Gilda Radner played a character on Weekend Update named Rosanne Rosanadanna. Search that name on YouTube to find golden nuggets of comedic history. Her rants became such a familiar shtick that on Monday morning everyone was reciting her routine in the high school hallway.

Every week Rosanne read a faux letter from a viewer on some social or political issue. I don't know about Gilda, but Rosanne Rosannadanna was about as ADD as they come. She'd respond to the question in a strangely unidentifiable accent, with ridiculous digressions, eventually deteriorating into a hilariously disgusting description of bodily functions or personal hygiene. Boogers and lint were always topical for Rosanne. Straight-woman co-host Jane Curtain just stared at her with an increasingly horrified expression, before demanding to know what any of this had to do with the viewer's question. To this, Rosanne always responded, "Well, Jane, it just goes to show you, it's always something. If it's not one thing, it's another."

Gilda died of ovarian cancer ten years later at age 42. She left behind a lovely memoire recalling her struggle with her terminal illness, an eating disorder, and the sudden disability and death of her beloved father when she was only thirteen. The book's title—*It's Always Something.*

So it goes.

A crisis is like any problem begging for a solution. But while normal problems wander in like a herd of grazing lambs messing up your lawn and eating your petunias, a real crisis leaps in like a lion, claws extended and teeth gnashing, ready to devour you.

What Not to Do

We've already discussed how people with ADD run into problems. Those same tendencies—acting without thinking, jumping from one thing to the next, blindly following your heart, ignoring how things work, taking the easy path, etc.—make it harder to select the correct off-ramp when you find yourself careening down the freeway of doom. Here are some common ways you might come face-to-face a with crisis and end up making things worse:

Entangle Yourself With Impulsive Responses. I pulled into my driveway one afternoon, fresh from the hardware store with several of those plastic shopping bags on the front seat next to me. Though environmentally unkind, you can conveniently overload them, then stick your fingers through all their handles and carry about five bags per hand into the house so you don't have to make a second trip. That's exactly what I did with my right hand. In my left, I'd wrapped the waist strap of the black fanny pack I use to carry my diabetes meds, billfold, phone, etc.

As I started to get out of the car, I felt the tug of the seatbelt against my lap. I'd forgotten to unbuckle. The correct crisis management strategy would have been to set everything back in the seat and start over, but I was eager to get inside and put my hardware treasures to work, so I chose the easy path.

I reached over with my left hand, dragging the fanny-pack across my lap, and unhooked the seatbelt, then started to lift myself out. Midway through the door, I found myself ensnared in the fanny pack, which I'd accidentally buckled around the seatbelt like a link in a chain. I fought bravely to uncouple its waist buckle with my right hand, which still held the five plastic bags. That caused the bags to swirl around the shoulder belt like anchor ropes entwining an underwater snare. I suddenly felt a great kinship with the poor sea turtles in Florida who are always dealing with these evil bags.

"Crap," I said in the PG-13 rated version of this story. "How did I get myself into this?"

Half in, half out of the car, I tried to release the bags by twirling them counter-clockwise around the belt. Instead, one of the bags, straining against the snare and the weight of its over-stuffed contents, tore open. I reflexively went to catch it with my left hand and instead dropped the rest of the bags and my fanny pack. A box of a hundred small screws broke open and scattered all over the floor of my car.

The more you entangle yourself in bad choices and short-cut exits, the more serious your crisis will become.

As I flopped back into the seat, tangled and frustrated, I experienced a moment of clarity about daily crisis management.

My clients enjoy this silly tale. Unfortunately, most messes are not as easily cleaned up as were the screws with the powerful magnet I keep in my garage. The more you entangle yourself in bad choices and short-cut exits, the more serious your crisis will become and the longer it will impact your life.

Run Run Away. People with ADD are prone to respond to crises through avoidance, procrastination, distraction, or, in some cases, literally just taking off—even if those strategies are what got you into trouble in the first place.

Because she was also fairly anxious, Melissa persevered in the face of obstacles that push back many people with ADD. But that same anxiety made her super critical of herself and her competency. The thought of a fourth nursing exam pushed her over the edge, even if not taking it would ultimately make her life worse. So, she tried to avoid what she feared most—continued failure.

Another version of running away that masquerades as a pretty neat trick is "doing something different." Some therapists even advise this to unstick clients who are so submerged in dysfunctional routines that they can't think of any new alternatives. But for people with ADD, doing something different won't solve a crisis unless it's the *right* something different, not just an easy one. Different doesn't always mean better, and a wrong solution usually makes your crisis worse. That adage "out of the frying pan and into the fire" is a bit of life instruction that dates all the way back to the fifteen century.

Get Addicted to Disaster. People with ADD sometimes respond badly to bad situations, because you're used to a certain level of chaos. You find turmoil fascinating and familiar and giving it up difficult and uncomfortable. It somehow seems easier to live within the swirling storm. You become fascinated with the novelty of a crisis or in the nature of crises in general, so you keep walking into the middle of one messed-up situation after another. I call this the death spiral. I mean that metaphorically, but I've actually seen it get dangerously close to the real thing.

A great example is found in the movie *Changing Lanes.* Gavin Banek (Ben Affleck) is a ambitious young attorney on his way to a New York City courthouse for a multimillion dollar probate hearing. He runs into Doyle Gipson (Samuel L. Jackson), a middle-class working man headed to the same courthouse to fight for shared custody of his kids. By this, I mean Banek literally runs into him, wrecking and disabling Gipson's car on the FDR Expressway. In a hurry, Banek tries to give Gipson a check for the damage, but Gipson, a recovering alcoholic, wants to "do things clean" by getting a police report and filing insurance. Frustrated, Banek takes off, leaving Gipson stranded on the road of life. Gipson is late to court and loses his case by default.

At that point, both discover that Banek has left behind an irreplaceable file needed for his court appearance. Gipson's anger at the loss of his children leads him to take the file hostage. Banek retaliates by hacking Gipson's credit history, just as he's trying to buy a house so his kids won't be moved to Oregon.

Midway through the day, Gipson sits alone in a bar, contemplating his deteriorating life and a full glass of whiskey. We sense impending doom. The scene fades to Banek's equally deteriorating situation. When we return to the bar, however, the glass of whiskey remains untouched and Gipson is on the phone with his sponsor (William Hurt). Though he doesn't take the drink, the day doesn't exactly get better. Gipson causes Banek to wreck his car. Banek tricks Gipson into melting down and getting arrested at his children's school.

Hurt shows up to bail Gipson out of jail and insists they go straight to an AA meeting, but Gipson refuses. They argue in front of the jail. "So, you finally hit rock bottom," Hurt says. "Today you almost killed a guy, tomorrow you might go all the way. Keep doing the next wrong thing, you could start a religion, convince the sober to drink, don't tell them to keep each other alive with hope! What you saw today is that everything decent is held together by a covenant, an agreement not to go batshit. *You broke the contract.*"

"I didn't have a drink!" Gipson protests.

"Well, wow! Thank you for sharing." Hurt waves his arms, frustrated with Gipson's refusal to follow his recovery plan. "You didn't have a drink today! What an inspiration."

"That's the point isn't it?" Gipson shouts back.

"God!" Hurt turns away and steps toward the curb, then spins back to confront Gipson. "You know, booze isn't really your drug of choice, anyway."

Gipson stares at him, blankly.

Hurt nods. "You're addicted to chaos. For some of us it's coke. For some of us it's bourbon. But you, you got hooked on *disaster.*"

Only when you realize you've become fascinated by chaos, can you find a legitimate exit strategy.

Changing Lanes is a powerful allegory for how to take a rapidly deteriorating, out-of-control, downwardly spiraling crisis and make it worse. Only when you step back and realize you've become fascinated by chaos, can you find a legitimate exit strategy and get motivated to take it. In fact, that's exactly how Gipson and Banek finally resolve their mutually assured destruction.

The Advantages of Audacity

Since the chaos of a crisis lands right on top of the chaos in your head, people with ADD enjoy only a few advantages. At the top is courage. Having little anxiety is pretty helpful in situations that call for raw audacity. Some of the most gung-ho Marines I've met had ADD. They were able to stand up and remain calm in situations that would terrify the rest of us. That only works, however, because the military trains young people to know exactly what to do in a wide variety of crazy scenarios.

Because it is so familiar to them, many (but certainly not all) people with ADD can tolerate the chaos of crisis more easily than the rest of us. When things spin out of control, your anxiety goes up just enough to listen to instruction, but not enough to fall apart. This can make you an awesome first responder. Many of the medical professionals with ADD I've worked with specialize in emergency medicine or work as EMTs. They love the novelty and excitement of facing crises that would drive the rest of us over the edge.

Principle 7: When Things Go Down the Drain, Don't Make Them Worse

Whether you're facing a large lion crisis or a small toothless alley cat one, seek an exit strategy that makes things better, or at the very least, does not make them worse. Here's a nine-step crisis management system to get you started. You'll want to walk through these steps in order. You may not need every one in every crisis, but consider each carefully before skipping it. Since this list won't fit on your wrist, copy it to your smartphone by scanning the QR code above, so you're ready to go when you hear the lion roar.

1. **Try To Remain Calm.** No matter what the crisis, you can't make a good decision while panicking. Carefully consider all the principles you've learned thus far, and several yet to come, before proceeding.

2. **Buy Time.** Crises often come with a clock or some factor that pressures your decision. Melissa couldn't practice nursing until she'd

passed the board exam. Gipson was going to lose his kids in a few days if he didn't buy a house. Banek was about to lose millions of ill-gotten dollars. Yet, pressured decisions are usually bad decisions. Do what you can to slow things down without putting your exit at risk, then use that time wisely to think through and follow the rest of the steps.

3.   **Get to A Safe Spot**. This can be literal, like pulling over in a parking lot to determine just how lost you really are on the Los Angeles freeway, or figurative, like stepping back from the trauma of your crisis so you can consider your options. Some crises don't lend themselves to this, but as any lifeguard will tell you, it's hard to save anyone if you can't keep yourself safe.

4.   **Define Nature and Scope**. There are many exceptions, but most crises aren't as bad as they seem at first. Rationally assess how immediate your crisis is, what it involves, and how much it threatens your situation. Be careful not to fool yourself into under-responding. It's a tough needle to thread. You need enough anxiety to solve the problem, but not so much that you become immobilized. Unfortunately, as with anything, practice makes perfect.

5.   **Consider How You Got to This Point.** Philosopher George Santayana famously said, "Those who cannot remember the past, are condemned to repeat it."[38] If you don't know how you got here, it's easy to take the wrong exit or keep doing the same thing over and over again, expecting things to change. Honesty in self-reflection is always important, but in a crisis, it's crucial. If it's your fault that things are spiraling out of control, own up. If you're too full of pride, shame, or self-deception, you can't help but make everything worse. More on that in Chapters 8 and 9.

6.   **Figure Out How Things Work.** Any advice or instruction you can get is a godsend during a crisis. In fact, a lot of my therapy with ADD people is helping them manage small disasters so they don't become big ones. Sometimes you won't have time to get live advice. Depending on the crisis, check the Internet for wise information on how to cope. It's saved me many times. Vet crisis instructions well, even if you're pressed for time. In a crisis, bad advice always makes things worse. Gipson knew who to call in *Changing Lanes*, even if he didn't like hearing the critical truth in his sponsor's words.

---

[38] The Life of Reason: Vol. I, Reason in Common Sense

7. **Discern the Right Exit from the Easy One.** You'll never be more tempted to grab the first solution you see than when you're face-to-face with doom. Do a fast pro and con list, even if it's just in your head. Typically if a solution looks too good to be true, it probably is, so vet your exit as carefully as you can within the time constraints. Reject any plan that includes avoidance, shortcuts, schemes, illegalities, unethical behavior, gambling, borrowing more money when you're already in debt, and so on. Ideas that are bad when you're not in crisis, are twice as bad when you are.

8. **Act.** Once you know what to do, do it. It's fine to buy time to think a problem through, and holding your decision so as not to make things worse is a smart position. But procrastination can be just as dangerous in a crisis as impulsivity. So always act wisely, but do act.

9. **Conduct A Post-Crisis Review.** If you're forced to deal with a crisis, you might as well get something from it. The only way that's going to happen is if you go back over what happened and see what you can learn. This should include understanding how to avoid a repeat performance, what you should have done differently in handling it, and what you did well that you'll want to repeat in the future.

Everyone is expected to create as few problems as possible and fix the messes they do make. What happens when you become incapable of managing life's ups and downs or get addicted to chaos? When you get a reputation as a hot mess or drama king/queen, difficult and high maintenance, or worse, manipulative, dishonest, and fake? You break the covenant. And it's all downhill from there.

In the next chapter we'll see just how far down that hill people with ADD can go, when they stop paying enough attention to who they are and how they're treating others.

CHAPTER 8

RESPONSIBILITY

Man is condemned to be free; because once thrown into the world, he is responsible for everything he does.

— Jean Paul Sartre

"I didn't mean for it to go down that way. Really, I didn't." Leandra kneaded the soft side of her weird furry purse. "It isn't like I *told* Stone to stab Xavier."

"Oh, please," I said. "This guy got stabbed because of your bad decisions."

"In the arm." Leandra flashed her I'm-in-trouble smile. "Let's not make this any more tragic than we have to."

"It sliced open an artery. He could have bled out before the ambulance got there."

"I know." She sighed. "But it's in the past. Nothing I can do about it now."

"It was only three weeks ago, Lee. And yes, due to the laws of physics, you can't go back in time and change what happened. But you still have to take responsibility for your part in it or else stuff like this will just keep happening."

"No it won't. I've learned my lesson this time." She offered up a sincere, wide-eyed look.

I folded my arms across my chest and offered a grumpy one in return. "Okay. Tell me exactly what you think you've learned? Because I've heard you say that about two hundred times, and so far, you're all talk."

"Well..." Her gaze darted around the room. "I guess I've learned...uh. I think I need to...I should have texted Stone to see where he was before me and Xavier went—"

"How about never dating two different guys, one of whom is a gangster, at the same time ever again?"

"Well, there's that." She giggled.

"It's not funny, Lee."

"Obviously. But you know how I get when I do something wrong. I'm not laughing about what happened. I just have to keep up a good face. It's embarrassing to be into so much effed up shit."

I sat quietly, trying to look exasperated with a girl whose special power was disarming people's exasperation. We'd been down one wrong path after another since she was fifteen. It took Leandra two stints in juvenile detention at seventeen, the first for sale and distribution, the second for assaulting a police officer, before she finally agreed to be tested for ADD. While medication had proven a miracle, she still moved effortlessly from meteoric success to disastrous misstep. One semester she'd get a 4.0 GPA in college and find a great job. The next she'd drop out, get fired and go straight back to trouble, usually in the form of a boy. Sometimes she was a victim of violence. Other times, the offender.

We sat staring at each other for at least a minute before she finally broke the edgy silence. "What?"

"Do you *ever* get tired of us not getting anywhere?"

"All the time. Nothing ever works right for me. I mean, really, what were the chances that Stone would be at that particular mall at the very moment Xavier and I pulled up? Zero. Eff my life. I just have the worst luck."

"You make your own luck, Lee. Every day in every way."

She dropped her gaze to the floor and her voice softened. "Please don't say that. I mean...I know you're right, but just don't say it. I'd rather—"

"Make another excuse?"

"I'm not making excuses. You know I never mean any of the things I do. They just happen."

"I don't care what you don't mean to do or how stuff just happens. I care about what you *do* mean to do, about what you make happen."

"But, I wasn't responsible. I didn't even know Stone had a knife on him. That's why he's in jail and I'm not."

"But you associate with violent people, Lee. I've told you about a hundred times that I worry you'll end up dead."

"And it's a terrible thing to say every time you say it!"

"Then you cleaned up your act and started dating a real live tax-payer, Xavier, a guy you met in class. Except you never got around to mentioning your life in the game—"

"I haven't sold drugs since I was in high school."

"You're still with Stone, so you're still in the game. You don't get to be a halftime gangbanger. When Stone saw you two together at the mall, his inner jealous fourteen-year-old boy came storming out, grabbed a knife and stabbed Xavier—"

"In the arm."

I let out a sigh and furrowed my brow. "I'm done."

Leandra looked up. "Excuse me? What do you mean? You can't be done."

"Every week you come in here and tell me another engaging tale of bad behavior, like you're coming to confession and I'm your priest. There's always another crazy effed-up mess you've gotten yourself into."

"What can I say, Wes? I'm a bad, bad girl." She batted her long, dark eyelashes. "But I want to be better. You know I do."

"And then you say that and I actually think you mean it and you probably do—at that moment. So, I give you a penance, which is basically listening to me lecture you about how unethical and lacking in empathy you've been that week, and—"

"Whoa there, buddy." Her voice felt more serious than the words themselves. "I passed Psych 101. I know where you're headed. I'm *not* a sociopath."

"Prove it. Because I'm not so sure anymore. I hear your confession and I want to believe you're remorseful, so then I absolve you of sin and you go out the next week and do the same thing again, or in Xavier's case, something worse. And while we're on the subject of gentleman callers, let's not forget Scooter, the man with the Harley and the generous pocketbook."

"That's on you, Wes. You told me I needed to start dating a better class of men. Scooter's a big step up."

"Were you planning on telling him about Xavier, Stone, and the whole stabbing situation?"

"Stop it." Her voice broke. "Just stop. Please."

"You can't just randomly decide who you want to be and then impose that on the rest of us. When you do that, people get hurt."

Leandra rubbed her forehead for several moments, then cupped her chin in her hands. "Scooter said something the other day. He said, 'Do you know how hard it is for you to want something on Monday, I get it for you on Wednesday and you punish me for it on Friday?' I didn't get what he meant until now.

"And what did you tell him?"

Tears welled up in Leandra's eyes. "I told him, 'Do you know how hard it is to *be* one thing on Monday, something different on Wednesday, and something completely different on Friday?' God, what's wrong with me? I feel like a multiple personality or something."

"That would be a nice excuse, wouldn't it?" I knew from years of experience with Leandra that as much as I felt her pain, I couldn't back down now. Caring about someone and showing empathy for her struggle, isn't the same as caving in and letting her sidestep the inevitable pain of consequence. "Except you don't have multiple personalities. You have ADD and that's only an explanation. It's not an excuse. Until you force yourself to be more consistent in life, I can't help you."

"But, I need your help, Wes. Do you know how hard it is to admit that? You're like, honest with me and I kind of trust you. Which I actually hate, but still—you're the only person in my life who isn't a douchebag."

"Which is also your responsibility." I paused and softened my voice. "Listen, Lee. I'm not giving up on you. But I'm not willing to see you until you decide that you're ready to see me and actually listen to my advice. I won't keep enabling you by making you think you're getting better, when you're not. That's me taking responsibility for what I do."

Leandra sat quietly for longer than I imagined possible, before letting out a frustrated groan. "Fine. Whatever. I never really wanted to be here in the first place. Then you suckered me into liking you."

"Who suckered who, Lee?" I smiled. "But now I have to let you go because I care too much about you to keep playing along."

Leandra scoffed. "Nice way to show you care."

"It is, in fact, the only way."

"So..." She gathered her purse and her jacket and stood up to leave. "How am I gonna know when I'm ready to come back?"

"I have no idea." I stood and opened the office door for her. She followed me through and into the empty waiting area. "But I'm looking forward to hearing all about it whenever you do come back. Just be sure you don't show up one minute sooner than you're really ready."

"This is so unfair." She reached over and gave me a little side-to-side hug. "But thanks." I couldn't tell if her tone was serious or sarcastic.

I hugged her back, feeling more deeply than I could afford to confess, how much I would miss her. "Go make some better luck. Okay?"

"Whatever." She wiped her eyes on her sleeve and left.

Is This Chapter For Me?

Hopefully not. Hopefully, a chapter about personal responsibility is better suited to that ex-boy or girlfriend you so wisely dumped. Or maybe it will serve only as a review of issues you nailed down a long time ago. Truth be told, however, we all struggle with responsibility from time to time, though perhaps not as wildly as Leandra. I not only use the ideas in this chapter with my clients, but I apply them to my own life, just to be sure I really am who I think I am one day to the next. Responsibility is something we all face individually and together. So, before you skip on to the next chapter, ask yourself and your people if you:

❏ Downplay your own role in situations that turn out badly.

❏ Let others do for you what you should be able to do for yourself.

❏ Complain that no matter what you do, things never turn out right, so why try?

❏ Use diagnosis as an excuse rather than an explanation for your problems.

❏ Claim hopelessness or helplessness to avoid responsibility.

❏ Don't seem to think or feel the same way about yourself, your beliefs, or your people from one day to the next.

❏ Move on quickly and avoid thinking about things you've done wrong, or obligations you've left unfulfilled, because dealing makes you feel too bad about yourself.

Coping with your influence on your own life and the lives of others is key to living successfully with ADD. If you've got personal responsibility mastered already, I salute you. If not, then this chapter is for you. Read it in the spirit it was intended—to help you become the responsible person you want to be.

Free Will 101

Among the most underappreciated movies I've seen is *Minority Report*. It's adapted from a short story by Philip K. Dick, on whose work the classic sci-fi film noire *Blade Runner* is also based. Directed by Steven Spielberg and starring Tom Cruise, critics called *Minority Report* a masterpiece, but at the box office it was beaten out in its first week by *Scooby Doo The Movie*.

I wish I were kidding.

I suggest you rent it—*Minority Report*, that is, not *Scooby Doo*—but I can sum up the theme of the movie in a single line of dialogue: "You can choose."

Tom Cruise plays John Anderton, a police officer in 2054 Washington DC. He serves in a special unit that arrests murderers *before* they commit their crimes. They use three mutated humans called precogs hooked up to a futuristic gizmo to predict what crimes are about to happen. Then, as luck would have it, Anderton is himself foreseen as a murderer just thirty-six hours into the future. Or is it luck? Perhaps someone's pulling a futuristic frame-up. Anderton *had* been asking a lot of questions about irregularities in another investigation. Either way, Anderton must now escape his own colleagues, go undercover, and try to discover and change whatever circumstances will lead up to the crime, thus preventing himself from committing it.

But is it actually possible to change his future or is he destined to fulfill the prophecy of the precogs? See the movie, find out, and apply it to your life.

Each day you must prove that your destiny is in your own hands through every choice you make.

Although a tad less dramatically, each day you must answer this same question for yourself. You must prove that your destiny is in your own hands through every choice you make. We call this "free will."

Sounds cool, doesn't it? You're free. You have a will. You can choose.

Except, as Sartre points out in the opening quote, free will is also scary. It requires us to accept responsibility for all our choices: our mistakes as well as our successes; our failures alongside our good deeds. Because many people with ADD grow up feeling they're not very good at life, they tend to either ignore or deliberately avoid the responsibility of ultimate choice.

Who's Really in Charge?

"Wait a second psychology guy," you say. "Aren't we really controlled by our brains? I mean, that's where every single thought, feeling, behavior, and word comes from. Just how free are we, really?"

Good point. Your brain does store every memory, generate every emotion and idea, and allow you to interact with and manage your world. That's not only true for you, but also for your pet cat, a dolphin, and every other creature that has a brain. What makes us different is that we have a larger cerebral cortex relative to the rest of our brains. That part of the brain handles many of our unique human skills, ideations, language, and problem solving.[39] Animals respond mostly to instinct, impulse and very basic conditioning. So do we, except our big forebrains allow us to go beyond instinct to have a higher consciousness of ourselves and our world. That in turn allows us to influence our brains to say, do, think, and feel what we want to; to direct and redirect our needs and impulses and how to pursue them. Simply put, *you can choose.*

Because it causes problems with executive function and metacognition[40], ADD makes it harder for you to mediate your experiences, both internal (needs and impulses) and external (what's happening all around you). That makes you feel more at the whim of those experiences and less like you're choosing what to focus on, take in, and do.

Stimulant medication is called that because it stimulates the part of the brain that lets you do everything I just described. Medication levels the playing field so you can successfully wrestle with your brain to get it to do your bidding, instead of the other way around. Lots more on that in Chapter 13.

Free will lies at the core of psychotherapy for ADD and every other problem that crosses my threshold. If you don't believe you're free to choose, you aren't free to change. If I don't believe you have free will, I won't see you in therapy because you can't give "informed consent[41]." Or, if I believe you are free to choose and you choose to harm others, I won't see you either. I'd just be helping you become better at being bad.

I'm not into that.

Leandra saw herself and her world as guided by fate. I stuck with her as long as I did because I believed she could reconnect with her own free will and finally get real. If she realized she was choosing to be bad, she could choose not to be. She'd come tantalizingly close many times. That's the thing about free will: you have to use it or lose it. You can see how that came out for Leandra in the Epilogue.

---

[39] www.sciencemuseum.org.uk/whoami/findoutmore/yourbrain/howdoesyourbrainwork/whatarethepartsofyourbrain/whatmakesthehumanbrainunique.aspx

[40] No, metacognition isn't another character from *Minority Report*. It refers to the way we understand and think about our thinking and learning. It's basically thinking about thinking, and truth be known, that's what this whole book is about!

[41] The ability both to understand the nature and quality of psychotherapy or medication and to consent to receive it.

Perhaps you've been told that you need to be more responsible. That means taking charge of your destiny. We actually use the term in two slightly different ways, both of which are critical for people with ADD.

Responsibility: Take Care of Yourself So We Don't Have To

Used this way, responsibility means "able to respond" to what needs to be done in your own life without excessive[42] help from others; managing your own affairs in an age-appropriate manner. The older you get, the more responsibility society expects you to take. This could be as simple as cleaning up after yourself so your mom or roommate or spouse doesn't have to, paying your bills, making and keeping appointments, or holding a job.

Taking care of yourself sounds awesome when you're fourteen, yearning for freedom from parental authority. You want to make your own decisions and live life as you see fit. But responsibility isn't about freedom. It's about independence. Never confuse the two. We only become free to do as we please if we spend the time and energy to create our own space in the world. Freedom isn't free. It's quite expensive, actually.

After about a week, taking care of yourself isn't all that interesting, which makes real responsibility challenging for people with ADD, especially if you're used to a pretty cushy life at home with Mom and Dad and a lot of disposable income. It involves working, saving money, keeping obligations, paying bills, and so on. In the long run, however, irresponsibility is a whole lot harder.

Research shows that adults with untreated ADD are in worse shape financially, educationally, and socially.

Short of a critical illness or debilitating accident, failure to take age-appropriate responsibility by your mid-twenties is about the worst problem anyone can face. In fact, I've seen many responsible young adults bounce back from physical health crises. Irresponsible ones struggle endlessly as victims of their own ineffectiveness. We even have a word for people at the extreme low end of this spectrum. We call them incompetent[43].

Incompetent people are dependent on family, spouses, their kids, or the government—for their survival. People with ADD are especially at risk for this

---

[42] Everyone needs support now and then, including responsible people. There's a big difference between interdependence (working together as a team) and dependency (being constantly needy).

[43] I'm using this term in the common, pejorative sense. Psychologists also use this term to legally define people as so impaired by mental illness, cognitive impairment, or dementia that they lack capacity to make rational choices and must be cared for by others. That's not what I mean here.

if they don't get adequate treatment as children or teens. This isn't just a Dr. Wes-ism. The research shows that adults with untreated ADD are in worse shape financially, educationally, and socially when compared to the rest of us.

Yikes. When you look at it that way, things don't seem very hopeful, do they?

So, let's not look at it that way. Instead, consider that the best thing about having ADD is that *you are not its helpless victim.* We know what to do to make your life better, or else I wouldn't keep working with kids and adults and watching them succeed. I wouldn't have written this book. You can't choose to not have ADD, but you can choose how to treat it.

You don't have to end up as anybody's statistic.

Responsibility: Face Up to Your Screw Ups

The second definition of responsibility means to accept accountability for your mistakes, admitting to yourself and others, "I did that. I contributed to this problem." Of course you can take responsibility for your brilliant, creative solutions too, but that's easy and comfortable. Failure? Not so much.

We've all screwed up. Most mistakes are minor. Others, like getting one of your several boyfriends stabbed, are not. Think of mistakes as a special type of crisis—the result of not understanding something, not thinking it through before acting, or not caring (focusing) enough to plot a better solution. Taking responsibility for screw-ups is one of the most important elements of living in society. In fact, we have a name for people who chronically, deliberately, and severely shirk accountability for their harmful behaviors. We call them "sociopaths"[44].

Although we diagnose it as a psychological problem, sociopathy isn't really like other mental disorders. It's about being bad, knowing you're bad, and continuing to be bad even when you see the negative consequences of your actions.

Even if you avoid responsibility and, at times act, against social convention, people with ADD aren't usually sociopaths. You don't mean to hurt anyone, you just find the expectations and customs of our world frustrating and difficult to follow. It's like the ocean of life is so big and your boat is so small, out there adrift on the waves. So you search for any way to get to shore, and if you have to break some rules to get there, that's just how it goes. When you do hurt someone, you may feel genuinely sorry.

---

[44] Psychologists have actually used the term "Antisocial Personality Disorder" for many years to diagnosis sociopaths, but that term confuses the general public, who think it means someone who doesn't like to be around other people. That's something completely different. Many psychologists still use the term sociopathy for greater clarity, as I am doing here.

Unfortunately, others probably won't view your mistakes with such charity, especially when you create havoc with your bad choices, your failure to follow instructions, or your meandering. They'll just get angry and tell you you're irresponsible. That makes it harder for you to face the music. So you further avoid responsibility and try hard to care less what others think of you because it hurts. That in turn makes people see you as even more irresponsible and so on. Eventually they just give up and decide you're bad.

That's why Leandra got nervous when I started talking about ethics, empathy, and remorse. She knew she was short on all three. I included her in this book not because most people with ADD go on to develop sociopathy, but because she's the extreme example that makes a broader point. Unfortunately, you never know where flawed thinking, impulsivity, and poor decision making will take you. So, sociopathy is worth mentioning. Think of me as the Ghost of Christmas Future. When I fly into your bedroom and haunt your dreams tonight, ask me, "Spirit, is this the future as it will be or as it might be?"

Bet you can guess the answer as I hover over your fitful sleep. "The future depends upon you. Wuhahaha...."

Psychological Integrity

In Chapter 5 we discussed ambitence, a style of coping and decision making in which people move randomly back and forth between emotion- and thought-based problem solving. Many people with ADD have this style, leaving them and everyone else confused and off-kilter. Or, as Leandra put it so well, it's hard to be one thing on Monday, something different on Wednesday, and something completely different on Friday.

A core part of responsibility is being predictable from one day to the next.

A core part of responsibility is being predictable from one day to the next. That allows everyone to count on you to do and say what you mean, and mean what you say and do. I use the term "psychological integrity" to describe that kind of consistency.

I'm not talking about moral integrity. We'll discuss that in Chapter 9. Here, the word "integrity" is about structure; how things hold together. If a building lacks integrity, it could collapse at any moment. If you lack psychological integrity, you won't be consistent in thought, feeling, and behavior from one day to the next. Nobody can predict what you'll do next. The structure guiding your life might collapse at any moment.

Whether you're introverted or extroverted, you're still interconnected with others, engaged in a complex and delicate social fabric with family, friends, and community. We can sense each other's level of psychological integrity. Those who have it seem the same whenever we meet them—not in a boring, vanilla way, but in a stable, solid one. We trust someone we can depend on and we gravitate toward him or her. We feel uncomfortable around people we can't predict, even if we find them entertaining, and we rarely like or have faith in them.

Karma Chameleon. You've heard the adage, "What goes around comes around," or if you prefer to paraphrase the Christian Bible, "You reap what you sow." Our goal every day in life should be to create more solutions than problems and to take honest responsibility for both. To pass on good, you have to be a consistent and authentic person day after day. When you make mistakes, you must own up to them and set about a plan for change.

The biggest threat to Karma is something I teach all my ADD clients and their people. It sounds kind of harsh and un-Karma-like when I call it "The thing we hate about ADD people." Although I named it that with my tongue firmly in my cheek, if you have it, this particular characteristic will cause you more problems with others than anything else. It can get you fired or divorced. It might even get somebody hurt. So, I gave it that name to get people's attention.

Now that I have yours, here's the thing we hate about people with ADD: *You seem to have infinite tolerance for your own chaos and none for anyone else's.*

No matter their age or severity, clients recognize intuitively what I mean by this, and none are offended. Occasionally, a client agrees with my premise but adds, "Actually, I don't like my chaos, either." But what I'm really saying is that no matter how much you like or hate your chaos, you're always more willing to put up with it than you are with ours. That's very apparent to the rest of us, and we don't respond well to it.

No matter how much you like or hate your chaos, you're always more willing to put up with it than you are with ours.

Here's how this works. It's hard enough for folks with ADD to organize their minds, their space, or their lives. Even when you're getting oh-so close, everything always seems right on the edge of entropy. So there you are, all knee-deep in chaos, and along comes everyone else in the world, teachers, bosses, bus drivers, parents, friends, dating partners, the government, The Chicago Cubs, and what do they have the audacity to do? They thoughtlessly pile their own chaos right on top of yours. And you don't like it.

"No way!" your people cry out. "I'm constantly adding structure, not chaos, to the life of my [son, wife, employee, etc.]. I'm not the chaotic one!"

They really believe they're trying to help, but that's not how you, the ADD person, sees it. You either want everyone to do things your way, or leave you alone to do them the way you want to. This is because you don't actually see your world as chaotic, or if you do, you see your chaos as comfortable, like an old familiar, slightly annoying friend. Your chaos makes sense to you, even if it causes your life to run as inefficiently as a 1967 Cadillac.

So if everybody would just quit organizing you, things would turn out fine, right? Sorry. There's more to it than that. We each bring our own idiosyncrasies and unique ways of being to our relationships. Maybe we're very clean or very messy, overconfident or insecure, introverted or extroverted. Maybe we love to work or hold a job just to pay for our leisure time. None of these ways is right or wrong, but a huge part of negotiating relationships is learning to accommodate[45] and assimilate[46] them, so we all feel we're getting a fair deal and contributing equally. We call this "reciprocity." It's how Karma works. We give what we get and get what we give.

If you have ADD, however, accommodating and assimilating others' ways of doing and being can be hard. Be honest. Wouldn't you rather have everyone accommodate or assimilate your weird stuff? We're all like that. It's a form of what we call the "self-serving attributional bias," where we assign good things to ourselves and problems anywhere else we can find. Or as my mom used to say with a tone of irony, "My dirt is clean dirt. Your dirt is dirty dirt." But just as with anything uncomfortable, people with ADD have a harder time than the rest of us tolerating all this give and take. It feels like a huge burden, making obligations even harder to handle.

Not only do you ask the rest of us to keep our chaos to ourselves, you also ask us to unconditionally accept yours and you take it as a personal affront when we don't want to. Or to paraphrase my mom, you think *our* chaos is chaotic chaos and *your* chaos is comfortable, carefree chaos. This upsets the rest of us to no end. It is "the thing we hate about ADD people."

For example, Leandra constantly complained that she couldn't trust others, yet she was deceptive herself. She thought her bosses terribly unfair, but called in or didn't show up when she was sick or hung-over. She would no-show an appointment at noon, then beg to see me at 7:30 p.m., as I was closing the office for the day. With me and everyone else, Lee trusted her winning smile and infectious charm to get her out of any mess her chaos had created.

For a while, that worked. Ultimately, it did not.

---

[45] In a cultural context, accommodation means changing your perspective to allow differences between yourself and others to continue.

[46] Adapting yourself, your relationship, the person you're in the relationship with, or all three to change how you operate.

Avoiding Avoidance...Again

There are many ways people with ADD attempt to avoid both forms of responsibility. Here are the most common.

Self-Deception. Lying to yourself is called "denial." It means ignoring or minimizing things in your personality or behavior that, if you acknowledged them, would require you to change. I think Leandra really did feel sorry for what happened to Xavier and her role in it, but she didn't let it touch her deeply enough or cause her enough anxiety to change. Any time it did, she reminded me (and herself) that she didn't hold the knife, so the stabbing wasn't really her fault.

Excuses. This one will really irritate your people because excuses are the exact opposite of personal responsibility. Unless you're unusually good at making them, excuses let everyone in on the fact that you're unreliable. Unfortunately, ADD itself is often seen as an excuse and some people with ADD use it to avoid responsibility. A diagnosis is an explanation, not an excuse. It tells us what to do to help you. It doesn't absolve you for your choices in life or explain away the mistakes you make.

Fatalism. People with ADD have terrible luck. They end up with the worst teachers, parents, bosses, roommates, friends, and dating partners known to humankind, while the lucky people get all the awesome breaks in life. I know this because they tell me all about it, every week.

Fatalism means your future is determined by stuff that's beyond your control. It can come from feeling powerless in the face of too many demands, but more often it's another method of avoidance. Your people hate it when you complain about bad luck or "circumstances beyond your control." They see it as a copout that not only excuses your errors, but demeans their efforts at success, especially if you blame them for your bad outcomes.

That said, there can be a grain of truth to this excuse, but it comes not from bad luck, but bad organization. For example, college students with ADD tend to enroll late in classes, leaving them with leftovers taught by professors with low student ratings and reviews. In seeking work, you may gravitate toward "easy path" jobs, which, not incidentally, your bosses gravitated toward, too. Thus you end up as an ADD person being led around by other ADD people, which is mutually frustrating for folks intolerant of other's chaos and too tolerant of their own.

In dating, patience is a virtue. Yet, people with ADD may glom onto the wrong partners because you jump too quickly and too early in the relationship, or end relationships too soon because they are stable, but boring. Even family can generate a lot of tension and frustration. Your parents may blame themselves for your condition and you may be happy to join that bandwagon rather than owning your problems. Because ADD frequently delays or makes more difficult the transition to adulthood, your parents may stay involved in your life longer, so it's likely you'll find more fault with them than your non-ADD friends who need less support.

In attempting to reacquaint you with free will, your people can accidentally make you feel even *more* powerless over your ADD. Frustrated with your chaotic ways and desperate to shove you down a better path, parents, friends, teachers, and dating partners release an endless stream of negative commentary. Any of these sound familiar?

- "Why can't you understand?"

- "You'd do so much better if you'd just apply yourself."

- "Finish what you started before going on to something else."

- "What were you thinking?"

- "Why can't you get it together?"

- "You are so lazy and irresponsible!"

- "Focus!"

Your people don't mean to be hurtful. They obviously care, or else they wouldn't spend so much time and energy redirecting you. In fact, if you tone down the judgment a tad, any of the above might be good advice. But hearing those words day in and day out, judgment attached, only sharpens your sense that you're controlled by your brain rather than the other way around.

In many cases, the supposed terribleness of your teacher, lover, parent, friend, or boss is in the eye of the beholder and not very helpful. Blaming everyone but yourself ultimately makes you a puppet, which in turn leads directly to....

Defeatism. When facing the "terrible cards dealt them by fate," people with ADD may decide to give up. In fact, failure to persist is a key element of ADD. You lose hope, surrender and accept whatever comes your way. In therapy I call this "collapsing in a heap" and there are a hundred ways to do it. An example is Leandra attributing her behavior to being a "bad, bad girl," as if this were an irreversible part of her personality, rather than a choice.

If your people find your displays of hopelessness are only designed to get you out of a fix or gain sympathy, their hearts will quickly harden. Worse, they'll start using the "M-word" to describe you: "manipulative." Attempting to avoid responsibility by collapsing, shedding crocodile tears, or begging for "one more chance" will get you cast in this light. Second only to sociopath, manipulative is about the worst thing anyone can call you.

The Advantages of Externalizing Blame

People with ADD enjoy exactly one advantage in the area of personal responsibility. I hesitate even mentioning it, because I'm not sure how helpful it really is in a book on how to succeed in life by bargaining in good faith with your destiny. But since the next chapter is about radical honesty, I should probably practice it myself.

Psychologists who study attribution[47] find that people who internalize credit for their own successes and externalize blame for their failures are happier than people who blame themselves for their own shortcomings. Yes, you read that right. They're telling you to do exactly what I told you not to do.

Since people with ADD tend to follow that advice on instinct, it stands to reason they would feel happier than other people, doesn't it? I have, in fact, found that to be true. Sort of. A "don't worry be happy" attitude certainly comes in handy when you need to sidestep failure and push on to success.

Unfortunately, this thinking can go terribly wrong, specifically when your happy illusion prevents you from changing your life for the better. Leandra was always cheery, even in the face of disaster. Her rejection of her portion of responsibility for the stabbing made her feel less sad. It also made her look pretty darn sociopathic and left her vulnerable to further chaos because she couldn't identify the lesson she'd learned and apply it to future situations. So, as advantages go, externalizing blame is pretty dicey. Use your mentor to gauge when to let go of personal responsibility and when to recognize it as key to your survival and success.

Principle 8: Take Personal Responsibility

It's the hardest path you'll walk in life, but psychological and moral integrity, and respectability are the only real roads to success. Responsibility is the most fundamental sign of maturity. No matter how old you are, you can't be a grown-up unless you follow this principle. Here's how to get started.

Add These Two Equations to Your Tattoo List. They'll remind you of how responsibility works and what happens if you take the easy path to avoid it.

Responsibility → Independence → Freedom

Irresponsibility → Dependency → Lost Control → Incompetence

---

[47] The process by which we explain and give meaning to behavior and events going on around and within ourselves. For example, if I like you, I'll cut you more slack than if I don't like you.

Get Help. Thanks for buying this book. I sincerely hope it kick-starts your journey, but if you're more than a leaner, it's no substitute for meds and therapy. In fact, clinical experience and research demonstrate substantial risks of letting ADD go untreated,[48] including irresponsibility, impulsive action, and questionable shortcuts that lead to bad conduct and even criminal behavior.

If you're a parent and hesitant to move forward on treatment for your child, consider this: we only get one chance to grow up. After the age of eighteen, it's harder to learn the life lessons you should have learned as a child, and they come with greater consequence. Too many parents underestimate that risk, hope their kids will outgrow ADD, and wait until things get bad. Others "don't believe in ADD," think it's "over-diagnosed," or "don't want their kids on those meds."

ADD doesn't care if you believe in it or not. It's no more faith-based than are diabetes or kidney stones.

ADD doesn't care if you believe in it or not. It's no more faith-based than are diabetes or kidney stones. While it's often misdiagnosed, it isn't overdiagnosed and even if it were, is that a reason to deny your child a treatment that he or she needs? Success in life for your child is not about politics or population statistics. Don't lose the chance for your child to benefit from assessment and treatment.

If you missed out on treatment as a child or teenager, I'm sincerely sorry. I see this every week. It's difficult to meet smart, creative, interesting adults who've failed out of school, relationships, and life, and now feel terrible about themselves. But it's also exciting, because once they come in for help, many like the folks in this book, take charge and create the lives they want and deserve.

Practice Chaos Karma. No matter what you do or where you turn, you must learn to accommodate and assimilate other people's needs. If you can't, you'll keep getting into one messed-up situation after another and you won't be able to depend on others to help you out. In practice this means:

- Recognize and manage your own chaos so it doesn't slop out onto everyone else. Make a list of what really frustrates your people when dealing with you. Take one item at a time and set up a system to change it. If you leave your clothes on the floor, find the easiest method to get them into the laundry. If you get too caught

---

[48] This only applies if you really have ADD. There is great risk in taking medication for a disorder you do not have, just to sharpen up your studying.

up in your own life to pay attention to your partner, put a note on your calendar to send a cute text or go on a date.

- Have reasonable expectations for how much chaos others can take and don't push them farther than they can go. I refer to this as not "overtaxing" them. The more your people feel you're protecting them from your zaniness, the more they'll respect you and the more they'll support you and your efforts.

- Tolerate the chaos of others. People will be far more forgiving of your chaos if they feel you're accepting of theirs. Describe diplomatically what irritates you about them. For example, if you're coming off stimulant medication at 5:00 or 6:00 p.m., you're likely to be irritable and fatigued. That's the worst time for anyone to ask you for anything. Instead, schedule times to talk with family or your partner when medication is fully in or fully out of your system. We call that "quiet time."

- Keep a secret ledger of things you do for others and what they do for you and keep both sides in balance. Don't show it to anyone. They'll misunderstand your motives, which must be pure. The goal is to be reciprocal in the relationship, not to call in old debts.

- Give people a reason to like you. Look for ways to add value to the lives of others. If people see you as benevolent[49], they'll more readily accept your errors and shortcomings. If they start seeing your mistakes as irreversible, you're in big trouble, because they'll give up on you regardless of how charming you are.

Make Your Own Luck. French scientist Louis Pasteur said, "Chance favors only the prepared mind."[50] That's a great one for your tattoo list. It perfectly defines the relationship between luck and effort. While Pasteur was referring to scientific observation, his point implies that if you prepare yourself well, you'll recognize the unexpected opportunities life throws your way and be able to better counter its obstacles.

Be Where, When, and What You Say You Are. Be accountable to your people. Everyone's late sometimes, but when it becomes a pattern, you'll be seen as irresponsible. Use religiously the calendar app and notifications on your phone and always schedule yourself to arrive fifteen to thirty minutes ahead of time. Then when you're late, you'll still be early. Yes, you'll do more waiting, but if you use that time to meditate you'll find yourself more at peace

---

[49] Keeping their best interests at heart and not just your own.

[50] Lecture, University of Lille (December, 1854)

and more organized in your thinking. Be careful not to overschedule yourself. Impulsivity and novelty lead ADD people to keep adding "one more thing" to their calendars or to-do lists. That causes you to run behind and leaves you feeling constantly overwhelmed.

Don't hold yourself out to be someone or something you're not. I've worked with ADD people who feel so badly about (or just bored with) who they really are, that they embellish. That's a great way to be tossed out of any social group. Even family won't put up with that kind of nonsense for long.

We all need privacy, but if you can't be honest about where you are or who you're with, something is either wrong with you or the relationship in question, whether it's work, family, or romantic. For example, if you have to lie about going to a bar with friends, you're either an alcoholic in denial, avoiding your dating partner, or dating someone too rigid in his or her expectations. Figure out which it is, but don't lie and say you're visiting your old Aunt Margaret.

Slow Down. Sometimes the responsible option is not the obvious one, so you have to take a moment, meditate, and think things through. If you don't know, think of what a wise person would do—your mentor, Jesus, your grandma, or Buddha.

Don't Leave Home Prematurely. If you're under eighteen, consider remaining in your parents' home for an extra couple of years. If you're currently on your own and not doing so well, think about moving back. The research says that people with ADD mature at least two years later than their peers. Age says nothing about your maturity and competence. Responsibility does. Leave home when you're independent, not when you're free.

If you or your parents can't stand you moving home, let them set you up in the dorms or a very inexpensive apartment in exchange for turning over your finances for a couple of years. As you gain maturity and responsibility living on your own, they can pull back.

Watch Out for Sex. No, I don't mean you should see how many opportunities you can find to have it. I mean watch out for sex as you might an express bus that is about to run over you in the street. I'm not moralizing here. I do sex therapy and I like helping people have productive, positive sex that they'll enjoy throughout their lives.

Sex is one area of life that only ends up being fun when you treat it responsibly.

For many people with ADD, however, sex is too much about urges and not enough about judgment. Sex is one area of life that only ends up being fun when you treat it responsibly. That's because careless sex produces unwanted pregnancies, pushing off impulsive choices onto a new generation of innocent little babies who didn't get to give informed consent in the matter.

While we're on the subject, never intentionally get pregnant just to avoid dealing with life. If you don't have ADD, that sentence will make absolutely no sense to you. In fact, it probably makes little sense if you do have ADD. How could having a baby, even a well-planned one, help anyone avoid life? Babies *are* life. Complicated life. When we're truly ready to be parents, we like that kind of complication and we accept the obligation that goes with creating it. Yet, I've seen many teens and young adults with ADD imagining a baby as the easiest solution to the problem of career choice, college, or general life planning.

Here's how it works. Parents *say* they're not going to support a teen or young adult's unplanned pregnancy. But when a cute little baby shows up, its mother (and at times, its father) will have a parent's financial and emotional support for years to come, which frees the baby's parent to put off a normal transition to adulthood. In twenty-two years I've never seen this come out well. There are few ways you can impact your world more directly than in your sexual conduct, and here, the easy path is *never ever* the right one.

Show Genuine Remorse. No matter how responsible you are, you're going to mess up. We all do. Being sorry for your mistakes is not the same as collapsing in a heap. In nearly every case, true remorse requires you to do five things:

1. Whenever circumstances allow, acknowledge the harm you've done, listen closely to how others feel about it, and unconditionally validate their views.

2. Own the nature, quality, and wrongfulness of your behavior.

3. State that you are sorry for the specific role you played in the situation. *Never* say you're sorry that the other person feels badly or thinks you've wronged them. That's no apology at all.

4. Enact a plan to make amends to those you've harmed, unless doing so would cause greater harm.

5. Specify a realistic plan for change. This may involve change in you, in the relationship, or both. Never promise anything that you aren't committed and able to do. That just makes things worse.

Here's a quick example of how genuine remorse would sound in Leandra's voice, if she were able to express it:

> I didn't stab Xavier, but I did put him in danger by having a side-relationship with him while I was still involved with Stone, and

not warning him. My carelessness contributed to him being stabbed. I am genuinely sorry for my role in what happened. I'm going to testify about what I know of the incident, cease contact with Stone, and never date two guys at the same time again, especially if one is dangerous. I told Scooter it's not safe for him to date me at this time.

While you may "always want to be *someone* you're not" from one day to the next, the most important thing you can do on the road to personal responsibility is strive for psychological integrity. That requires you to find a set of beliefs and learn to live consistently within them.

That brings us to Principle 9.

CHAPTER 9

RADICAL HONESTY

A man got to have a code.

— Omar Little, in HBO's *The Wire*

"It's gotten to the point that I can't trust anything Don says." Jackie folded her arms and turned away from her husband sitting on the couch next to her. "I mean, I could understand if he lied about having a secret lover, but it's never anything that exciting."

"I'm not detail-oriented enough to hide a mistress," Don said in an attempt to lighten the moment. It didn't work.

"It's stupid things like whether he paid the electric bill, which he didn't this month, or if he filled up my car with gas like I asked him to, which he didn't."

Don let out a nervous chuckle. "I feel like I'm twelve and my mom caught me in the middle of the night with my best friend in my bedroom playing Pokémon with a flashlight. She was like, 'It's Friday. If you wanted Keith to spend the night, why didn't you just ask?' I just started making stuff up. 'I didn't know he was coming over. I forgot. His mom had to go the hospital.'" Don shook his head. "It's just always been like that."

Jackie stared at him, her expression stuck between befuddled and furious. "Then why do you do it? Especially if you know for certain you'll be caught. It's insulting when you say you've vacuumed and I see cat hair and crumbs on the floor." She turned to me. "I need to know if he's a pathological liar."

"He's not."

"Then what's wrong with him? We've only been married six months and I find myself Googling 'annulment' one minute and 'ways to get away with murder' the next."

"Are you serious?" Don's eyes grew wide.

"No." A slight grin creased Jackie's lips. "It's too late for an annulment."

"You knew Don had ADD when you married him, right?"

"She knew," Don interjected. "I told her the day we agreed to be exclusive, just like you said I should. "

"He did." Jackie sighed. "But I just thought ADD meant not paying attention and being disorganized. I figured I'd have to keep him on track, but I didn't know I couldn't trust him."

"But if the two of you dated for a year," I said. "You had to see some of this before the wedding."

"I guess." Jackie glanced down and fiddled with her necklace. "But, he was still trying to make a good impression back then. Now, he thinks I'm stuck so he can just be himself, whoever that is. I mean, it's not just lying. He eats my yogurt and doesn't replace it when he goes to the store. He moves stuff and tells me he didn't, then sits there trying to remember where he didn't put it. Nonsense like that. He makes promises and doesn't follow through, then he goes and covers it all up. I mean, if nothing is real with him, then what keeps him from having a secret lover?" She leaned back against the cushion and rolled her eyes. "How does ADD explain all that?"

"It's that thing you said about Don wanting to make a good impression. Nothing is as uncomfortable for people with ADD as disappointing their loved ones and feeling powerless to fix it. So they try hard to put up a good front, even if it means staging a ridiculous cover-up."

Jackie's mouth fell open as she turned back toward Don. "Is that true?"

"Pretty much," he said sheepishly. "I've always felt like I don't measure up, so I try to keep everyone from seeing me that way. But I also lie to avoid getting into it with someone I care about. Like with my mom, I didn't tell her Keith was coming over because I was afraid she'd say 'no' and we'd argue. I didn't want to feel bad or make her feel bad. It just seemed easier to have Keith sneak in my window. Then, when we got caught, it seemed easier to say anything to try and get out of it."

"But…" Jackie stammered, uncharacteristically speechless. "That doesn't make sense. How can lying make a good impression on anyone?"

"It can't," I said. "And Don knows that. But, as he said, it's easier than confronting failure. So if he procrastinates, or doesn't vacuum, feed the cat, or remember your birthday, his automatic impulse is to avoid dealing."

Jackie nodded, thoughtfully. "But if he feels bad about what he's done, then why doesn't he just correct it? It's like he has no compassion for how it hurts me."

"Close, but not exactly," I said. "It's not a lack of compassion. It's a lack of empathy. He's so caught up in the chaos up here," I tapped the side of my head, "that he doesn't always connect to the feelings of others. He feels badly about what he's done, but he's able to push it away more easily—to compartmentalize it."

"That's exactly how it is," Don said. "I know lying hurts you, but I—I don't know—I can't let myself really feel it inside. All I feel is, um…"

"Ashamed?" I asked.

"Yeah. That."

"This is where it gets complicated," I said. "For most of us, shame drives us to take responsibility for our actions and set things right. But Don can't really differentiate the discomfort of doing something shameful from being a shameful person. So he puts it all in a box and locks it away."

"You're saying he can't let himself learn from his own bad behavior…" Jackie's voice trailed off to a murmur. "He can't learn."

"He *can* learn," I said. "It just takes extra effort, courage, and willpower. Facing up doesn't come naturally to him. He has to be intentional about it."

Don leaned forward and put his head in his hands. "Before you and I met, Wes was trying to get me to do this thing he calls 'radical honesty' where you always tell the truth no matter what, and I was trying to do it, but—"

"Actually," I said. "While dating Jackie, you only did the puppet show version of radical honesty, not the real thing. Which was itself dishonest."

"I know." Don spoke so quietly I could barely hear him. "But that was hard enough. I just thought that if I were really real with you, you'd see I'm hopeless and you'd give up. So, I sort of did it good enough to get by because I didn't want to be alone."

"You trapped me by pretending to be someone you're not—an honest person. Everything with you is spin. I'm in advertising. I understand spin. But I know the difference between marketing and reality. Do you?"

Don sat quietly, his head bowed.

I turned to Jackie, though I intended the message for Don. "Radical honesty isn't just telling the truth about yogurt or mistresses. It's about living every aspect of your life honestly and with discipline every day. It's about showing the world your real character, because you trust who you are and what you believe in and you're straight with others about it."

Jackie crossed her arms and stared at her husband. "You've been working on this since before we met, yet you can't even be honest about what radical honesty is?"

Don wiped his eyes on his sleeve. "I guess I'm a work in progress."

"Listen," I said. "Jackie's not asking for a whole lot here. She just wants to know the real you, not the puppet show version."

"But that person is useless," Don said. "You once told me, 'Be yourself is the worst advice you can give some people.' Don't you think that applies?"

"No," I said. "Because I don't believe the real you is a huge screw-up. I think that's just you collapsing in a heap. Jackie only asks that you be a person who puts forth consistent effort to change and improve. That's how the rest of us have to live life. Every day we ask ourselves, 'Who am I?', 'What do I believe in?,' 'How do I make my behavior match those beliefs?' And then we get up and do it."

"He's right." Jackie's voice softened. "I don't need you to be perfect, Don. I know you have a good heart or else I wouldn't have married you. I need you to work on living your life that way."

"It won't be easy," Don said. "But I'll try."

"Whoa." I raised my palm toward Don in a stop-gesture. "Is that really what you meant to say?"

"Sorry." He closed his eyes, reciting. "I meant to say that I'm going to make it happen. I'm going to practice radical honesty, even when it's hard."

Before he could open his eyes, Jackie reached over and kissed him on the cheek. "That's all I needed to hear. How can I help him, Wes?"

"Let's start with a little ritual. Jackie, every time you have a conversation in which Don might be prone to dodge the truth, I want you to say, 'I know you ate my yogurt and didn't replace it. Please don't make any response. Don't even move your head back and forth a little. Just think really carefully about what you want to say. You can give me a hug and run to the store and get me more yogurt or you can try and cover it up for no good reason and piss me off. Decide what you really want to do and get back to me.' Then leave the room."

"Okay…" Jackie seemed a little puzzled. "But I already do that."

"No you don't," Don said. "You come at me a hundred miles an hour, on fire, accusing me of stuff, and I instantly see my mom and think, 'How am I going to get out of this?' Before you know it, I tell you that the cat opened the refrigerator, ate your yogurt, and hid the empty carton at the bottom of the trashcan."

"I see your point," Jackie said.

"If you lay out the solution up front for Don and give him time to think about it, he'll do the right thing more often than not."

"I can make a good decision if I can stop and think," Don said.

Jackie grabbed his hand. "I'm glad we came today. I didn't know what to expect, but I think we found things we can both work on."

Is This Chapter For Me?

It depends. As with personal responsibility, living honestly is a lifelong pursuit, so a chapter on the ethical treatment of others should have something to offer us all. In fact, early readers found it valuable whether or not they had ADD. Because they struggle with moment-to-moment decision making, persistence, and discomfort, some people with ADD find honest living to be a challenge. Others push back the inherent difficulty of honesty and live in harmony with their people and society. In determining which description fits you best, ask yourself and your people if the following attributes describe you:

- ❏ You're straightforward from one day to the next, saying what you mean and meaning what you say.

- ❏ You make an ongoing, honest, and accurate appraisal of yourself, your conduct, and your effectiveness at life, particularly where others are concerned.

- ❏ You're interested in what others think of you—not in an anxious, self-conscious, conforming way, but in a way that shows good citizenship in your family, community, work, and friend group.

- ❏ You're unlikely to cheat, steal from, manipulate, or deceive others.

- ❏ You're known to be a safe person to be around, both physically and emotionally.

❏ You're capable of showing empathy, understanding the experiences and feelings of others, and tolerating their differences as you do your own.

This checklist is reverse scored, so if you have lots of checks, it's time for another victory lap. You're well on your way to a life of radical honesty. This chapter should validate what you're already doing well and give you some additional food for thought. If your people instead see you as thinking, feeling, and acting the opposite of the attributes in this list, this chapter is critically important for you.

Attaining Character

The Big Kahuna (1999) was shot in the Hyatt hotel in Wichita, Kansas, one of my several hometowns. Based on the stage play *The Hospitality Suite*, it follows Larry and Phil,[51] two salesmen attending an industrial convention to schmooze "The Big Kahuna." He's the president of a company that might place a huge order for their line of lubricants. They're joined by young tech guy Bob (Peter Facinelli), sent to showcase the brains of their company. The sale is critical to Phil and Larry's future.

The three host a reception in their tiny hotel suite, but The Kahuna never shows up. Or so they think. Dejected, they debrief their disastrous evening to figure out what to do next. Only then does Bob realize he's actually met the man while tending the bar. The Kahuna cleverly switched nametags to avoid being hassled by salesmen. In fact, Bob talked at length with The Kahuna about the recent death of the man's dog, and in turn, Bob received an invitation to his after-party at a nearby hotel. It's the perfect connection. Phil and Larry send Bob to the party, instructing him to put their business cards in The Kahuna's hand and simply tell him that they need a few minutes to talk with him the next morning before he leaves town.

Bob sets off on his mission, leaving Larry and Phil to a remarkable late-night dialogue about the nature of existence and God. In fact, this discussion sets the subtle theme of the entire movie as Phil, recovering from alcoholism, depression, divorce, and even thoughts of suicide, shares his recent struggle to understand who he is in his fifties and what life has left for him.

Bob returns from the party just before dawn. Religiously devout but self-righteous, he admits that he never actually discussed industrial lubricants with The Big Kahuna because he didn't want to exploit their new friendship. He instead took to witnessing about his Christian faith. Bob sees nothing wrong with this and, in fact, defends it as noble. Tired, fearful, and frustrated, Larry

---

[51] Kevin Spacey and Danny DeVito in stellar performances.

explodes. They argue bitterly, culminating in an absurd wrestling match on the floor of the suite.

After Larry collects himself, he apologizes and exits the room, leaving Bob and Phil alone for what turns out to be an extraordinary exchange. I often show this clip on the big TV in my office:

> Phil: There's something I want to say to you. And I want you to listen very closely, because it's very important. The man we just chased from here—
>
> Bob: We didn't chase anybody.
>
> Phil: The man who just left the room a moment ago is a very good friend of mine. Is it because I've known him for a long time? Well, there are a lot of people who I have known for quite a while and some of them I wouldn't let wipe my dog's ass. Others I can take or leave. They don't matter to me. But Larry matters very much. The reason being, I can trust him. I know I can trust him. He's honest.
>
> Bob: Is he honest or is he just blunt?
>
> Phil: He's honest, Bob. He's blunt as well. That sometimes is part of being honest, because there are a lot of people who are blunt but not honest. Larry is not one of those. Larry is an honest man. You too are an honest man, Bob. I believe that. That somewhere down deep inside of you is something that strives to be honest. The question that you have to ask yourself is, "Has it touched the whole of my life?"
>
> Bob: What does that mean?
>
> Phil: That means that you preaching Jesus is no different than Larry preaching lubricants. It doesn't matter whether you're selling Jesus or Buddha or civil rights or how to make money in real estate with no money down. That doesn't make you a human being. It makes you a marketing rep. If you want to talk to somebody honestly, as a human being, ask him about his kids. Find out what his dreams are, just to find out, for no other reason. Because as soon as you lay your hands on a conversation to steer it, it's not a conversation any more. It's a pitch. And you're not a human being. You're a marketing rep.
>
> Bob [Tearful]: Forgive me if I respectfully disagree.
>
> Phil: We were talking before about character, you were asking me about character and we were speaking of faces. But the question

is much deeper than that. The question is, "Do you have any character at all?" And if you want my honest opinion, Bob, you do not. For the simple reason that you don't regret anything yet.

Bob: You're saying I won't have any character unless I do something I regret?

Phil (chuckles): No, Bob. I'm saying you've already done plenty of things to regret. You just don't know what they are. It's when you discover them—when you see the folly in something you've done and you wish you had it to do over, but you know you can't because it's too late. So you pick that thing up and you carry it with you to remind you that life goes on. The world will spin without you. You really don't matter in the end...then you will attain character because honesty will reach out from inside and tattoo itself all across your face. Until that day, however, you cannot expect to go beyond a certain point.

See *The Big Kahuna* to fully appreciate the impact of this scene and how it fits the point of this chapter. Attaining character is a lifelong process of discovering your flaws and letting them truly change the whole of your life. Two things make that harder for people with ADD.

Psychological Integrity

The first obstacle is that lack of psychological integrity I mentioned earlier. If you can't pull your psychology together from one day to the next, it's harder to pull your morals together. You could follow a rigid religious or moral code, but how often have you seen someone raised in a strict home fall into a life of foolishness as an adult, because he or she has never made a personal choice to really sign on? To have any bearing upon your life, a moral code must be integrated into it, not painted on the surface. Good parenting will help guide you, but you still have to do the work in late adolescence and young adulthood to make it your own. And bad parenting doesn't excuse bad conduct. Either way, you must first believe in the importance of a code to guide your life, and then develop one that makes your life work better.

The Tricky Nature of Shame

For people with ADD (and quite a few without it), the second barrier to radical honesty is shame, or, more correctly, the improper role of shame. Shame has gotten a bad rap in pop psychology, particularly with John Bradshaw, who saw "toxic shame" as the root of just about every psychological problem. However, that perspective ignores the role shame plays in shaping proper conduct.

So let's clear up our language. There is such a thing as functional shame. It's our conscience telling us when we've done something wrong. In an effort to make kids feel good about themselves, we often shield them from the consequences of their actions and the sense of conscience that should accompany them. That leaves many kids growing up feeling too unashamed for their own good. To attain character, as Phil describes it, you have to allow your shortcomings to teach and thus protect you from further harms you might commit. Letting those regrets touch the whole of your life requires that you actually *feel* something. Something a lot like shame. If you don't, then you lack empathy for the harm that you cause to yourself and others.

> *Functional shame is our conscience telling us when we've done something wrong.*

The kind of shame Bradshaw made famous comes not from regret but from self-hatred—the feeling that you're responsible for things that aren't your fault; that you are a bad person, flawed beyond repair. A common example is childhood abuse, which causes dysfunctional, toxic shame for something no child could cause or want to happen. A big part of recovery from child abuse is shifting the shame from victim to offender. If you are instead the abuser, you need to feel shame or you won't see any need to change.

A powerful illustration of this fine distinction is found in HBO's *The Wire*. After accidentally killing his young friend Sherod with a hotshot of poisoned heroin intended for his nemesis, street addict Bubbles turns himself into the police and confesses to Sherod's murder. When the confused officers step out of the interview room for a moment, Bubbles hangs himself. They return just in time to cut him down and save his life.

Later, Waylon, Bubble's sponsor in Narcotics Anonymous, visits Bubbles in a locked psychiatric ward at the county hospital. As Waylon arrives with Kima Greggs, a detective who has befriended Bubbles, he explains the suicide attempt this way: "Shame is some tricky shit, ain't it? Makes you feel like you want to change and then beats you back down when you think you can't."

In an acclaimed script filled with profound, beautifully written dialogue, this line stands out. Waylon asks Kima and us to consider the good and bad of shame. How it both motivates and limits us; how we need and fear it.

Self-Esteem and Self-Efficacy. Functional shame (what makes you want to change) and dysfunctional shame (what makes you think you can't) are easily confused by people who have ADD. That makes it harder to live honestly. Like Don, you get busy dodging self-loathing, when you should simply be taking responsibility—accepting the functional shame that really is yours to deal with.

But why is this so much harder for people with ADD? In Chapter 4, I said that ADD and depression often go hand-in-hand. As you grow up struggling to make your brain do what you tell it to, you learn not to feel very good about yourself. Most people call this a problem of "self-esteem." I'm actually not a huge fan of that term. Like so many pop-psychology concepts, it started out as a useful idea, caught on with the public, and is now a cliché.

Self-esteem is supposed to estimate how you value yourself compared to others (attractive, smart, interesting, worthwhile, etc.). I've met exceptions, but if you ask most people with ADD about their self-esteem, they'll say it isn't high. In fact, very few non-ADD people will tell you they feel really great about themselves. Self-esteem has become a commodity that we're supposed to have a certain amount of, so not having that amount becomes one more reason to feel bad about yourself. I've come to see the concept as overused and trite. Let's give it a rest, at least for this book.

> *Self-efficacy is the belief you have in your own ability to succeed. It impacts how you approach goals, tasks, and challenges.*

Instead, let's talk about "self-efficacy." Originating in the work of psychologist Albert Bandura, self-efficacy is the belief you have in your own ability to succeed. It impacts how you approach goals, tasks, and challenges. This should sound a lot like willpower and waypower and how they create hopefulness (Chapter 4). That's because self-efficacy is the "I think I can" part of hope. When someone says, "Believe in yourself," they're really saying, "Trust your self-efficacy; your ability to be effective."[52]

Self-efficacy affects more than the big stuff, like, "Am I good at school?" "Can I hold a job?" It impacts little details like, "Can I pass Calculus?" "Am I effective in social situations?" If you believe you're always prone to failure, as many ADD people do, you build a reserve of dysfunctional shame that replenishes itself, even as you try to cover it up. For example, Don messed up. Jackie got mad at him. The next time he messed up, he remembered how that felt. So, when Jackie caught him, he lied to avoid his own shame, which made Jackie even angrier. At each step, he picked up one more thing to regret. Rather than learning, he just became more and more ashamed and prone to cover-ups until he gave up trying to be more honest and responsible.

Eventually your people will get so frustrated with you that they'll want to divorce or kill you, which makes you feel even more ashamed and ineffective. So you care even less and appear even less competent. That's pretty much the definition of hopelessness. No will. No way. Collapse in a heap.

---

[52] Remember, a belief in your own self-efficacy is only useful if it's based on a rational appraisal of your abilities (Chapter 4). Otherwise, it's more like wishing.

This process can start happening as early as kindergarten or pre-school, and unless your parents got you involved in some darn good treatment back then, it just keeps on happening. Of course it's not always as terrible as I make it sound—particularly if you're also really intelligent, a bit anxious, or just an ADD-leaner. But even then, success may require so much effort that the easy path feels like a better alternative. Melissa's desperate struggle in Chapter 7 to graduate college and pass her nursing exam is a great example.

The Advantages of Poor Character

There aren't any. There's no upside to an absence of honesty and moral integrity. I could stretch a bit and propose that ADD people who are skilled at lying might be better at covert operations in the CIA or something, but that job requires *greater* psychological and moral clarity than just about any other. Besides, as Don pointed out, being good at deception requires the ability to be careful and detail-oriented.

Principle 9: Practice Radical Honesty

A code for living can be a complex work of philosophy or very simple, like joining the Marines and following orders. It could be religiously based or secular. No matter where it comes from or how you create it, your code should consider what I refer to as *The Three E's*—Ethics, Empathy, and Excellence in Behavior.

Ethics. In philosophy, ethics seeks to answer the question of how people should act. It systematically examines morality by proposing and defending ideas of what is right and wrong and applying them to issues of conduct. The word comes from the Greek word "ethos," which means "character." Your job in living a radically honest life is to apply ethical reasoning to questions of how you should act as a mature, successful, responsible adult.

That's easier said than done, even if you don't have ADD, because ethical questions are often complex and difficult. For example, as a society, we all agree that murdering someone is wrong. Or do we? Do you consider abortion murder? What about capital punishment? War? Self-defense? Stand your ground laws? Euthanasia? Even a commandment as cut and dried as "Thou shalt not kill" leaves a surprising amount of room for debate. But what's most important for you, here and now, is to systematically consider what you see as right and wrong and apply that in your daily life.

"Wait," you ask with that philosophical look in your eye. "Does that make the answer to every ethical question, 'It depends?'"

No. We call that "moral relativism," which suggests that right and wrong are just abstract concepts that cannot be applied outside of a given situation. A great example is the old adage, "If it feels good, do it." Talk about the easy path. While ethical conduct varies from situation to situation and from culture to culture, and often requires interpretation, many rules of social engagement are widely agreed-upon. But unless you join up with the USMC or the Jesuits, who expect a strict adherence to their standards, you're not free to avoid ethical reasoning and decision making.

I could write a whole book on this. Perhaps I will someday as a sequel to this one. But for now, our main goal in this chapter is to: (A) imagine what a right life path might look like, (B) give you some tools to find it, and (C) make it as easy as possible to follow. So, I'll try and make my ADD ethics talk simple. Here are the high points:

- **Don't** deceive, cheat, or steal from others.

- **Do** seek what is good, right, virtuous, and just. Sometimes that's obvious. Frequently it is not. Figure it out and act accordingly.

- **Do** reject what is evil, wrong, vicious and unjust. You won't get this right one hundred percent of the time. Your job is to stay on the lookout so you minimize your regrets and apologies and learn from every one.

- **Do** accept the inconvenient reality that you exist not only as an individual but as a part of a larger community. When you make a decision for yourself, you make a decision for everyone. Individuality is a myth. We're all interdependent.

- **Don't** threaten or harm anyone except when a greater harm would be done if you did not. You're rarely justified in using excessive force—just enough to protect yourself and others from harm.

- **Do** be loyal to those with whom you share a social contract, and follow through on your obligations to them. I know this already showed up in Chapter 3, but without it, you can't experience or convey real honesty. Phil said Larry was his friend because he was an honest man; he could trust him. He found Bob to have no character at all. Larry fulfilled his obligations. Bob did not.

- **Don't** let anyone question where they stand with you. Being "nice" is not the same as having character. In *The Big Kahuna*, Larry isn't actually very nice. He's sort of annoying. That's why we're surprised at the end when Phil shows such admiration for him. Bob seems like a very nice, respectable, Christian fellow. But as the story unfolds, we see that what really counts is underneath the surface. Be nice whenever possible. But don't let nice become a thin veneer covering a deeper dishonesty.

- **Do** practice beneficence. That means helping in a way that is actually helpful, rather than just making you feel better about yourself or because you feel sorry for someone. Bob shared his faith with The Big Kahuna, not because sharing it met that guy's need, but because it met Bob's. The opposite of beneficence is enabling or codependency. A good example is giving a street addict money because you feel badly for him. Beneficence is about thinking. "Following your heart" is rarely beneficent.

- **Do** be patient with the differences of others and strive to embrace them. However, because it is a gift, patience must follow the rule of beneficence and not validate bad behavior. Never let yourself be abused or treated unethically. Nor should you enable alcoholism or drug addiction among your people.

- **Don't** exploit or manipulate others. Phil, a professional salesman, notes, "As soon as you lay your hands on a conversation to steer it…it's a pitch." He's telling Bob to be straight forward and honest in his persuasion. Manipulation is when you spin things in order to influence people *outside of their awareness* or to make something seem different from how it really is. Jackie felt manipulated by Don because he said anything to keep her from being upset. That prevented her from authentically knowing him. She felt swindled.

- **Do** contribute to your community. Many ethical guidelines are about avoiding wrong and preventing harm to others. This one is about doing something right. We all get a lot from our schools, families, and communities. Return the favor. Besides being good in and of itself, there's that whole Karma circle. What goes around really does come around.

When you're having trouble holding yourself accountable to these ethical standards, ask your people for help. That might get extreme at times, particularly if your dishonesty has gotten out of control. I've developed a few techniques that will keep you on the straight and narrow path. Be brave and share this list with your people and see if they'll do a little tough love with you.

- **Do The Exercise That I Did With Don and Jackie.** It slows down the lying process, giving the ADD person a chance to think things through. It also reminds him or her that lying is usually a greater affront than the act being lied about and it greatly improves the emotional tone of the conversation. The secret is preventing the ADD person from answering before he or she has thought it through. As soon as one commits to the lie, it's far more difficult to reverse the process.

- **Find A Good Polygrapher.** No, I'm not kidding. Some lies are worse than others and require greater certainty of the truth. That's what lie detectors are for. Besides, the very possibility has a profoundly sobering impact on the critical moment of choice—do I lie or not? It's worked many times when nothing else has.

- **Escalate The Consequences.** I have a particularly harsh technique for families with children and teens who habitually lie and won't stop despite severe consequences. The family agrees to start "strategically lying." The liar knows this is coming, but can't quite believe it. A few weeks later, the family plans something great, like a vacation to Disneyworld. They let the liar believe they're really going until the last minute and then admit that the whole thing is a fabrication. Tears and screaming ensue, but after three or four of these ordeals, the liar *feels* what it means to be deceived. This clinical intervention takes something in one's head (the truth matters) and puts it in the heart (being lied to hurts). Besides, if a liar can't learn to tell the truth any other way, I guarantee someone, someday will pull a non-clinical version of this ordeal with far worse consequences than disappointment.

Empathy. This means understanding and experiencing the feelings of others as if they were your own. If you cry with a friend because her father has died and you imagine for a moment how it would feel if it were your dad, you're experiencing empathy. It also means feeling anger at injustices done to others. It means feeling happy with your friends when they succeed, even if you're a bit jealous. Or, as we just discussed, knowing how it feels to be lied to. Most importantly, empathy means experiencing how your behavior impacts others. We call this "perspective taking."

Empathy also implies caring for others and considering their needs at least as much as you do your own. Because many people with ADD don't naturally pick up on the little details of human interplay, you may not feel a lot of natural empathy. You may even feel socially impaired because you just don't get other people very well. Fortunately, there are workarounds that allow you to express empathy, even if you aren't really feeling it.

A minister came to see me several years back. His son had recently been diagnosed with ADD and he thought he had it too. In our intake session he shared, "None of my parishioners know how much I don't care about what they're talking about in my office. I mean, I want to care. I just don't feel it. I just don't connect. For the first time I see my son really making that kind of connection and I know what's wrong with me."

I asked how he could possibly get by as a pastor without showing empathy for others. He said, "Oh, I *show* empathy. I sit there and nod and look very concerned and people believe I really am. But I don't *feel* it. That takes concentration and I don't have any to spare. I'm thinking about my sermon and how we're going to pay for the new pew cushions and my tee-off time at the golf course and my grocery list..."

Sienna (Chapter 6) struggled with feelings of selfishness. Even as she was well-liked, her friend group and girlfriend were often frustrated with her lack of feeling for others. She believed deeply in the value of empathy, but she didn't experience it. I encouraged her to worry less about that and more about forming empathic responses. We spent many hours discussing how that looked in numerous day-to-day encounters.

It turns out that it's more important to act with empathy than to feel it.

It turns out that it's more important to act with empathy than to feel it. So, here are some rules for empathic conduct:

- **Do** unto others as you'd have them do unto you. The Golden Rule is famous for a reason. But to make it work you must imagine yourself on the other end of the stick and ask, "How would I want to be treated?" Always hard and uncomfortable, this meditation will rarely steer you wrong.

- **Do** consciously consider the feelings of others. While you're in Golden Rule meditation, ask, "If I were in this situation, how would I *feel?*" Envision similar situations you've experienced to give yourself a few clues. Your wise mind knows this stuff. Use it.

- **Do** treat others fairly, kindly and with compassion. That does not imply being someone else's doormat. Act assertively, but in a diplomatic and intentional way.

- **Don't** forget to say "thank you" whenever warranted. If there's one thing people really despise, it's an ungrateful person. Speaking of which...

- **Do** forgive. You'll be needing it yourself one day and you'll be more likely to get what you give. Besides, life's too short for vindictiveness.

Excellence In Behavior. There sure is a lot of "I don't care what people think" going around social media these days, much of it delightfully profane. Young people are stating their independence from criticism and doubt. It all sounds so confident and full of self-efficacy. It's not.

It's a cocky denial of our social interconnectedness. You can't afford to ignore what others think, though you need to sift out what is useful and what is crap. Unfortunately, a great deal of the crap that people want to not care about is the result of other people taking no responsibility for their free speech or ethical conduct. That's what excellence in behavior is about—making what you say and do intentional, owning what you believe and living your life in a way that makes you proud, not arrogant.

Sound lofty? It's not. It's super practical.

Here's a passage from my book *Dear Dr. Wes: Real Life Advice for Teens*[53] to explain what I'm talking about. The book, and its companion for parents, is based on our weekly *Double Take* newspaper column, coauthored by a sixteen- to eighteen-year-old selected from an annual writing contest. In one of our best columns, we revisited the issue of teen suicide. Rather than offering a list of symptoms, we suggested assuming every teen (or adult) is at equal risk of suicide and deserving of encouragement. In her half of the column, high school senior Samantha Schwartz offered some raw insight into her personal struggle toward excellence in behavior:

> I'm no Gandhi. I've slipped into bashing someone so excruciatingly annoying that I convinced myself he's brought it upon himself. We need to realize that just like academic intelligence, there is social intelligence, and some people just aren't very gifted. They have trouble picking up social cues, so they behave in ways we find odd or irritating. I'm still developing patience for these people. Sometimes what I say feels like word vomit—awful things flowing out of my mouth without my control. But I do have control. It's a matter of training myself to think before I speak.
>
> My mom once had a notepad with yoga's Principles of Mindful Speech written on them. I think they're dead on. We're supposed to ask ourselves three questions before we say something: Is it kind? Is it true? Is it necessary? When tempted to pile on complaints about someone, thinking through these questions can help slow down the thought process and let the right words come to the surface.

---

[53] www.dr-wes.com

It's definitely a challenge, and I don't always succeed. However, when I feel guilty for talking badly about someone, I try to reverse it by looking for something I like about her and complimenting her on it. I see it as tipping the scale of someone's day slightly toward the positive. We all weigh our days subconsciously, counting up the good and bad things to give it a final rating.

Those days add up.

The three rules Samantha mentions come from yoga, a discipline of mindfulness. Here are some additional tips for intentional communication.

- **Do** pause. Learn to count two or three seconds between sentences. Avoid running all your thoughts together.

- **Do** consider what you mean to say and how it will sound *before* opening your mouth. Consider both your words and your tone.

- **Don't** start an argument that has no purpose. Instead, meditate a couple of minutes. Consider that the First World War started without any clear goal and ended with 20 million people dead. And what was the outcome of The First World War? The Second World War. Know what you're getting into before you get into it.

- **Don't** convey contempt—the belief that someone is beneath consideration; worthless; deserving of your scorn. Marital expert John Gottman, PhD can predict whether a marriage will succeed or fail. He's not a fortuneteller. He's done the research and compiled a composite of variables that kill marriages (and many other relationships, I've found). At the top of his list is contempt, conveyed through anger, insults, degrading comments, and stonewalling. Mindful communication conveys respect for the person, even when you profoundly disagree with him or her. It doesn't mean liking someone. It means treating him or her with dignity.

Radical honesty is no easier than it sounds, whether you have ADD or not, and you won't get it done by the end of next week. Only after I finished the addition on my house (Chapter 4) did I know how to build an addition on a house. So it is with character: you finally get it right at the end of your life. But, don't let that discourage you. Living life intentionally with Ethics, Empathy, and Excellence of Behavior isn't a goal. It's a process. The more your people can witness your progress, the more they'll admire your character.

And the more you'll admire it yourself.

CHAPTER 10

THE JOY OF ORGANIZATION

Happiness is when what you think, what you say, and what you do are in harmony.

— Mahatma Gandhi

"Is it really that hard to just put your dishes in the dishwasher, Kylie?" Mr. Simpson kept adjusting his hair, keeping it in perfect alignment with his head. With his neatly pressed suit and shined shoes, he looked nothing like the father of a discombobulated nineteen-year-old girl. But he certainly sounded like one. "When you live under our roof, you have to follow our rules. Cleaning up after yourself is one of them."

Kylie grimaced, somewhere between despair and eruption.

"Let me guess," I said. "Neatness doesn't come naturally for you."

"Not hardly." She sniffed, pulled another Kleenex from a box on the table beside her armchair, blew her nose, and then stuffed it under her left thigh, even though the wastebasket was about thirteen inches from her right one. "Sorry, Doc. Allergies."

"Her mother has given up on her," Mr. Simpson huffed. "Which is why she didn't come today. That doesn't help, of course, but who can blame her? We just want Kylie to be happy, but we've sent her to therapy several times with no discernable results. Now, she's dropped out and moved home and we don't know what to do with her. At bare minimum she needs to show respect and keep herself clean. It's a matter of good character."

"Seriously?" Kylie blinked her dark brown eyes. "So, I guess Dr. Wes's cat has amazing character, huh? 'Cuz she's over there licking herself like there's no tomorrow." She pointed at Grace, my office cat, cleaning her paws on the other couch. Kylie lifted her own arm, stuck out her tongue and licked it from her inner-elbow to the back of palm. "There, Dad. I'm a fully functioning human now. Aren't you proud?"

I jumped in before he could answer. "How do *you* define character, Kylie? In people, I mean. Cats have their own code of conduct."

"I don't know." She thought for a moment. "Like, being a good friend. Or caring about the environment. I marched for victims of sexual assault last year and I like animals. Here kitty kitty kitty." She patted her knee.

Grace yawned and went back to licking her paws.

"Actually, Kylie, you only registered to march," Mr. Simpson said. "Then you stayed out late with friends the night before, missed your alarm and no-showed the event. It was your mother who marched, without you."

"At least I signed up."

"And what about holding a job?" Mr. Simpson continued. "Apparently that's not in your definition of a 'fully functioning human' either."

"A job is no thing," Kylie deadpanned. "I'm starting a new one tomorrow. I can get two jobs a week."

"And you do!" Mr. Simpson's face turned red. "I don't know how she does it. She'll get fired at lunch for calling in to work or showing up twenty minutes late and have another job by supper."

"What can I say?" Kylie offered a grim smile. "A girl's gotta be good at something."

It was pretty obvious why Kylie never lacked employment, despite a terrible work history. She was the most interesting person I'd met that month; adorable in a dark and enigmatic way that made others curious to know what was going on in her head.

"Can you make your cat sit on my lap, Dr. Wes?" Kylie's tone was flat. "Her fur looks really soft. I love cats with soft fur, they're so—"

"Over here, Kylie." I wagged my finger to draw her attention off Grace. "Can I ask you a strange question?"

"Why not." She patted the floor near her feet. "Here kitty kitty kitty."

"Do you know where your bras are?"

"What?" She sat up, and her eyes grew wide as they refocused on me. "Wait. How could you know about that?"

"A guy's gotta be good at something." I glanced at the growing wad of Kleenex peeking out from beneath her skinny jeans. "I'll wager that you go through bras like no other girl. And…" I closed my eyes, pretending to see into a secret dimension of lost garments. "Most of them are currently stuffed under your bed…and one is hanging on a coat hook on the back of your bedroom door."

"That's amazing," Kylie said, unsmiling. "But, sadly you're mistaken."

"No, he's not." A wry grin crossed Mr. Simpson's face. "Actually, they're under the couch and hanging on the doorknobs in the dining room. She's so immodest. She'll come home and just yank her bra off and down her sleeve in front of anyone and fling it anywhere." He tossed an invisible bra toward Grace's couch. "And she spends more money annually at Victoria's Secret than I do on my country club dues, because she won't use the lingerie bag we bought her."

"And you're so smart about lingerie, huh Dad?" Kylie wrinkled her nose.

"I am. I have four daughters. And none quite like you." He glanced my way with a look of pride. "Emily is attending Yale this year, and she uses her lingerie bag with every wash. I had to ask her mother to take over Kylie's laundry. At nineteen years of age! Kylie washes the same things twice because she doesn't keep track of what's dirty and what's clean. A terrible waste—"

"Fine. I'll just quit wearing bras." Kylie shuddered and raised her hands to her underarms like she was doing the funky chicken. "I hate how they feel. I wouldn't wear one 'til I was like fifteen and about a C-cup and finally the school was like 'You *have* to do something about her.'" She mimicked the tone of a frustrated principal.

"Ah yes, the St. Bartholomew's scandal." Mr. Simpson said. "I'd tried to forget. Everyone in the parish was gossiping about your breasts. Kylie was once fired from a job because she kept coming in without a bra."

"Hey, at least I wear clothes, which I actually hate almost as much as underwear. If I had my way, we'd all be nudists. Here kitty kitty. What's wrong with her? Can I just go pick her up?"

"That's not how I'd go about it," I said. "Grace prefers a more nuanced—"

"Kylie! Leave the cat alone," Mr. Simpson said. "Why is she like this?"

"She's a cat," I said.

"No! Not her." He pointed at Kylie. "Her! Why can't she be just a little bit normal?"

"You said she had ADD." I glanced over the testing they'd brought to their first appointment. Kylie was diagnosed at age eleven and retested a month ago, right after her junior college crash. "I'd say she fits the bill pretty well. It's common for ADD kids to be sensitive to irritations, tags, bras, noise—"

"School," Mr. Simpson said. "Work, people, life. Her roommates couldn't deal with her so they sent her packing."

"Probably," I said. "But I'm worried about how depressed she is."

They both just stared at me.

"I'm not depressed." Her monotone was reminiscent of Eeyore in *Winnie the Pooh*. "I'd be the life of the party if my friends weren't so perky and like, OCD all the time."

"To be perfectly frank," Mr. Simpson said. "She's never been a good friend, yet she expects everyone else to be, which is quite off-putting in a young woman."

"Whatever." Kylie rolled her eyes.

"Well if you're not depressed my dear..." I flipped through the thick chart of materials her other therapists had accumulated over the years. "Then you must not understand your situation very well. 'Cuz there's some pretty depressing stuff going on in here."

"Hmm." Mr. Simpson nodded and pursed his lips. "I've always wondered if this whole ADD business was just covering up something deeper."

"No." I made my stop-sign hand. "It's the other way around. Kylie has ADD all right. Her testing is clear. What's depressing is how much it's impacting her life; causing her to fail at everything. She's nineteen and while her peers are off at college, she basically has no point or direction in life. Who wouldn't be dark and irritable all the time?"

Tears began streaming down Kylie's cheeks. "I thought this was supposed to make me feel better! You're just giving me all these new labels and calling me a failure and saying my life is pointless. I want to go back to Dr. Raja. She'd never say something like that." She grabbed her purse and stood up.

"Wait, Kylie." Mr. Simpson reached across the arm of the couch and grasped his daughters hand, his first show of tenderness since we'd started. He cleared his throat as she stood silently before him, head bowed. "Listen, Honey. I need to say something to you. Of all my girls, I love you the most. Do you know why?"

She glanced at him without raising her forehead. "No."

"Because you need the most love."

Kylie eyed the door, hesitated and then, instead of leaving, threw herself down on the couch next to her dad. She leaned into him and began to sob. I could barely hear her halting whisper, "I'm sorry Daddy. I don't mean it. I just hate myself so much because I want you to be proud of me, like you are with Emily, Jordan, and Madison. I'm just such a screw-up. I want people to like me and I don't know how to make them like me. Even Mom and Dr. Wes's cat don't like me. But please—just don't give up on me."

Mr. Simpson put his arm around his daughter and let her cry on his fresh-pressed shirt until it was dirty with tears and mascara. He spoke gently. "You aren't a failure, Honey, but you do always fail. Not because you're not smart and talented, because God knows you are. It's because you don't spend the time and effort to learn how to succeed, with school, with friends, with us. You have to get yourself together and try."

"I do try Daddy, but it always just comes out a big mess." She opened her eyes and tried to wipe his shirt clean of wet black muck, which only ground it in deeper. "God. See what I mean?"

"I like you, Kylie," I said matching her father's gentle but firm tone. "And I believe you mean what you're saying. So I'm going to do you a favor today."

"What?" She pulled a dirty Kleenex from her pocket and wiped her eyes.

"I'm going to tell you the secret of happiness."

"There is no secret of happiness," she said. "Not for me. Everything is just disappointment and pain and being second best, or twenty-fifth. I'm like an old shoe that doesn't fit anyone right. So you throw it away."

"I don't know much about shoes," I said. "But I do know about happiness and there is a secret and you need to know it."

I picked up Grace's catnip mouse and tossed it onto Kylie's lap. Grace stood up and eyed her prey.

"Here kitty kitty kitty." Kylie dangled the mouse above her knees.

Grace lept off the couch, dashed under the coffee table and jumped up on Kylie's lap.

"Hi cat!" She cuddled Grace's face gently in her palms.

"Things don't just happen because you wish them to," I said. "You have to make them happen. That's where the secret of happiness comes in…"

Is This Chapter For Me?

That's hard to say, because even figuring out if you're happy or not requires a clear definition of happiness and a lifetime of self-examination. Parents, like Mr. Simpson, love to say, "We just want you to be happy, dear," usually when they're trying to make something you don't want to do sound like the path to nirvana. But if you ask what they mean by "happy," most admit they've never given it much thought. It just sounds really nice. We're all suckered into simplistic notions of happiness as sustained ecstasy or mellow bliss. If that were true, we'd see opiates as the preferred path to joy, instead of dangerous, addictive drugs.

Happiness doesn't come from a pipe or a bottle. While people with ADD can get a lot of benefit from stimulants, they aren't happiness in a capsule either. You may find temporary joy in food, sex, recreation, entertainment, adventure, art, video games, and humor, but real happiness comes from having purpose and meaning, and the free will to fully engage in life. It means identifying and pursuing wholesome wants, while protecting yourself from cravings; achieving something and sharing a connection with others.

In deciding whether this chapter is for you, consider the following:

❑ Do you often feel overwhelmed by your own chaos and that of others?

❏ Do you at times find your physical and mental life so disorganized that it makes you feel depressed?

❏ Do your people often comment that you lack time management?

❏ Do you avoid organizing because the job has just gotten too out of hand?

❏ Has chaos caused you to fail in school, lose jobs, upset your family, or blow relationships?

❏ Do you have too much of everything (stuff, ideas, friends, etc.)?

❏ Do the anxious people (or leaners) in your life have to create organizational systems for you?

If any of these sound like you, read on. The secret of happiness really isn't as complicated as it sounds. This chapter can give you some great ideas on how to get started on the path to a happier, more organized life, and why that can be especially hard for people with ADD.

Lost in The Clutter

Kylie's young adulthood had fallen into disarray. She had no will and no way, leaving her hopeless and others treating her that way. She felt unguided, unaccomplished, and socially isolated. She lost independence when she had to move home. For her, therapy would become a process of digging her out of the clutter of a failed life plan, irresponsibility, broken obligations, disappointed loved ones, and missing bras. Kylie needed to get her life organized.

Disorganization seems easier and more comfortable than order. It can even be kind of entertaining.

For people with ADD, disorganization seems easier and more comfortable than order. It can even be kind of entertaining. But, if you want to get anything done and get along with others, organization wins hands down. That's becoming truer each day as our world grows more complex and demanding. I suspect that's one reason we're seeing more people diagnosed with ADD than ever before. Life no longer forgives poor focus, low motivation, and difficulty following through and taking responsibility.

A Little Out of Place. For many people with ADD, things don't seem to end up where they belong. Used tissues are a great example. They somehow end up in the vast emptiness of couch cushions instead of the trash can. You're watching *CSI* or playing *Call of Duty* or coming to see me in therapy, and you just can't quite get Kleenex in the trashcan. Promises to self and others that you'll "throw them away later" are soon forgotten and they remain imprisoned in their sofa tomb for eternity, or until we get to dig them out, which we find pretty gross.

A similar fate awaits dirty dishes and pizza boxes under beds, bras hanging from hooks in hallways or cereal boxes piled on the kitchen counter next to the stack of dirty coffee cups. Disorganization is why people with ADD end up with piles of stuff in their homes, offices, or cars. It's why you own several hammers and a flock of scissors. You accumulate extra stuff that ends up surrounding and concealing the things you need but can't find.

Many ADD people don't like to open and close drawers or cabinets, and they really hate hangers. So, clothes end up in piles on the floor, one clean, the other dirty. Except, the piles have no labels and get mixed up, so you have to apply the smell test to trace which should be worn and which should be washed, or you just give up and wash everything again.

Storage. Filing paper documents is boring, complicated, and time-consuming. You have to put labels on the folders to know what's in there, and then put them in alphabetical order and move them from one drawer to the next as you fill one up, only to realize there are more "M" files than "Q" and "E." If you go digital and scan all your documents, as I'll suggest later, you still have to create an electronic filing system, then protect it from prying eyes with a password and from catastrophe by backing it up. Yet, the effort is well worth it. Once your filing system is in place, you'll always be able to access what you need, effortlessly. If you don't have a system, important things pile up and get lost amongst the unimportant things.

You'll find this same sort of clutter with big, poorly organized items in garages, storage units, basements, closets, or in extreme cases, warehouses. You spend twenty years tossing stuff somewhere, without rhyme or reason, then one day, you have to deal with it. Maybe you're moving. Maybe your spouse is threatening divorce. You've hit a wall of junk. Literally. You see it and feel like giving up. You might even end up diagnosed with depression. I've seen it happen.

Critical items like keys or smartphones easily disappear in the chaos, creating disasters ranging from lost time on the hunt to lost money for replacement. Cars misplaced in lonely parking lots can make you late or, in some cases, put you in danger. Forgetting kids at the mall or at school can range from embarrassing to negligent. Losing homework or work product is especially irritating after you've spent the energy to do it and then have to do it all over.

Health and Nutrition. Growing up in an age of processed food, you may not realize how much organization it takes just to feed yourself properly. Anyone can hit a McDonalds drive-thru. It takes little effort to get burgers and fries handed through your car window. As with any easy road, however, a high-calorie, low-nutrition diet isn't the right one. It takes time, organization, and patience to eat right, so people with ADD may face some nutritional challeng-es. Since exercise is rarely interesting or easy to schedule, you'll get less of it over a lifetime if you don't get organized to do it. Lost or forgotten medica-tions can have serious health consequences, and missed contraception can easily become one of the most serious acts of disorganization imaginable.

Driving. Earlier we discussed this as a metaphor for life, but disorganized driving is literally a problem for many people with ADD. This includes inattentive curb checks, speeding, getting lost on the freeway, running stop-lights, texting while driving, running out of gas, and serious accidents, all of which can lead to tickets, injury, and lost time or money. By the way, this isn't a Dr. Wes-ism. It's proven out in the research.

Relationships. It's easy for ADD people to lose friends in life's clutter. If you have good social skills, you may end up with more friends than you can manage, leading you to neglect them all. Or you may get bored with one friend when another comes along or when you start dating an interesting new partner. Friends start feeling rejected, trash-talk you to the larger friend group, and pretty soon you're *persona non grata*.

Time Management

Like Kylie, people with ADD may not have problems getting jobs, but you often have problems keeping them. That might be due to poor attendance or self-sabotaging a job you don't like, but it more often results from bad time management. That includes failing to prioritize what needs to be done, to meet deadlines, to know where you're supposed to be at any given moment, and to set aside enough time to complete a task. Every week in my office, someone shows up at the wrong time or on the wrong day for an appointment. We send reminders, but even when they're confirmed, sessions get missed.

Another common problem is over-scheduling. It's a lot easier and more interesting to schedule something than to actually do it. You may find yourself adding "just one more thing" to your to-do list or calendar over the course of a day, then blowing several off at the last minute because you can't fit every-thing in. Underestimating how long things will take to do is a big part of why people with ADD are habitually late. Bad time management also impacts social life by making it less likely you'll show up for obligations. That in turn makes you a less desirable friend and dating partner.

What's In Your Head?

The most serious clutter is all in your head. While it varies a lot from person to person, the most obvious sign of internal chaos is your language—how you form your thoughts into words, struggling to communicate basic ideas, directions, or concepts. Others may look puzzled and ask, "What are you talking about?" or "What's going on up there?" while smacking you in the forehead. Yet, no matter how much you try, you can't quite get your words to say what you mean. I can usually tell when clients are off medication by how they communicate in session. Their thoughts aren't well connected, they can't finish their sentences, and it takes forever to get through a story or example.

Most of us listen to our internal dialogue as we sort our thoughts and feelings. You may instead organize your thoughts by talking out loud and listening to what you have to say. I actually mentioned this as a useful strategy in Chapter 7. While it might help you to gather your thoughts and make better sense to yourself and others, just remember *we can hear you*. This is a big reason why many people with ADD have few secrets. We know more about what you're thinking than is probably in your best interests, because you keep telling us. It also irritates your people when you yammer on about some tidbit of thought that might best be kept to yourself. Talking to yourself is a fine idea, but it's usually best done in private.

The Advantages of Disorganization

Many people with ADD can deal with chaos unencumbered by an organized plan. You're so disinterested in order that you can just go with the flow. When that doesn't turn out badly, it can be kind of refreshing. If you have good social skills and are responsible to your people, others may actually find your disorganization lighthearted and entertaining. Nobody can guess what will happen next in your life. If you arrange a project or host an event, it may lack structure, but people will feel at home and at ease, as long as you don't overtax their tolerance for chaos. A great example is the famous party scene in Holly Golightly's tiny apartment in the movie *Breakfast at Tiffany's*.

If they have most of the other principles in place, ADD parents tend to be better at picking their battles and letting the little things go—a key element in raising kids. Clean rooms and made beds create an endless stream of argument and frustration in anxious homes. Parents with ADD put organization in second (or fourteenth) place, after finding adventure, spending time together, or having spontaneous fun. That can certainly create problems, particularly if things like school aren't prioritized, but it can also reduce stress, anger and discord, allowing the household to run chaotically but without excessive emotional reactivity.

While chance favors only the prepared mind, ADD people can actually wander into some interesting opportunities. That's precisely because you don't worry much about what you're doing, when you do it, or how it might turn out. Sienna traveled through Europe on her way to Africa. I kept after her to get her couch surfing plans made, so she'd have a place to sleep. Instead, she just winged it at the last minute, and in doing so, met some very interesting people and gained a wealth of (mostly positive) experiences.

Principle 10: The Secret of Happiness is in How You Organize Your Life

It seems like the secret of happiness should be something really spectacular— like meditating toward a higher state of consciousness or maybe a gluten-free diet. Or perhaps something trite yet unattainable, like, "look on the bright side," "seek your true love," "have courage, "be proactive," or, "give yourself choices." Each of these sage tidbits are drawn from popular literature on happiness. Some actually appear elsewhere in this book, (attributional style, self-efficacy, hope, discipline, meditation, etc.).

I must admit that when I finally had to think through the path to happiness, "get organized" seemed a little anticlimactic. But a catchy mantra, no matter how much you practice it, can't create happiness unless your life is organized so you can have real choices, be proactive, eat a good diet, or find true love. You must be intentional to find a right path, and courageous to choose it over the easy one. Any bright side you look on comes from what you set into motion, not from imagining it. And when you create disasters, looking at them as opportunities won't fix things or even make you feel better if you don't take responsibility for them or learn anything by going through them.

All your stuff, tangible, emotional, and psychological, has to fit together. That's the whole point of wanting versus wishing, thinking versus following your heart, and so on. Organization means needing something and being able to find it or feeling like your life is "in the flow," with new opportunities building on past successes. That's how you pull yourself together to get things done; to develop self-efficacy, hopefulness and ultimately happiness.

It's that simple. Getting there? That's harder. So, here are my best tips for organizing your life:

Use Workarounds. A key part of organization is making the right path easier to follow. Stop. Read that again. I do *not* mean you should take the easy path or find a shortcut. I mean you should find ways to make difficult things more doable, thus making it more likely you'll start and finish them.

As an example, let's return to the Kleenex problem one last time. People with ADD should own more wastebaskets than anyone else. I have four in my office. My son, Alex, cleans it each week and always complains about how many bags he has to empty. But people with ADD never leave Kleenex in my couch because a basket is always in arm's reach. Your goal is to make it so easy to throw your Kleenex away that you cannot justify couch stuffing. This also works well for dirty clothes hampers, laundry baskets, and recycling bins.

Sadly, I didn't discover this brilliant idea. While designing Disneyland, Walt Disney visited other amusement parks and counted the number of steps guests took to get to a trash can. He observed that if the cans were more than thirty steps from a guest, that person would toss his or her garbage on the ground.[54] So today, when visiting any Disney park, a trashcan is sure to be there, calling your name. In some cases, literally. Disney even has talking robot trashcans that wander around and interact with you. Wow. Wouldn't it make the right path even easier to follow if your own trashcan came to you?

Live a Minimalist Life. Minimalism is a powerful tool of organization that seeks to prevent chaos before it starts. Its origins are found in the teachings of the Greek philosopher Epicurus who held that an untroubled life was a happy one, and possible only through carefully considered choices. About 2400 years before I wrote the same thing in this chapter, Epicurus proposed seeking only what is basic for life, happiness, and bodily comfort, and using everything else in moderation or avoiding it entirely. This shows up repeatedly throughout history. In the 1850s Henry David Thoreau wrote of simplicity in *Walden*. The Shakers built a whole religion around it, leaving behind a famous hymn known as *Simple Gifts* that extols its virtues.

Creating your own minimalist life requires you to study the difference between needs and wants and to focus primarily on your needs (Chapter 5), though that difference may not always be obvious. Some would see a smartphone or tablet as a want, but in the next section, I'll argue that people with ADD need those devices to get organized. Limiting wants is critical to cutting down clutter. Minimalism also means limiting the stuff you have to think about and do, and even what you say. The less of anything you have, the less organizing is required and the faster you'll get stuff in its proper place.

---

[54] www.disneytrivia.net/park_pages/wdw_mk_facts.php

There are lots of little, mindful choices along the path to minimalism. Here are some tips to help you make them as you start digging yourself out.

- **Get Rid Of Stuff.** This can be tough for people with ADD because stuff is super fun to acquire and really boring and uncomfortable to throw away or sell. Throw-away stuff ranges from junk mail and unused coupons to clothes you can't wear and need to donate. It means using Ebay, Craiglist, and garage sales to sell that boat you're frustrated with or that vacation cabin you use three weeks a year and worry about the other forty-nine. It's fine to keep family heirlooms or special gifts, but sentiment quickly becomes an excuse for keeping everything. The best motto in striving for minimalism is to "Give 'til it hurts." You'll be astonished at how short-lived your sorrow will be, particularly as you bask in the glory of your success.

- **Set Up A Filter for Snail Junk Mail.** You probably have a state-of-the-art spam filter on your computer. Create one for your snail mail. The minute a stack comes in, sort out the 98% that is junk and send it straight to the trash, recycling, or shredder bin.

- **Shred.** If you have confidential material, take it to an office supply store like Office Depot. They'll destroy it while you watch and it's cheaper than maintaining your own shredder. This works great for documents you've scanned into your computer, as long as you don't need the originals. If you're in business and have a lot of material, hire one of those mobile scan and shred services.

- **Don't Carry What You Don't Need.** A large purse seems helpful, but filling it up just means you have more stuff to take out, sort through, and lose in the cushions of my couch. Often, a client goes into her super-purse to find, say, a prescription bottle so I can learn what medication her prescriber selected. Soon my coffee table is piled with thirty-five random items. "Oh," she exclaims as she pulls out an extra set of keys. "I wondered where those were last night when I locked myself out of my apartment!" Usually, the only thing that's not in there is the prescription bottle. Many ADD guys seem to have this same problem with their cars and backpacks.

- **Throw Away Obligations.** Mindfully dispose of commitments that you're not fulfilling—a relationship you're not ready for, a volunteer position you can't manage, or a job you aren't doing well. Don't take this lightly, because obligations are important and you should never give up on something or someone without trying. However, it's usually more honest to gracefully resign something than to keep doing it badly. If you're leaving an unsuitable job, get another before quitting and give at least two weeks notice.

Systematize What You Have Left. Once you've gotten rid of as much stuff as you can, develop the least cluttered method of storing what you need. While at Epcot my daughter, Alyssa, and I wandered through the Innoventions House of the Future[55], probably because it was air conditioned. What we found, however, was Gladiator,[56] the most amazing system of wall storage I'd ever seen. I went home and bought it. It wasn't cheap, but it's been well worth the money. All my tools now hang quite nicely, ready for use. Here are some other ideas for organization that I've tested over the years with clients. Some may not work for you, but many will.

- **Schedule Short Times to Clean and Sort.** Whether it's your car, locker, backpack, closet, storage unit, etc., keep it organized a little at a time in short increments, just as I described building the addition on my house in Chapter 4. That way you'll never get overwhelmed with the task.

- **Hire an Anxious Person.** When it comes to throwing stuff away or organizing your garage, basement, warehouse, or schedule, no one is better than an overly organized college student. I've used this strategy many times with overwhelmed ADD adult clients and it works like a charm. Likewise, parents have hired college students to organize their ADD teens and young adults. It not only brings the labor you need for big jobs, but the anxious person's orderly nature forces you to be more organized and to stick to the task at hand. You might also want to have your car detailed once or twice a year. They pick up all the debris and put it in nice plastic bags so you can sort what needs to go and organize the rest.

- **Shelves and Hooks.** Toss dressers and get inexpensive shelves from Ikea, Sam's Wholesale Club, or Costco or buy more expensive ones at furniture stores. Then pile to your heart's content and never push a drawer or close a cabinet again. Sloppy? That's in the eye of the beholder, but shelves are certainly more efficient and

---

[55] This is now called Vision House with an environmentally friendly theme.

[56] www.gladiatorgarageworks.com

using them beats having piles of laundry lying everywhere. If someone comes to visit, neatly stack the piles and tell them you prefer that cool department store look. This also works great in the garage or basement. In your closet, forgo hangers and use as many hooks as you can fit. Hooks are faster and make it easier to find things. You won't be able to store as many garments, but if you got rid of enough stuff, you won't need that much space.

- **Put Things Away.** People have told you to do this for years, but finally making it happen requires minimizing clutter and creating a good organizing system. Then, you'll *experience* the joy of finding what you're looking for, which will reward you for your ongoing organizational effort. When I rebuilt the motor of my Toyota 4Runner, I put the nuts and bolts in freezer bags and wrote what they held together on the outside. I tagged each part with notes on how it should be reinstalled. The motor went back together perfectly and started on the first turn, giving me a feeling of success I can remember to this day. That wouldn't have happened without good organization.

- **Seek An Expert's Opinion.** Buy a book on organization or take a class. I have several books listed on my website to get you started. Or you can go even further and get an organizational consultant who does this for a living. That's a big ticket purchase, but if you have the resources, it could really pay off.

Join The Digital Age. Early in the Facebook era, I worked with a girl whose friend pranked her by logging onto her profile and posting my client's status as "I'm pregnant." My client only noticed this after her minister called her mom to ask if there was anything he could do, like marry her and her boyfriend. I asked my client if she might want to consider giving up on the whole social media revolution.

Technology can save you or lead you down an endless path of distraction.

"No, Wes." Her voice was surprisingly calm for a girl who had recently learned of her virtual pregnancy via a hysterical text message from her mother. "Facebook is a tool. You can drive a nail with a hammer or you can hit yourself in the forehead with it."

That sage advice is ten times as true for people with ADD. Technology can save you or lead you down an endless path of distraction. Here are my tips for keeping your technology hammer aimed at the nail and out of your forehead:

- **Choose Your Devices Wisely.** In the near future, your laptop, smart phone, and tablet will all exist in the same device. You'll add keyboards and screens as you move through your day. Until then, you'll want all your devices to talk to one another. Apple's iCloud and/or Google make this possible and, if you're even slightly tech savvy, fairly easy. As we discussed in Chapter 6, however, instructions matter. So, select a platform, understand how it works, and learn to protect it from intrusion and loss.

- **Schedule Your Life.** In *The Seven Habits of Highly Successful People*, Steven Covey touted the critical value of calendaring. Today, smartphones, tablets, and computers have sophisticated calendaring apps.[57] By linking them through an Internet cloud they can all share information. If you feed them correctly, they can tell you where you're supposed to be at any given moment and provide a visual picture of your week, so you can easily see what's coming up and how full your schedule is. This keeps your time organized, reduces confusion, and improves your punctuality. If you set audible reminders you'll have an electronic friend, hollering at you just when you need it most. I schedule every hour of my week, including dinner dates with my wife and vacation itineraries. That may sound lame, but we're having a blast hitting every ride at Disneyworld, while less organized people are waiting in line to ride Dumbo.

- **Notes And Lists.** I plug what I need to do into calendar events, like "Go to Home Depot" or "Ride Rockin' Rollercoaster" on Thursday at noon. Some people prefer to-do apps so they can check off what they need to get done. It makes them feel good to see what they've accomplished. I dictate or type notes on my phone when I'm attending a conference or preparing a TV appearance. I can pull them up on my computer later when I need them in the office. I also enter serial numbers for appliances and machines I own, so when I'm buying parts I can look them up easily.

- **Digital Storage.** Convert every paper document you own to a digital format or, in the case of books, just buy them that way.

---

[57] If you really hate technology, there are still plenty of old-school day planners just waiting for you to fill them up with ink pens. Many of my clients prefer them.

Whenever anything important comes in the mail or at a meeting you attend, scan it and name the file something descriptive like, "HomeMortgageContract 0904135[58]." If you're a student, and your profs don't already use an interactive online system, scan every paper you're given and toss the original in a bin for recycling *after* the semester ends. If you store your digital data locally, you'll want to have a cloud backup system like Carbonite to keep it safe offsite. I actually gave away all my file cabinets last year and I can find anything I need quickly and easily on my office network.

- **Email Statements.** Why waste time scanning paper documents if you don't have to? Your bank, credit card companies, and most vendors have joined the digital age. They'll happily stop mailing paper statements any time you ask and send you everything electronically instead. That moves key paper documents from your kitchen counter to your computer without having to digitize them yourself.

- **Recording Pens.** I haven't actually tried this technology, but I have clients who swear by it. These pens are made by Livescribe and require a special kind of notebook to use. Neither pen nor paper are cheap, but when you use them together, everything you write is digitized so it can be stored and displayed on your computer. The pen also records the audio of your meeting or lecture and synchronizes it with your writing. Study closely the online reviews of each model, as they seem to vary greatly from one to the next. Email me and let me know what you think.

- **Digital Cameras.** That little eye in your phone or tablet is good for more than selfies and videos of cats falling off tables. Only after I finished the motor in my 4Runner did I realize I should have taken digital pictures of how certain parts looked before I removed them. I have a good memory for things like that, but there's no substitute for a high-res image of something you need to remember. Now that we have cameras on all our devices, we can store thousands of images of documents, whiteboards, parking spaces—anything we use to organize ourselves. While looking for office space, I photographed "For Lease" signs, then pulled up those images on my computer and checked their location tags on Google maps.

---

[58] That number is the date code for September 4, 2013.

- **Email Submission.** Computers and tablets are ideal for ADD people, particularly students, who lose work before it gets turned in. Just write your report, spreadsheet, or PowerPoint and email it to your teacher or boss. I realize this isn't exactly a newsflash in the business and college world. But if you're in middle or high school, you may need an accommodation to allow email submission and even some college professors won't accept email submissions without one. If you must do an assignment on paper, just scan or photograph it and hit send. Email gets stuff turned in and creates a record of all completed work. That will come in handy many times a semester and deprive you of the infamous "dog ate it" excuse.

- **GPS.** Maps and navigation are all about detail and organization, so many people with ADD find themselves directionally challenged. Devices like Google Navigation, Garmin, or Tom Tom aren't perfect, but they're pretty helpful. Beyond just getting you where you're going, GPS accurately estimates your arrival time, particularly if you have the traffic feature[59]. That lets you give honest and accurate estimates of when you'll be where you're supposed to be instead of underestimating your travel time and showing up late. Use GPS even for routes you know well, and you'll quickly discover how useless speeding really is. Unless you have an hour-long commute down a low-traffic freeway, driving ten miles over the limit won't get you to work more than a few minutes early. If you're cutting it that close, you have some serious time management issues you won't be able to address by racking up speeding tickets. And if you really love speeding, you really need to use your...

- **Cruise Control.** Never buy a car without this technology, and if it breaks, fix it. The cost is usually less than a single speeding ticket. Most people think of using cruise control only on the highway. I use mine on other streets I know well where the speed limit is at least 45 miles per hour, there's no traffic, and few stoplights. Done correctly, this allows you to avoid speeding and attend to the road.

---

[59]At the time of this writing, traffic is where Google has Garmin beat. Nobody beats Google Traffic because Google is constantly spying on your cell phone, so it knows how many phones there are in a given mile, and when that hits a certain number, their computer system knows traffic is backing up. Creepy, huh? And amazingly helpful.

When you're out on the highway, always use your cruise unless weather or traffic conditions make that unsafe.

- **Fun Tech.** Social media, video games, and gaming apps are for entertainment and nothing more. Yes, you can learn to fly a plane or shoot zombies, but those skills are of limited utility. You can get your message out or meet people from all over the world on Facebook and Twitter, but does that get you a job or keep you in school? For people with ADD, fun tech is usually a distraction. Enjoy it, as you would a delicious dessert, but don't consider it healthy or vest your future in it. Too many people do.

Master Your Day. In the chaos of daily life, it's easy to lose control of all the little things that make our days better. When you add them up they have a greater influence on your happiness than just about anything else. Here are the lifestyle choices that consistently give people with ADD the most trouble:

- **Sleeping.** One of the worst mistakes anyone can make is failing to set aside enough time for good sleep. For ADD people, it's even easier to procrastinate going to bed or to avoid it altogether. What could possibly be more boring than sleeping, unless perhaps you have fascinating, vivid dreams. On the other hand, some ADD people use sleep as a way to avoid stressful or uncomfortable situations. In either case, the goal is the same: fit the sleep you need into your schedule. And by the way, researchers consider naps evidence of unhealthy sleep. Painful to hear, I know. The only exception is the "micro-nap," a ten- to fifteen-minute siesta you grab mid-afternoon. Feel free to schedule that one into your day.

- **Waking up.** For many people with ADD, mornings are hard, especially if you have problems sleeping. In addition to taking your stimulant before you actually get out of bed (see Chapter 13), you may want to buy a super alarm clock to rouse you without offering any snooze options. Several are available. The best of them won't shut off until you perform a certain task. One shoots a spinning top into the air. You have to find the top and insert it into the clock to shut off the hideous screaming alarm. Another, invented at MIT, jumps off the table and rolls around the floor. There's even a smartphone app that requires you to get up and spin around a few times before it will shut off. They may sound ridiculous, but these gadgets make sure you get going in the morning. That's usually the most critical organizational task you'll perform all day.

- **Diet and Exercise.** Every weekday my calendar says, "Genesis" between 1:30 p.m. and 3:00 p.m. That's not a reading assignment for Sunday School. It's the gym where I swim. If I didn't put it on my schedule, something would come up and push it aside. I also set time for breakfast and lunch to be sure I don't skip those, too. It's easy to turn important things into options if you don't make time to do them.

- **Friend Groups.** People with ADD do better with a few close friends rather than a complex social network. However, the company of a large group of friends can be super entertaining, so extroverted ADD people tend to gravitate toward relationship clutter. Instead, try to choose a few good friends wisely and keep the drama and distraction to a minimum. You might also keep a few acquaintances, but be careful to clarify the limits of your obligations to those folks so you aren't expected to engage in more social life than you can manage.

- **Private Time.** No matter how extroverted, people with ADD require time and space to decompress, meditate, and refocus. The more sensory problems you have, the more important this will be. I've written letters to get young people into private dorm rooms so they can be naked or quiet or messy and whatever else they need to be, without offending a roommate. Even more often, I request private testing rooms for exams. We've also used noise-cancelling headphones as a workaround, though this can create concerns about cheating in testing environments and some jobs make their use impossible.

- **Substance Abuse.** Regardless of your opinion about the joys and sorrows of drugs and alcohol, their recreational use demands self-regulation and intentionality. Not surprisingly, research shows that ADD people are at a greater risk of substance misuse. If you wish to partake, do so occasionally and moderately. If you find that drugs and alcohol are making things worse for you, follow Principle 7, get help and keep yourself from going down the drain.

- **Contraception: Women.** Regardless of how well your calendar works, young women with ADD should forget daily oral contraception and go straight to Depo Provera (a three-month shot), Implanon (a tiny implant that goes in your arm), or the Nuva Ring (a vaginal insert). The College of Obstetricians and Gynecologists is all about the Mirena, an IUD that attaches to a your cervix. That sounds great, but we'll see if they stick to that recommendation in the next few years. No client I see has had any luck with Mirena, and they're expensive to insert. Nevertheless, any of these methods is safer than relying on a daily pill. If you must use an oral contraceptive, set a very annoying alarm on your smartphone to go off every day at the same time, carry your pills with you, and understand the correct use of emergency contraception.

- **Contraception: Men.** There's an old saying, "pack your own parachute." It means that you should never trust anyone else to do something that your life depends on. Here, it means wearing condoms, unless you can personally verify your partner's *correct and consistent* use of contraception. Every month or two I meet a frustrated young father who didn't do this and seems puzzled at the inevitable pregnancy.

Disorganization works the same way as other decisions. Subtle daily chaos is sort of like the zombie apocalypse. It starts out small and isolated, then grows until it takes over and destroys your world. That leaves you feeling overwhelmed and often, as we saw with Kylie, depressed. It leaves your people frustrated and argumentative. In fact, that's often how ADD people end up in therapy in the first place. Some aspect of your life becomes so disorganized that you and those around you can't face it any more.

Thankfully, you have the power to push back this particular apocalypse and reorder your life to produce a happier, more productive future. That's especially fortunate, because you'll need all the organization you can muster to take on our next big challenge: Love.

CHAPTER 11

LOVE AND OTHER RELATIONSHIPS

You're not perfect, sport, and let me save you the suspense: this
girl you've met, she's not perfect either. But the question is
whether or not you're perfect for each other.

— Psychologist Sean Maguire in *Good Will Hunting*

"Let me try and explain." Todd seemed to be choosing his words
carefully as his wife, Nikki, filled the wastebasket I'd placed right in
front of her with tear-laced Kleenex. "We did have a strong sexual attraction,
but it was more than that. I'd always dated these really pretentious girls and—"

"He's always comparing me to some old girlfriend. One his parents would
have approved of." Nikki rolled her eyes. "I'll never be good enough."

"I don't think that's where Todd was headed," I said. "I think he was about to
say that he liked you because you *weren't* pretentious."

She blew her nose. "I don't even know what that means. We didn't need big
words in styling school. That's how Todd talks at law school."

"Don't be so hard on yourself," I said. "Hair styling is a good gig, Nikki. You
get paid pretty well and you make people happy. Attorneys never make anyone
happy."

Nikki chuckled and glanced at Todd from the corner of her eye. "'Cuz they
can't take a joke or have fun or even smile. Todd holds it over me that I'm not
as smart as he is."

"That's not true," Todd said. "I never say you're not smart, just that you don't
have a lot of…" His voice faltered. "Never mind."

"Say it," Nikki daubed her eyes. "You say it at home all the time. Don't act like somebody you're not, just 'cuz we're in his office."

Todd cleared his throat. "Nikki doesn't have much common sense. I used to think of her as bubbly and idiosyncratic, and maybe a little ditzy, but now I get so frustrated with her because she doesn't apply logic to any situation, or if she does it's some kind of private logic that I don't understand."

"That's so unfair. I told you I had ADD when we met, but you never took the time to really understand. I thought you were different, that you cared about something more than just having sex with me, but you didn't. Then once we had the baby, you got stuck with me."

"Do you feel stuck, Todd? I asked.

He hesitated. I understood Nikki's insecurities about how their relationship had gotten to this point. Only twenty-one, she was cute and shapely and already back to her pre-pregnancy size three, less than six months after delivery. She'd undoubtedly had her choice of casual partners before her rushed marriage to Todd, a guy who probably never expected to bring his stylist home to meet his parents, let alone tell them that they were engaged.

"Be honest." Nikki's voice cracked. "You're sorry you married me. You're sorry we had Nathan. I'm too much for you to deal with."

"I'm not sorry," he said firmly. "I've grown to love you more than anything, Nik. Nathan too, but if you really want me to be honest here, then yes, you are too much for me to handle at times."

"Todd, you know my rule here," I said. "Tell me your goal for starting conflict with Nikki. Her goal is obvious. She wants to know whether you're giving up on the marriage. What's yours?"

"My goal is for her to understand that love isn't enough. I need to have a *partner*. It can't just be me pulling the load. She has to be more serious."

"Whether you agree or not, Nikki, is that a fair goal for an argument?"

"I guess it's fair, but I *am* serious."

"You're not." Todd took a deep breath. "You're a mom now. You have to act like an adult. You chose to have the baby and I supported you in that. I married you because I want to be with you and I think we could be a good team, but being a mom and a wife means you can't go out with your girls every weekend. You don't get to be that kind of twenty-one-year-old."

"No, because you want me to act like *your* mom did or something!" Nikki's voice was bitter. "Just because I have a kid now, I can't have any time to just be myself? Is that how it is?" She shook her head. "You try carrying a baby around for nine months and then having post-partum depression and never sleeping. You didn't spend your twenty-first birthday in labor instead of playing drinking games and—"

"Nikki!" Todd erupted. "Why can't you see the big picture here?"

"Stop." I spoke sharply to protect them both from another pointless, over-emotional fight. "Nikki, Todd has hung in there ever since you came in with post-partum depression. When you weren't sleeping he was up with the baby on rotating shifts so you could get some rest. He bottle-fed breast milk. He took off a semester from law school and his family pitched in money so you could take a longer maternity leave."

"So, you're saying he's right? That I have to just give up my whole life because I'm a mom now?"

"Yes," I said. "Being a parent and a spouse pretty much means that you don't exist as an individual anymore. Really you haven't since you got into an exclusive relationship. You have to take others into account—"

"Well, eff that." She pulled another Kleenex. "I didn't sign up for that."

"Actually, you did," I said. "You have to give up some of what it means to be an individual for a greater good." I turned to Todd. "But that also includes coming to some agreement on what's okay for Nikki to do socially. If she wants to go out one evening per week with friends and you can agree on a time she comes home, it would help her balance her life between being an adult and still having some fun while she's young."

"He gets to set a curfew for me?" Nikki fumed. "What am I, fourteen?"

"You're acting like it," Todd said. "This is how she always is, Dr. Wes. It's like I married a teenage girl."

"And it's like I married my dad." Nikki threw her last Kleenex in the trash and turned into the fight. "Except even he wasn't this controlling."

"Hold on," I said. "This is pretty much par for the course when ADD people, like you, Nikki, marry people who are anxious, like you, Todd. That's what I really meant when I said you did sign on for this. When you first came in you told me that you liked Todd because he's stable, careful, and he looks out for you on things you aren't good at. I have it right here in the notes." I tapped the screen on my laptop.

"And I said he's totally boring." She crossed her legs and folded her arms. "Did you write that in your notes?"

"Listen, if I weren't a little anxious, we'd both be screwed," Todd said. "My parents have already spent $400 this year in overdraft fees on our joint account. All of them yours. I had to take away your checkbook."

"I told you I'm not good at math."

"I check your car every morning to be sure you won't run out of gas so I don't end up driving into the city to pick you up from the salon. If it weren't for me, the rent wouldn't get paid and the baby wouldn't have diapers."

"That's not true! Nathan always gets what he needs."

"No, he gets what you need, Nikki." Todd nervously tapped the side of the armchair. "Which brings us to the secret credit card you took out at Target the other day. Did you really think I wouldn't find out?"

Nikki's gaze fell to her perfectly manicured toes and sequined flip-flops. "I don't know anything—"

"Stop, Nikki," I said sternly. "Take a breath before you utter a word and think very carefully about what you want to say right now."

"Yes," Todd said. "And before you do, remember that we have an identity theft protection plan that alerts me when anyone opens an account using either your social security number or mine."

We sat in silence for nearly a minute. "It was for the baby. You took away my check card and I had to get formula."

"*Nikki...*" My voice carried a skeptical tone. "Be truthful."

"I just bought a few small items, because—"

"Four hundred and ninety-eight dollars worth of small items?" Todd said smugly. "You like to spend money and then justify it by saying it's for him."

"See what I mean, Dr. Wes? He's so controlling!"

"Because you need to be controlled," Todd said. "You have no self-regulation. Dr. Wes said it himself."

"Time out, people." I raised both hands. "You're both right and you're both wrong, except neither of you knows which is which or why. So, who wants to recite the fundamental rule of survival when an ADD person marries an anxious one, because it's looking pretty important right now."

Neither said a word. They just sat there, facing away from each, arms crossed, like a pair of matching sphinxes.

"Seriously?" I said. "You two are so busy arguing that you somehow missed the most important thing I've ever told you. Since the baby is with your parents, Todd, I guess we're going to sit here all night if we have to, and start from scratch, because I'm not giving up on your marriage just yet and I'm not going to let you give up on it either."

Is This Chapter For Me?

Probably. Maybe it's just because I'm a couples and family psychologist, but I find that most psychotherapy involves learning how to love and be loved. Even if relationships aren't the initial complaint, much of a client's recovery involves connecting to and working with others. For people with ADD, that can get complicated, though I've seen plenty of ADD clients who have as their special power people and relationships.

In determining whether this chapter is for you, consider the following points. Be sure to include your people in this checklist, because this chapter is as much about them as it is you:

- ❏ Do others complain that they have a hard time knowing where they stand with you, or vice versa? Or does where you stand with others seem to shift from one day to the next?

- ❏ Do you try to be monogamous but often fail, leaving behind hurt feelings and broken promises?

- ❏ Do you easily get bored with relationships, even if (or particularly if) they are stable and long-lasting?

- ❏ Do other people seem to understand and respond to their partners, friends, and family members better than you do?

- ❏ Do loved ones tell you that you're emotionally immature?

- ❏ Are you particularly attracted to partners who "keep you in line" and organized, but call them "controlling" when they do just that?

If you believe that love never comes easy, you're right, and this chapter is for you. Here, I'll ask you to consider whether you're interested in or ready for monogamy and, if you are, discuss how to take your best shot at finding, getting, and keeping a relationship. I'll even suggest some ethically informed workarounds if you're just not the monogamous type.

By the way, all relationships are based on rules of obligation and social interplay. They only differ in purpose and intensity. So, a lot of what I'll discuss here also applies to your relationships with family and friends, and perhaps even coworkers or casual acquaintances.

Where Do We Stand?

When I was twenty years old, the range of romantic relationships ran from "friends who don't hold hands" to "married or darn close to it." In between, there were six or seven increments (e.g., steady dating, promised, engaged). Today, young adults and teens still have the same ends on that continuum, but there are now about thirty in-between points. That leaves a lot of people feeling pretty in-between.

An essential element of human interplay is actually knowing what kind of relationship you're in at any moment.

An essential element of human interplay is actually knowing what kind of relationship you're in at any moment and being sure your partner is on the same page. It's vital that you keep your connection to a given person down to one relationship at a time (e.g., friend, lover, coworker), and that you always know which label applies.

For generations, this need for order has led to the "Where do we stand?" conversation. That was hard enough with six possibilities. It's excruciating with thirty because it lowers the chances that you and your partner will end up on the same space on the board at the same time. That leaves a whole generation of young adults dealing with ill-defined relationships where nobody is really sure where anyone stands, resulting in too many couples who decide to "not put a label on it," or "keep things casual."

Many ADD people think they love this, because "no labels" seems to mean no obligation. However, over thousands of hours working on human interaction, I've learned that ill-defined relationships aren't liberating. They're just confusing. They keep everyone off-kilter and ultimately disappointed. We label relationships for the same reason we label clothes, cars, files, psychological problems, and everything else—so you can tell what you've got going on and communicate that to others.

Be very clear with yourself and your partner as to where you stand along every point of the relationship journey. Are you talking? Are you exclusively talking? Are you dating? Do you call each other boy- and girlfriend (or boy- and boyfriend, etc.). Are you just friends? Are you friends with benefits? Are you just sex partners? If you can't be clear where your relationship lives on the continuum, you're either headed for a heartache or about to cause one yourself.

The Problem With Monogamy

Historically, the great nirvana of the "Where do we stand?" conversation, the peak to which we all aspired, was exclusivity—dating one person and/or marrying them. For people with ADD[60] however, ultimate coupledom presents three titanic problems:

- **You Get Bored.** As we discussed way back in Chapter 1, doing the same thing over and over again is ADD torture. You yearn for novelty; to be Somewhere Else, or, in this case, with Someone Else. Exclusive relationships are by definition stable, which means they're inevitably less entertaining than meeting someone new every other night.

- **You Lack Psychological Integrity**. If you feel one thing on Monday, something different on Wednesday, and something completely different on Friday, you'll leave your partner's head spinning like a top. Or maybe just leave your partner.

- **You're Not Great At Mind Mapping.** This sounds really psychedelic, but mind mapping is nothing more than picking up on someone's expectations, perspective, and ways of doing things, and using that to learn how they think. It's the intuitive component of empathy and lies at the core of any successful relationship. Because you don't always notice small details, people with ADD can struggle to get this right.

Over the years I've come to understand that there are several sides to the whole monogamy issue and the only way to make an authentic choice to be exclusive is to understand that you don't have to be.

Monogamy is Good. I'll tell you my bias right up front. I'm a big fan of exclusive, long-term relationships. I think they work well from a psychological, sociological, and interpersonal perspective. But have you ever stopped to consider *why* anyone would voluntarily give up the ability to get sex and companionship from whomever they want in order to settle down with just one person? I get asked about this all the time, especially now that there are many more ways to be a couple than ever before as well as many lifestyle choices that do not require you to do so.

A scene from the movie *Shall We Dance? (2004)* explains my views on monogamy better than I can. The shocking plot twist of the film is the revelation that a man is in love with his wife. Nobody saw that one coming, which says a lot about the state of marriage today. In fact, Beverly, the wife (Susan Sarandon), is as surprised about it as we are. She hires a private investigator to track her husband, John (Richard Gere), precisely because she suspects he's having an

---

[60] And quite a few other people too. But this book is about ADD so I'll stick to the challenges you face with monogamy.

affair. He's not. He's just learning to tango from dance instructor, Paulina (Jennifer Lopez). No, really. She's just teaching him to dance.

After the investigator gives Beverly this crazy good news, he and she discuss the nature of marriage, which leads them to this wonderful exchange.

> Beverly: Why is it that you think people get married?
>
> Investigator: Passion.
>
> Beverly: No.
>
> Investigator: That's interesting, because I would have taken you for a romantic.
>
> Beverly: It's because we need a witness to our lives. There's a billion people on the planet. I mean, what does any one life really mean? But in a marriage, you're promising to care about everything. The good things, the bad things, the terrible things, the mundane things. All of it, all of the time, every day. You're saying 'Your life will not go unnoticed because I will notice it. Your life will not go un-witnessed because I will be your witness'."

Monogamy isn't statistically viable. Just look at the divorce rate. It's not biologically sensible because it limits the production of children. Legal marriage has economic benefits, but when it fails, it can have tremendous costs. It aids in the rearing of children, but solid single or divorced parents can do almost as well. Monogamy is prescribed by religious faiths, but that only works if you both believe in that doctrine *and* choose to practice it. Many people say one thing and do another. For me, monogamy really doesn't make a lot of sense unless you believe Beverly. And I do.

I'm not saying that everyone who's with someone right now must stay with that person forever. That's impractical given that a whole lot of people didn't know themselves very well or weren't thinking when they chose their partner. Moreover, all dating is practice and a critical part of that practice is breaking up. That may even mean a divorce or two, though you'll hopefully cut down on your total number of marriages by following the advice in this chapter.

Here's what I *am* saying about monogamy.

- Love is something you do, not something you just feel. No couple is meant to be together, but those who succeed *mean* to be together.

- It's worth time and effort to find a soul mate and to form a reciprocal, mutually supportive relationship, however you choose to define that as a couple.

- Monogamy is based on radical honesty and psychological integrity. You both need to be either in or out of a given relationship and stay that way over time.

- As an ADD person, monogamy requires you to cognitively override the joys of novelty and actively fight the ensuing boredom simply because you believe in the greater value of stability.

Monogamy will rarely feel right for people with ADD, except at the very beginning, when it too is novel. But if you choose wisely and intentionally, it can *become* right for you.

Or Not. On the other hand, in working with clients, I've learned that some people just aren't designed for monogamy, including some folks with ADD and ADD leaners. I don't mean they shouldn't be with the person they're with right now—though there are plenty of those too. I mean they're genuinely not interested in or very good at exclusivity and they shouldn't hold themselves out as monogamous. This may seem cynical or defeatist to some readers who love monogamy as much as I do. It's not. Monogamy just doesn't work for everyone the way I wish it did. And really, what *does* work the same for everyone?

If you're not sure whether you fit into monogamy or not, ask yourself the following questions:

- ❏ Do you affirmatively prefer dating multiple partners? When I said monogamy had to be an authentic choice made against non-monogamy, this is what I was talking about. You get to choose.

- ❏ Do you claim to be monogamous or avoid the question, then break up easily, cheat, or try to keep your partners at arm's length, even when you know they're falling in love with you?

- ❏ Once you've had sex with someone, do you quickly lose interest and never get it back, even if your partner wants to keep it going?

- ❏ Do friends or dating partners tell you that you lack emotional depth or that you're selfish in your relationships?

- ❏ Do you find that you're only good for about half a relationship; maybe sex or companionship or casually hanging out?

If you checked any of these, you probably shouldn't hold yourself out as monogamous. Instead, I propose that everyone—you, me, your family, and society—come to a peace about this. You may have very good reasons for choosing non-monogamy. As long as you've followed the principles in this book, act with psychological and ethical integrity, and are clear about that choice with all potential partners, you are expressing an honest identity.

Grow Up. On the other hand—because this issue seems to have an awful lot of hands—you may simply not be ready to settle down with one person at this stage of your life. Developmentally, many teens and young adults aren't as ready for monogamy as they may be later on. They may have many short-term relationships or several long-term ones before finding a soul mate.

For those with ADD, maturity is usually an extended journey. Give yourself time to grow, change, and complete your brain development before you give up completely on monogamy. By your late twenties, you might be ready to make a marital-style commitment. Until then, identify and practice what you want to be, but don't claim to be something or someone you're not.

Complimentary or Symmetrical?: ADD, Anxiety, and Love

In Chapter 2, I said most people lean either toward the anxious side or toward the ADD side; that anxious people (or leaners) care too much and ADD people (or leaners) don't care enough. That becomes really important when you start mixing your leanings with other people's.

In romance, people can pair off in one of three combinations: two anxious people (or leaners), two ADD people (or leaners), or one of each, like Nikki and Todd.[61] Over the years, I've found that how you pair off along this continuum explains a lot about your relationship. The farther each partner leans one way or the other, the more conflict ensues, unless they learn to map each other's minds and to accommodate and assimilate.

Of the three, the anxious-ADD dyad is without a doubt the most common[62], forming what family psychologists call a "complimentary" relationship. Sounds nice, huh? People complimenting each other. But what it really means is that one partner's strengths match the shortcomings of the other. Usually, complimentary relationships yield a hierarchy where the more skilled or functional person is dominant. That can work pretty well if the relationship is, say, parent-child, therapist-client, or teacher-student. But if you're supposed to be equals, as in a marriage, complimentary relationships can get dicey. That's why Nikki and Todd fought like a father and daughter and resented each other for acting out those roles.

Yet, equality in romance presents its own difficulties. People with similar strengths or weaknesses are "symmetrical." Think of business partners with the same number of shares and the same drive, experience, and financial resources forming a perfect synergy of effort. Or vice versa—two people with

---

[61] I also said about 25% of people with ADD have symptoms of anxiety, which really complicates matters, so let's ignore them for a moment in order to make my point.

[62] Meaning most common in my clinical experience. I haven't found any research on the incidence of these dyads, particularly at the sub-diagnosed (leaner) level.

a great idea and no money, no business experience, and no contacts. In each case, neither party is dominant, so both must pull together to use what they have to become successful. That might sound neat, but as it applies to ADD or anxious dyads, things are rarely that rosy.

Advantages and Disadvantages of Each Dyad

It doesn't make sense to identify advantages in how people with ADD love and accept love from others, because any advantage depends on whom you're matched with. Instead, I'll explain the strengths and weaknesses of each dyad.

ADD-Anxious Dyad. The magnetism between ADD and anxious people must be more powerful than I'd ever imagined, because so many couples, diagnosable or not, present for therapy this way. Think about it. How many couples (or friendships) do you see in which one partner is organized, conscientious, and prone to follow his or her head, and the other is free-spirited, creative, and always chasing a dream? Even if they're just leaners, you can see these personality contrasts and clashes. Apparently, opposites really do attract.

Yet, for any complimentary relationship to last, both partners must feel like they get something out of the mismatch of skills and personality attributes. For the ADD-anxious dyad, this means that the ADD person appreciates and responds to the anxious person's order and guidance and the anxious person is entertained and enlivened by the ADD partner's energy and spontaneity. Nikki caught Todd's attention by being "carefree, bubbly, and idiosyncratic." She liked him because he was so stable.

Unfortunately, these two are also typical of what goes wrong in an ADD-anxious dyad. As a relationship ages, we grow frustrated with the things we loved about our partner when we were dating them. Throw kids in the mix, and you find the extent of each partner's tolerance for the other's chaos. What starts out as a perfect love match of fascinating contrasts ends up with one frustrated master and one humiliated servant.

There's only one way to avoid that outcome. I call it the fundamental rule of survival for ADD-anxious dyads. You'll have to follow it every day in every relationship you get into. It requires a team effort, and it won't work if either partner doesn't do his or her part. Here it is: *The anxious partner must learn to tolerate the ADD partner's chaos and the ADD partner must learn not to overtax the anxious one.* It's no easier than it sounds, but at the end of this chapter, I'll give you and your partner point-by-point instructions on how to pull it off.

ADD Dyads. If they're just leaners, some ADD couples succeed by engaging each other's best qualities—art, music, innovation, creativity, etc. But at their worst, these couples compete for the highest score in a game of "the thing we hate about ADD people" (Chapter 8). Remember that couple in Chapter 5 who wanted to move to California and pursue careers in singing and brewing, without experience, money, connections, training, or family support? They were about the most ADD couple I've ever met. In a complimentary dyad, an anxious partner would point out how impractical that plan was, just as Todd curtly pointed out Nikki's lack of "common sense." In a true ADD dyad, nobody filters anything, and thus chaos rules the day. Sometimes the consequences are immense, as with an ADD couple I saw who, in their mid-sixties, bankrupted an established family business because neither could keep track of their once-sizable fortune.

Anxious Dyads. These couples can be very successful at raising a family and putting food on the table, especially if they're just leaners. They're like two determined oxen, side by side, pulling their family wagon across the prairie. While that sounds like the definition of a highly functional family, anxious dyads can bore each other to relational stagnation, drift, and distraction. Not infrequently, that leads to infidelity intended to either escape the marriage or liven it up and thereafter, separation.

An example is found in *Hope Springs* (2012) starring Meryl Streep and Tommy Lee Jones as Kay and Arnold. This uptight couple sits back and watches their sexless marriage descend into drudgery, until Kay undertakes a militant journey to resuscitate it. Though humorous, the film is so anxiety-producing at times that it's uncomfortable to watch, which is exactly how it feels to sit in on a session with an anxious dyad. You don't feel a sense of panic but instead a pall of dread pressing down on both partners.

And that's exactly why people with ADD (and leaners) find anxious partners and vice versa. Sometimes that's conscious. Usually, it's just an innate law of attraction to seek out someone who balances you out. How well that turns out may depend on how you handle the ideas in the rest of this chapter.

Principle 11: Love Intentionally

By definition, dating is the process of figuring out who you *don't* belong with. Read that again, because people usually get it backwards. Your goal in dating is *not* to make anyone into someone you want to date. It's to figure out if you belong with that person, and if not, to move on.

> By definition, dating is the process of figuring out who you don't belong with.

This usually gets mucked up right from the start of a relationship, when we're all a little ADD, following our hearts, ignoring details and red flags, and letting our love run like happy unicorns through a field of roses. We embrace surging sexual attractions and suppress concerns as to how well we're really matched, certain our passion can conquer whatever peccadillos it may bring with it.

We call this "falling in love." That's a super metaphor, isn't it? Love as a hole in the ground; you walking down the street, carelessly minding your own business. Suddenly, you tumble into it and can't get out. This accident-waiting-to-happen model of love almost guarantees you'll either end up with the wrong person or on the blunt end of an awkward breakup. Yet, that's exactly what we teach young people about love in our homes, music, media, folklore, and literature. No wonder we have a high divorce rate in America[63].

If instead you think of loving someone as an intentional act—something you do, not something you just feel—you can wisely shop for a partner as Alex shopped for toys (Chapter 5). Get to know a lot of people but keep it casual until something real develops. I'm all for good healthy sex, but try and hold off until you have a clear picture of what you're getting yourself into. That's not moralizing. It's a real world example of psychological integrity and radical honesty. It also gives you a better strategic position in the dating pool because you'll be taken more seriously and afforded greater credibility.

Sound boring? It's not, unless you find romantic disaster enchanting and empowerment dull. Best of all, approaching love this way removes the element of fate and makes it into something you can *learn* how to do.

Five Stages of Love. I once received a letter to my newspaper column asking for my definition of love. Answering it proved more challenging than I'd expected. Here's what I came up with. I use it to help all my clients love more intentionally, though I've added a few thoughts on where folks with ADD struggle at each stage.

1. **Attraction.** Your heart inspires you to be near someone, likely based on how they fit an attraction profile you've acquired and refined during adolescence and young adulthood. Try to make this more about how you and your partner match physically than a comparison to a well-airbrushed magazine model. Because ADD people seek novelty over stability, invest a little extra time at this stage. If you give it a chance and there's still no chemistry, the game's over. It's either a no-match situation or you and the attractive person are better off friend-zoned.

2. **Emotional Connection.** I like the term "talking" as it currently describes this stage of courting, because it involves communication. As you talk you may begin to feel something very personal with your love interest. Today, this is typically followed quickly by sex, which presses the issue of sexual compatibility early in the game. A mismatch of experience can try the patience of an ADD

[63] www.nytimes.com/2005/04/19/health/19divo.html?_r=0

person, particularly if you're the more experienced one. You may become frustrated with an emotionally reserved or cautious partner. Your lack of psychological integrity may also rear its head of uncertainty. Try not giving up too quickly, lest you miss your perfect match due only to impatience. Sometimes the "I-love-you"s are exchanged toward the end of this stage, which usually pushes things on to the next level. If a deeper bond doesn't develop, break up ethically by explaining that you were really feeling it and hoping the attraction would grow, but as you've gotten closer you don't see a real, consistent connection.

3. **Thinking.** Time for your head to get into this game. At this stage you build an intellectual connection with your partner. I don't mean you go to museums and libraries together, though that's nice. I mean you begin to map each other's minds. You weigh the pros and cons, consult with your mentor and your people, and decide if you and your dating partner are well matched. If you begin to see more cons than pros, break up by explaining that despite your emotional connection, the relationship isn't making your life better or more sensible. That's harder and more uncomfortable at this stage, which means you may procrastinate or go back and forth in deciding what to do. So work toward a good decision and then act on it.

4. **Spiritual Connection.** Here's where stuff gets real. Compared to the earlier stages, loving this way is like the difference between studying a great work of art and playing *Grand Theft Auto V*. You and your partner get to know each other ultimately, feel impossibly comfortable together, and understand each other's minds almost as you do your own. You feel uniquely matched with your partner, as if you fit together almost perfectly. Many people with ADD want to love this way, but the depth of obligation can crowd and overwhelm you. Because most of your relationship mysteries are already solved, there's little left to discover, which can tax your need for novelty. However, few relationships survive if they don't eventually get to this point. Once you're here, the biggest danger is sticking too long with a dysfunctional partner who can't really reciprocate, just because you feel so connected. When you break up at this stage, there's rarely any turning back. Get a therapist. You'll need one.

5. **Time.** All relationships are four-dimensional because all people grow, mature, and change over time. Sometimes that brings a couple closer. Other times, it creates distance. No matter how well the first four stages have gone, only time will tell if your love can

stand the test of time. You have to work at it for a while to get all the sexual, emotional, cognitive, and spiritual components aligned and keep them that way even when things get hard and problems must be solved. Because you aren't wired to be patient, time is the hardest accommodation for people with ADD in relationships or anything else. However, if you master time and listen to what it's telling you about the relationship, you'll eventually come up with a soul mate.

As you work your way through these stages of love (probably more than once), keep in mind that substance abuse is incompatible with good decision making. Yet time and again couples describe making one life-changing decision after another while one or both are drunk or high. Partying is partying. Love is love. Don't confuse the two or you may end up at the bottom of that hole I mentioned earlier, and not at the top of love's summit.

Obligation and Motivation. Back in Chapter 3, I said obligation was at the core of any relationship. When it comes to love, you can double down on that point. A core tenant of any relationship is that the least motivated partner always has the most power. ADD partners are wired to more easily walk away. That can be helpful when you're still shopping for love and don't want to commit too soon, but it can make it all too easy to manipulate an anxious partner. Manipulating or being manipulated in a power-mismatched relationship is one of the best reasons to end it.

Cheating. Infidelity violates several principles in this book. Cheating is a problem, not a solution. It's also kind of delusional. Affairs are exciting because they're affairs, not because the person you're having the affair with is fantastically better than the person you're obligated to. Nor is it ethical or wise to enter one exclusive relationship after another when you know you're not really ready to make any kind of commitment. That's just slightly more ethical than cheating, which brings us to a more ethical solution...

Polyamory. If you've thought all this through, tested the waters and found that you truly aren't interested in a one-to-one romantic life, then consider staying openly single or practicing polyamory—having more than one open romance at a time.[64] Practiced as intended, polyamory has established rules for how to manage multi-partner relationships. While I mentioned my bias toward monogamy earlier, radical honesty makes polyamory far more ethical than claiming to be monogamous right up until you see a new, shiny romance within your grasp and leaving your partner in the dust, or worse, using cheating as a workaround.

---

[64] www.merriam-webster.com/dictionary/polyamory

Polyamory is more complicated than monogamy. To make it work you have to honor the importance of instructions (Chapters 6) and ethics (Chapter 9). Nowhere in love are guidelines more critical than when you start tinkering around with the feelings of not one, but several partners. If you decide to proceed, do so wisely and with caution.

Breaking Up. This might not seem a very fun topic in a chapter on love, but breaking up is an essential part of finding a soul mate. If it weren't, you'd end up married to everyone you ever dated, which would be a huge pain, not to mention illegal.

Breaking up with someone can get as dicey for people with ADD as loving him or her in the first place. Sometimes more so. You may be impatient and give up on a relationship before it's had time to work. Or you may hang on too long, after things get toxic, because it's too uncomfortable to split up. You may become too dependent on the structure of an anxious partner, which causes that person to feel used. Or perhaps you're addicted to disaster (Chapter 7) and keep bad breakups going on longer than they should, just to keep feeling that familiar intensity.

I have a couple of rules for when you find yourself at the point of a breakup. Both are doubly true if that happens to be a divorce. They're intended for everyone, but people with ADD often have to be more intentional to make them work:

- **Never Break Up With Anyone You Don't Mean to Break Up With.** If you're really nearing the end of a relationship and you need your partner to take you seriously when you're asking for a change, it may be okay to offer a breakup or divorce as an authentic choice. Just don't use it as a threat to manipulate someone. And never bluff. Your partner might call your hand. Then, if you beg to stay, you've instantly become the more motivated and least powerful partner. If you go ahead and cover your bluff, you may have blown a salvageable relationship for no good reason.

- **Actually Break Up.** Next to an ill-defined relationship, an ill-defined breakup is the worst dating idea ever. It's called breaking up because it's broken. So, get the job done. Don't "take a break,"[65] and don't look back. You can stay friendly, especially if you're in the same friend group, but don't stay friends, stalk each other's Facebook, or follow your ex on Twitter. That's just an excuse to avoid the discomfort of doing what's hard, particularly

---

[65] A "break" is an excuse to date other partners while not fully ending the current relationship, which leads to more hard feelings and heartaches. I've never seen it turn out well.

when a new partner comes along and demands to know why you're still not over your ex. Today, breaking up means "delete." Use that function on your heart and all of your devices, lest you end up in a zombie relationship where you just keep hurting each other for no good reason. Better to move on and use the wisdom you've gained toward a better relationship down the road.

And now that we've discussed how to end a relationship, let's work on saving yours by returning to the fundamental rule of survival for ADD-anxious dyads. If you're in one, it comes not a moment too soon. So, let's start with your anxious partner's to-do list. Please pass this book to him or her.

Tolerance 101 For Anxious People. You don't have to lean very far to the anxious side to find yourself dating an ADD person or leaner. If you're diligent, conscientious, and well-structured in life, ADD won't make much sense to you, but it sure can be fun to watch. At least for a while.

Your ADD person is at his or her most entertaining in the early days of a relationship: creating spontaneity and fun in your life, taking you places you might never go by yourself—physically, geographically, culturally. But as the relationship progresses, you learn "the thing we hate about the ADD people"—your partner has infinite tolerance for his or her own chaos and none for yours.

The fundamental rule of survival says that to succeed in a relationship with an ADD person, you must raise your tolerance for his or her chaos. That should keep you busy for years to come. For this to work, however, your ADD partner has to follow the list at the end of this chapter to learn how not to overtax your tolerance. You can't *make* your partner do this. He or she has to value the relationship enough to choose to do it. And if that's not happening, you might want to reread the section of this chapter on breaking up.

> *To succeed in a relationship with an ADD person, you must raise your tolerance for his or her chaos.*

Here are my tips for building up your tolerance.

- **Practice Radical Acceptance.** You're in a relationship with an ADD person. Your partner has a neurological disorder that makes him or her care less than you do about almost everything. That's not an excuse, but it is an explanation.

- **People Want to Change, But Not Very Much.** That's true for everyone and especially for people with ADD, so don't expect your meticulous nature to eventually rub off on him or her. Your partner may feel satisfied with things you can't stand about him or her. Set clear but realistic goals for what you can't stand and must have, and help your partner achieve them. That will take a lot longer than you think it should. Put at the top of your expectation list...

- **Get Help.** If your ADD partner hasn't been diagnosed and treated, nothing is going to get better. That treatment should include you, medication, and therapy, all working together. A good therapist can help you both practice the strategies in this book while tossing in some others that he or she has learned along the way. John Gottman, PhD notes that most couples wait six years too long before seeking help. Don't be one of those, even if you have to make continuing the relationship contingent on therapy.

- **Develop Empathy.** Read this book as if you were your partner. Imagine what it must be like to deal with the many struggles of ADD I've shared here. The more you learn, the more you'll know when to push your partner hard and when to support him or her gently.

- **Practice Beneficence.** In Chapter 9, I talked about the ethic of beneficence—giving in a way that actually does some good. That means helping your ADD partner function more independently and effectively. Here are some examples: Picking up medication and putting it in a pill box so it's taken regularly. Setting up a calendar system and reminders for birthdays, anniversaries, appointments for doctors and therapists, date nights, vacations. Leading the way in financial planning. Designing couple's activities, so your partner just shows up and has fun.

- **Don't Enable.** This means doing something for your partner that creates dependency. It means getting gratification from over-functioning while your ADD partner under-functions.[66] These boundaries can be tricky, but here are a few examples of enabling: Repeatedly taking a forgotten phone to work instead of creating a system for remembering. Calling to be sure your partner took contraception on time, instead of helping her get on a low-maintenance method. Cleaning his or her designated space or doing laundry without negotiating a comparable chore in return. Funding impulsive purchases you don't agree with. Looking past violations of your relationship rules. Ignoring medication and therapy noncompliance.

---

[66] This is also referred to as "codependency."

- **Care Less.** Being tolerant means not taking your ADD partner's issues personally or reading into his or her behavior something deeper or darker than necessary. Your partner wasn't put on earth just to aggravate you. Pick your battles carefully and put all your emphasis on about three priorities, usually things like financial stability, employment, substance use, emotional and sexual connectedness, and time spent together. If you have kids, parenting should be on that list. Make everything else secondary.

- **Organize Your Partner's Life.** Setting up an organizational structure for your ADD partner (à la Chapter 10) is beneficent because it makes him or her more independent, increases your tolerance, and decreases conflict. If you work as a team, your partner should be appreciative. But if you quietly toss those Spiderman comic books that were supposed to go to auction back in 2009 and somehow ended up stacked by the night stand, you won't be an organizational hero.

- **Reach a Peace About Cleaning.** In the spirit of radical acceptance, understand that this battle is unwinnable and call a truce. If financially possible, find a living space that allows your ADD partner to have his or her own bathroom and den. Consider all common living areas yours. If you have a family room, give it to the ADD partner. Judge not the way your partner keeps his or her space as long as it does not constitute a fire hazard or breeding ground for rats. In return, the ADD people in your home must leave your space and any common spaces as neat as you want. If you've tried this for a year or two and it just doesn't work...

- **Live Apart.** I'm not kidding. The hardest thing people do is live together, as nations, cultures, or families. This is about ten times truer for ADD-anxious dyads, particularly when you get beyond the leaners. I've saved more than one marriage by having the partners buy both sides of a townhome and live separately. They get all the benefits of lovers and none of the problems of roommates. Besides, it's usually cheaper than the impending divorce that's always hanging around these stressed marriages.

- **Hire A Maid.** In Chapter 10, I suggested hiring an expert, particularly an anxious one. Getting a maid is cheaper than you think and it could save you a lot of wasted time and energy arguing. Many services will come in twice a week and clean your house while you're out, or you could hire a college student and have more flexibility.

- **State A Goal For Any Conflict You Start.** I illustrated this in Nikki and Todd's vignette. Only fight to solve problems, never to vent frustration.[67] For example, you might say, "I want to discuss something with you and my goal is to persuade you to set aside more time for us," or "My goal is to change our homework schedule so the kids' grades improve." If you can't state your goal as clearly as that, don't start the argument.

- **Honor Quiet Time.** No matter how well-stated your goal, never start an argument or share some important aspect of your day if your partner isn't able to pay attention. That will be worse early in the morning before meds have kicked in, ten to thirteen hours later, and during the first days of an extended stimulant break. Learn that rhythm and take it seriously. An ADD-savvy therapist can do wonders to coach you through it.

- **Make Things Fun.** ADD people are prone to boredom-breakups. Your only real hedge is to make the relationship as entertaining as it can be. You don't have to be a clown 24/7, but to keep things interesting, you'd better be up for some fun, and not just at the beginning. It's after you expect things to settle down that you have to keep looking for novelty to avoid stagnation.

When things get hard, try and remember why you liked your ADD partner in the first place. Frustrating as he or she may be, being the yin to his or her yang must have brought joy and meaning to your life at some point. Take heart in those memories. If you both follow the fundamental rule, this can be a pretty neat combo. On the other hand, if you don't like being that person anymore, maybe this relationship isn't for you.

To succeed in a relationship with an anxious person you must avoid overtaxing him or her with your chaos.

Those are the basics of how to reach harmony when in love with an ADD person. Now, it's your partner's turn. Return the book for a lesson on how to keep him or her from driving you over the edge of a very steep cliff.

Taxation 101 For ADD People. The fundamental rule of survival says that to succeed in a relationship with an anxious person or leaner, you must avoid overtaxing him or her with your chaos. If you've ever dated another ADD person, you know what it feels like to be overtaxed. That's why

---

[67] If you really do need to vent about something, be clear and say, "This isn't about you, but I'm upset. My goal is let off some steam about what a jerk my boss really is!" That way your partner won't take your emotional tirade personally and you're free to let it out.

ADD dyads rarely work. Both want to be the carefree partner and neither wants the obligation of being the conscientious one. So let's get started.

- **Practice Radical Acceptance.** You're in a relationship with an anxious person. That means they care more than you do about most everything and they have a limited tolerance for chaos. That's not going to change. Don't expect more than your partner can deliver, nor hold out hope that he or she will become more like you.

- **Develop Empathy for Your Partner.** Read this book as if you were your partner and think what it must be like for him or her to deal with someone who has ADD. Then ask your partner to help you put all my good advice to work. Anxious people are great at that and if your partner sees you're committed to taking action, he or she will be more likely to forgive the times when you fall short.

- **Get Help.** There's no shame in seeking a better way, only in refusing to do so when it's obvious you're hurting yourself or someone you love. When you make a decision for yourself, you make a decision for everyone, so your partner has the right to be involved in your therapy and med management. If you think you might have ADD and you haven't been diagnosed yet, don't wait another day, lest you end up alone. Sometimes a partner will get so overtaxed that he or she sends you to therapy by yourself, noting only, "You need help!" That's a mistake. Individual therapy for relationship problems is a fast ticket to a breakup, and ADD people often do better when they have their partners in session with them.

- **Remember That Your Partner is Benevolent.** Take a deep breath. Remember that your anxious partner has your best interests at heart. He or she isn't trying to limit your freedom or turn you into someone you're not. Your partner just cares a lot or maybe too much. Dealing with that is part of your relationship contract, just as dealing with your chaos is part of his or hers. Love your partner for the order he or she brings to your life, even when that feels like being controlled. And if I'm wrong about this—if your partner really is out to dominate someone and you happen to be the unfortunate target—break up. I've seen that happen and it *does not* end well.

- **Avoid Codependency.** By definition, relationships are interdependencies. The whole point of an ADD-anxious dyad is to invite someone you love to keep you on track in exchange for you bringing your lively, creative nature to the table. But that nifty dynamic has so many points of failure that it can collapse like a house of cards. You'll know codependency when your partner's attempt to help makes you more helpless and resentful. When you find yourself calling your partner "controlling," as Nikki did Todd, take a step back and ask yourself why anyone thinks you need to be controlled. Then reread Chapters 8 and 9, particularly the parts about externalizing blame.

- **Care More.** Tell yourself—actually say it in your head or out loud, if you must—"Putting away the cereal will take just five seconds." Then do it. Toss the Kleenex in the trash or at least pick them up off the floor after the big game. Show up to appointments ten minutes early rather than ten minutes late. Master the organizational tools from Chapter 10, not because they will make your life better (they will), but because organization makes life better for your partner.

- **Be Noticing.** Observe what your partner likes and how he or she likes it, then make changes to bring that about. As with everything ADD, it's not the big issues that make your life awesome or a mess. It's all the little ones. Care about those details, even if you have to plug them into your phone to remind you. Your partner will feel more loved and, in return, more tolerant.

- **Listen.** Next to being noticing, listening is the most important behavior you can perfect in a relationship. I know this is hard, so schedule time while your meds are in full force to just sit and listen to what your partner has to say. It's a critical tool in keeping a relationship running.

- **Be Less Messy.** Anxious-ADD couples fight more about cleaning and clutter than anything else. The further your partner leans to the anxious side, the more this will drive him or her crazy. Disorganization is to anxious people what scratchy tags, annoying sounds, having to rewrite something you've finished, or reading a super-boring book is for you. I've saved marriages by organizing homes so that people with ADD can reserve their own area, especially bathrooms, and keep it just how they want. But that only works if you keep your anxious partner's area just the way he or she wants it.

- **Do Your Part.** Draw up a list of what you and your anxious partner each contribute to the home. Perhaps he or she cleans the house and you mow the yard. Factor in the hours you work at your jobs and how much time you take for leisure. If you get to play video games, your partner should get equal time doing something he or she likes. Or you could hire help around the house, including a maid service for light housekeeping, a teenager to do lawn care, or a contractor to do routine maintenance. What matters is that your partner feels you both contribute equal time and effort. How you contribute should be up for discussion.

- **State A Goal For Any Conflict.** People with ADD often start fights just to express frustration, even when you're not frustrated with your partner. It lets off steam and calms you down. This is incredibly anxiety-producing for your partner and guaranteed to go badly. If you really need to vent about something that has nothing to do with your partner, then say, "I need to vent and I don't want to be alone when I'm talking to myself." That may keep your partner from taking your rant personally. If you really are frustrated with him or her, keep your venting to yourself. Only fight to solve problems.

- **Win The Struggle Against Boredom.** Speaking of venting, people with ADD may try to keep relationships fresh by making them overly dramatic and emotionally reactive, occasionally to the point of violence. Instead, find your emotional connection through adventure, sexual compatibility, and mutual interests. Manage your time apart so your time together is even better. Things will never be a 24/7 amusement park ride, but you can stay engaged. John Gottman, PhD has a thing he calls "bids and turning." One partner "bids" for the attention and involvement of the other and waits for the partner to respond. That can be either a turn toward (woo hoo!), a turn away (indifference) or a turn against (antagonism). Bid for your partner's attention and turn toward as often as possible.

Controlled and boring as your anxious partner may seem, there must be something you really liked about him or her in the early days, probably predictability and structure; knowing he or she would always be there for you, day in and day out. If you really don't like that anymore, get out and find someone who's a better match. Just be careful and remember what I said about ADD dyads. They move to entropy fast and there's often nobody filtering anyone's chaos. So think twice before ditching an anxious partner. If you both follow the fundamental rule of survival, you may turn out to be a pretty awesome couple.

The impact of ADD on marital-style relationships isn't just a Dr. Wes-ism. An article in the American Psychological Association Monitor notes, "Traditional marriage counseling often isn't very helpful unless ADHD is diagnosed and treated. Many people have tried going to therapists and marriage counselors who are not trained in ADHD and may overlook it as a source of potential problems in the marriage."[68]

To this I can only add a hearty, "Amen."

---

[68] www.apa.org/monitor/2012/03/adhd.aspx. The article cites Kevin R. Murphy, PhD, president of the Adult ADHD Clinic of Central Massachusetts and associate research professor in the department of psychiatry at SUNY Upstate Medical University in Syracuse.

CHAPTER 12

TESTING AND DIAGNOSIS

Named must your fear be before banish it you can.

— Yoda, *Star Wars Episode V: The Empire Strikes Back*

"It just seems really crazy that I'd have ADD." Kurt glanced over at his parents. "I mean I'm almost out of high school. Shouldn't it have shown up when I was like nine?"

"It does seem odd," said Kathy, his mother. "I was a stay-at-home parent. We had discipline in our home. He was never one of those little boys who tears around the house and climbs the walls."

"I actually hear that a lot," I said. "But you have to remember that most kids with ADD aren't hyperactive. They're just inattentive."

"I read that somewhere," said Jake, Kurt's father. "But why weren't we seeing problems with his grades and study habits before his senior year in high school? I think it's just senioritis. He's really ready to move on to college."

"Maybe," I said. The best way to get to an accurate diagnosis is to consider ADD alongside a series of alternative hypotheses. Though you won't find senioritis in the diagnostic manual, when a young person is about to turn eighteen, high school just doesn't seem that important anymore. "What do you think, Kurt? Are you getting antsy to leave?"

"Sure. But to be honest, I'm a little scared of moving out. I've been a big fish at Columbus High. I'm going to a big out-of-state school that has a lot of kids from cities like Chicago and New York. That kind of freaks me out."

"Is that normal for you?" I asked. "Being freaked out by a big change?"

"Not really," Kathy interjected. "Kurt's always been a pretty calm soul. There are only forty-five kids in his graduating class, so it's like one big friend group and he's always been the easy-going, even-tempered one."

"So, Kurt," I asked. "What's *your* theory as to how you might have come this far in school and only now just started wondering about this diagnosis?"

"I've thought about it a lot." Kurt paused for a moment. "Things have always come really easy for me. I'm our school's quarterback and the lead in our spring play next year. I never study, but I was always able to get As and a few Bs. I'm not trying to sound conceited, but I think I'm pretty smart. Or at least I used to think that. But this year, I had to take Calculus and Chemistry II and Physics and they're all advanced placement classes—"

"The recession really cut into business at my car dealership," Jake said. "We've only just recovered in the last couple of years. We need Kurt to test out of as many credits as possible to make college affordable."

"How did you end up taking all those classes in your senior year?" I asked.

Kurt shook his head. "I didn't listen to my advisor, or my dad." He glanced over at Jake. "I put things off sometimes."

"So, now that you're a senior and so much is riding on your performance, do you feel a lot of pressure to succeed?" I asked.

"Sort of, but not exactly," Kurt said. "But the work is just harder this year. I have to read the textbooks and the math doesn't just come to me like it did in pre-calc. And there's homework."

"You've never had homework before?" I asked.

"Not like this." Kurt took a deep breath. "I hate to say this, because to be totally honest, it's literally giving me nightmares, but I'm starting to realize my high school is just this tiny speck in this huge world, and not a very good one. I'm like the only person who's not going to community college. If I'm getting beat up now, what's going to happen to me next year?"

"Hmm." I leafed through his intake paperwork. "You said you're having nightmares. Are you waking up rested?"

"Yeah," Kurt said. "I mean the nightmares aren't all the time, and I have football after school so I'm pretty spent by bedtime."

I turned to Kathy and Jake. "Any relatives with ADD?"

The couple exchanged glances. "Kurt has two cousins who have it," Kathy said. "And maybe..." Her voice trailed off.

"Kathy and I met at Columbus High," Jake said. "We went to college together, but she didn't continue."

"I just wanted to marry Jake and be a homemaker," Kathy said. "Or at least that's what I told myself."

"I love Kathy more than anything," Jake said. "She's my soul mate and an amazing mom, but…she's kind of forgetful and disorganized and she could get lost in our driveway." He chuckled. "But she's an awesome cook and so creative. She has a new idea for an online business just about every week. But getting anything going? That's a different story."

"Guilty as charged." Kathy sighed. "Some of the things I've read about ADD do sound a lot like me. Nowadays it just seems like everyone is on meds or getting diagnosed and that kind of scares me. What ever happened to just putting in a little more effort? If Kurt just spent an hour a day studying, his grades would go right up. I didn't need to be on any of that stuff and things turned out fine for me."

Jake's eyebrows arched slightly.

Kurt took another deep breath and let it out through his nose. His face looked tight and serious. "Dad's right. You're a great mom and maybe ADD doesn't mess with you or stop you from being satisfied with who you are. But if I do have it, it isn't going to fit with who I want to be. This isn't about an hour a day studying. I want to go into architectural engineering and that isn't going to come easy for me. I don't want to have some ADD label either, and I sure don't want to be on meds, but things are different than they were in your day, Mom. I have to do what I have to do. I have to find out if I have this."

Is This Chapter For Me?

It depends. If you believe you have an accurate diagnosis and everything you've read in this book and others sounds about right, you can probably skip this chapter. Otherwise, consider the following:

- ❏ Have you wondered if you might have ADD, particularly after reading the first eleven chapters of this book?

- ❏ Were you diagnosed, but you still aren't sure because nobody actually tested you or spent much time interviewing you?

- ❏ Has medication seemed to have the wrong or opposite effect on you?

- ❏ Are you concerned that you might have both ADD and anxiety?
- ❏ Do you want to be more conversant about diagnosis and testing before you go to a mental health provider?

If any of these apply, this chapter is for you. I'll give you the lowdown on how to get a good, test-based diagnosis without overpaying, and I'll throw in a couple of thoughts on treatment and alternative therapies to get you thinking.

The Big Conspiracy

ADD generates more debate than global warming, most of it based on politics, emotional reactivity, and ill-informed opinion.[69] I'm not speaking out of school here. Back in the late 1990s, I too was an ADD-doubter. Who could blame anyone for thinking something was up? It seemed a little too convenient that big pharmaceutical companies, increased prescription drug benefits, and an uptick in ADD diagnoses all fell from heaven at the very same time. There had to be a conspiracy in there somewhere. Toss in schools supposedly demanding that parents chemically restrain kids, and shortened attention spans due to video games, TV, and the emerging Internet, and it seemed pretty obvious that big corporations were turning us into drug fiends, like the pacified masses in Aldous Huxley's *Brave New World*. At one point, even Bill and Hillary Clinton got on the anti-ADD bandwagon.[70]

Except for one tiny problem. A whole lot of children, teens, and adults diagnosed with ADD were taking stimulants and learning early versions of the techniques I've described in this book, and they were getting better.

As a therapist, I'd been trained to assign most problems to poor parenting, poverty, multigenerational family dysfunction, violence, and a host of other environmental influences. I was taught to view psychobiological explanations as deterministic[71] and therefore unhelpful in therapy. But none of that thinking seemed to make ADD people better, without actually treating them for ADD. Those who were treated as I describe in this book, dealt better with life problems, even horrible ones like child abuse and outplacement to foster care. Those who weren't, got worse even when their life stressors were comparatively minor. Many, like Leandra (Chapter 8), came from pretty good homes. Yet they seemed to gravitate toward trouble like a compass points north. That only increased their stress and decreased their ability to cope.

The conspiracy wasn't adding up anymore.

---

[69] Check out www.adhdaware.org and www.additudemag.com to clear up a lot of myths about ADD.

[70] www.pbs.org/wgbh/pages/frontline/shows/medicating/readings/brainpolitics.html

[71] Determinism denies or minimizes the ultimate importance of free will.

At the same time, I saw the world becoming more complex and difficult to manage, and that wasn't working out very well for people with ADD. Things really are different now from when Kurt's mom and I were in high school. Education, work, and life are more complicated and demanding. If you can even get a job in a factory, you don't just operate an impact wrench or drill press. You interact with technology. In high school, you learn complex math—whether you need it or not. I began to see why people who'd never needed an ADD diagnosis or treatment before, now sought help. Some were folks I'd grown up with, and they seemed to be doing a whole lot better with treatment than they were back in the day, without it.

Today, I consider both biology and social influence in getting to know my clients. Nobody is a disembodied brain floating about, disconnected from external influences. But neither are we rats in life's maze, subject only to social learning and environment. We are products of our world *and* our wiring. We can't be human or humane without both.

Over-Diagnosis and Misdiagnosis. At the heart of the conspiracy theory is a belief that ADD is "over-diagnosed," meaning that more people are getting labeled than can possibly exist in the population. Except we have no idea how many ADD people there are in the population, so we can't know whether it's over-diagnosed or under-diagnosed. So any opinion on that topic is just that, somebody's theory.

We do know that a lot of people aren't diagnosed who should be, because they keep showing up on our doorsteps, getting evaluated and benefitting from treatment. Others show up, get evaluated, but don't qualify for diagnosis. And if everything is done right, that's exactly how it should be. Unfortunately, all too often, everything is *not* done right.

It's too easy for people to get diagnosed, whether they should be or not. So the issue isn't over-diagnosis. It's misdiagnosis.

A lot of people are diagnosed and on medication who've never been properly evaluated. At least one per week shows up in my office, describing how another professional "eyeballed it" rather than doing any testing or conducting a thorough interview. Often, a prescriber spent a few minutes in an exam room hearing the client rattle off a list of symptoms he or she found on the Internet or gave a quick checklist before offering up stimulants. That makes it too easy for people to get diagnosed, whether they should be or not.

So, the issue with ADD isn't over-diagnosis. It's *mis*diagnosis.

Principle 12: With ADD You Go From Where You Start

In life, things turn out better when you start them correctly. In treating ADD, that means getting a good diagnosis before deciding on medication or therapy. So, let's go back to the opening vignette. Could you tell whether Kurt had ADD or not? Oh, come on! Twelve chapters into this book and you still can't spot an ADD person a mile away? He couldn't focus. Didn't study. Procrastinated taking hard classes until senior year, at which point his underlying weaknesses began to show through. His mom was at least a leaner and he had two cousins with ADD diagnoses. What are you missing here?

Nothing. I'm just messing with you to make a point. When we left the vignette, I had no idea whether Kurt had ADD, senioritis, a lower IQ than he thought, inadequate planning, or hadn't been challenged enough in his small high school. A whole lot of cases that come my way are no more obvious than this. Even if I were 90% certain, I still wouldn't have called Kurt's diagnosis this early in the process; not without more information and testing. You'll see how that turned out for Kurt in the Epilogue.

Good evaluation and accurate diagnosis go together like a horse and carriage. While that doesn't rhyme quite like the old Sinatra classic, you really shouldn't have one without having had the other. And if you try, you actually can squeeze my version into the tune. Or you can just keep reading and learn what it takes to get your evaluation horse *before* the diagnosis carriage.

Seek A Highly Qualified Professional. You want to begin with a psychologist or other mental health provider who specializes part of his or her practice in the assessment and treatment of ADD. You don't want to leave something as important as a mental health diagnosis to anyone else. You might try asking your physician for a referral, but you'll often do better searching the Internet. *Psychology Today* has a pretty good national directory called "Therapist Finder" that will come up at the top of any Google search in your community. Then, check the provider's website and be sure he or she has the training and experience to do a real ADD evaluation at a reasonable price.

Interview. Before testing, the evaluator should visit with you for at least an hour and sometimes two, depending on how complicated your case appears to be. I illustrated a small sliver of that interview in the opening vignette. This combines with the testing I'll describe next to provide an accurate diagnosis.

Every evaluator has a style for conducting these, but unless you're about six years old, he or she will want to investigate how you've gotten this far without treatment. Some of that conversation may seem cagy, almost like the provider doesn't believe you. None of us wants to incorrectly diagnose someone who is just drug seeking. But what we're really trying to understand is your level of impairment, particularly whether you might just be an ADD-leaner. Even if you have ADD, that's not enough to justify treatment. It has to cause you problems in functioning. That's rarely difficult to prove, but a thorough examination of the issues we've discussed all through this book is necessary to make the puzzle fit together.

Getting a good diagnosis shouldn't take forever, but neither should it be a fifteen-minute checklist, a prescription, and a fond farewell.

Be patient. Getting a good diagnosis shouldn't take forever, but neither should it be a fifteen-minute checklist, a prescription, and a fond farewell. If your evaluator is doing his or her job correctly, that will also include ruling out other causes for your symptoms, so before we move on to testing, let's take a look at several of what we call "differential diagnoses" for ADD.

Sleep Deprivation. Notice how I got really interested in Kurt's sleep the moment he mentioned nightmares about his educational future? That's because bad sleep can also yield symptoms of inattention and poor concentration. However, a lot of correctly diagnosed kids and adults have what I call "ADD-Related Insomnia[72]," especially after the onset of puberty—poor sleep due to ADD rather than the other way around. So, if sleep plays *any* role in your symptoms, you need to correct that first.

I sent Kurt home with an iPhone app called Sleep Cycle[73] that costs about a buck. It uses the accelerometer in your smartphone to graph your sleep pattern based on how much you move around in bed. Deep sleep paralyzes your body, so your phone can tell if you're lying still or thrashing about. I use this app a lot myself, and the graph is pretty accurate. The percentage the app assigns to your sleep, however, makes no sense to me. This kind of data isn't good enough to make a sleep diagnosis, but it does offer a cheap screening tool to see how bad your sleep might be, before spending the time and money on a sleep study.

Kurt was young, in good shape, and had a good body mass index for his height and weight. For those not so lucky, I also recommend a weird little app called Sleep Talk Recorder for both iPhone and Android. It's intended to preserve for posterity all those fascinating things you say while sleeping as your unconscious mind processes the day (Chapter 5). That could be fun, but for our purposes, all we care about is your breathing. After you wake up you can play back the soundtrack and listen very closely. Snoring is easily the most

---

[72] While this shows up all over the non-scientific literature, it is not a recognized disorder but a Dr. Wes-ism. I've seen it many times and heard about it from colleagues.

[73] They now make Sleep Cycle for Android, along with another app called Electric Sleep and a new one called SleepBot.

boring podcast you'll ever listen to, but you should be able to monitor your breathing and hear if you're waking up due to shortness of breath. This could be a sign of sleep apnea. I used this app to catch my own nightly breathing problems, due to oversized tonsils that somebody should have removed when I was about nine. Now I use a cool mouthpiece that opens up my airways and keeps me in deep sleep.

These apps are better at telling you your sleep is bad than at confirming that it's good. If you sound like you're having breathing problems, or your graph looks like you toss and turn a lot at night, consider a formal sleep study. Ask your doctor, but I suggest the newer take-home kits. They gather data in the privacy, convenience, and familiarity of your own bedroom, rather than a sleep lab. I've referred a number of clients to both forms and all preferred the take-home system.

Anxiety. I also got interested in how pressured Kurt felt to succeed. Yet, each question I asked that might lead toward concerns about anxiety came up short. Your evaluator should consider three possibilities, though in just one interview, it's hard to prove which applies.

- **Anxious-ADD.** You should be diagnosed with both ADD and anxiety, as we've discussed often in this book. In my experience, this is the most common scenario when a person is showing symptoms of both conditions. Your therapist should get this on the books and pass it on to your prescriber, because your medication management will be more complicated. You'll have to manage the anxiety before you can benefit from stimulants. In fact, if you really have both problems, stimulants are likely to make you worse. Sometimes, that's how we realize you have a mixed condition, but usually an evaluator will have a good hypothesis about this after one or two interviews.

- **ADD Primary.** ADD is causing your anxiety symptoms. In my experience, this is the second-most common situation and pretty hard to discriminate from the above scenario. However, you'll know quickly if you start taking stimulant medication and your anxiety goes away. More commonly, however, the prescriber starts you on something like Lexapro[74] and a stimulant, and after a few months you find you're able to manage just fine with only a stimulant.

---

[74] A selective serotonin reuptake inhibitor (like Prozac or Zoloft) that is used to treat moderate anxiety.

- **Anxiety Primary.** Anxiety is causing your ADD symptoms. This is the least common scenario in my experience, but I have seen it among people who have really bad anxiety. Here you're so tightly wrapped that your mind never stops running and you can't focus on anything but what's worrying you. This may even get to the point of obsessions and compulsions, which distract you from getting anything done. An experienced evaluator may hypothesize that this describes you, but it's hard to prove without a medication trial. If taking something that resolves your anxiety, like Lexapro, also resolves your ADD symptoms, you fit this category.

Mood Dysregulation. Speaking of complicated diagnostic and treatment conditions, I've worked with a lot of teens and young adults with mood disorders like Bipolar I, Bipolar II and Cyclothymia. Mood dysregulation is a whole book in and of itself, so for the purposes of this one let's just say that some people who seem to have ADD, especially those with hyperactivity, either have one of those other disorders or they have *both* ADD and mood dysregulation. Your evaluator should study this carefully and rule out a mood disorder before proceeding on to an ADD diagnosis.

Unfortunately, particularly among young people, these diagnoses can get complicated because the symptoms of ADD and mood dysregulation overlap and obvious full-blown manic episodes are less common in teens than irritability and hypomania. If it turns out that you have a mood disorder, you can't be treated for ADD until that's in check, or else you run the risk of making your condition worse with stimulant medication.

Substance Abuse. Some of you aren't going to like this, but substance abuse, including those cultural faves marijuana and alcohol, can generate ADD-like symptoms. I'm not talking about recreational use. I'm talking about the heavy, frequent use that's increasingly common these days, particularly among young adults and teens. I didn't ask Kurt about this in the opening vignette because his folks were still in the room, but we did talk about it privately. He used alcohol and marijuana occasionally and, with rare exceptions, moderately. Those incidents were confined to non-school nights, and he was putting in plenty of time studying, not just hitting the bong.

Marijuana is so revered now that any criticism, even of heavy use, is considered about as credible as the belief in evil fairies. Any research that supports anything other than the grandness of the herb is dismissed by its many avid fans. So, I'm not going to get into that debate in this book. I'm just going to say that every week someone comes into my office asking to be evaluated for ADD, while admitting they drink heavily or smoke a boatload of weed. Some actually claim marijuana is helpful for treating their ADD.

Before any professional can accurately assess you for ADD, the effects of substance abuse must be ruled out. You can see that as thoughtful clinical wisdom or dangerous propaganda wrought by reefer madness. But you won't find many prescribers willing to chase heavy substance use with stimulants or therapists willing to treat ADD when they think your real problem is drug or alcohol use. Some won't even continue the conversation once you tell them you're drinking or getting high every day.

With those competing diagnoses out of the way, let's move on to one of the most important and least understood aspects of a well-rounded evaluation.

Testing. For psychologists, it's kind of shocking to learn that not every evaluator uses a valid and reliable testing system that compares you with a standardized sample of people your age and gender. Yet, it's rare for someone to come to me with a good testing profile. That not only means their diagnosis is less robust, but also makes it nearly impossible to get educational and work accommodations. So, good testing is worth the time, energy, and money.

In my office, we use the Conners-3 instrument for children and the Conners Adult ADHD Rating Scales (CAARS) for adults[75]. Both can now be administered through a secure online form, so respondents can complete it anywhere in the world that has Internet service. The Barkley Scales[76] are also good, valid, and reliable and operate much the same way. The Vanderbilt Assessment Scale[77] is often favored by pediatricians, but it's nothing more than a checklist of symptoms from the diagnostic manual, with no reference to a norm group. We don't use it.

> *Testing for ADD is unusual in that it includes not only your responses, but those from at least two observers.*

Testing for ADD is unusual in that it includes not only your responses, but those from at least two observers who know you well. For pre-college students, that usually means a parent and an educator, though finding a knowledgeable teacher gets harder once you leave middle school. By college, you'll have to rely on a roommate and/or best friend, unless you go to a very small school with a low teacher-to-student ratio. Typically a parent still serves as the other observer. If your parents are divorced, have each complete separate forms, and include a third non-parent observer. If the testing profiles come back with one minority report—either high or low scores—you'll want to find a third observer to balance things out.

---

[75] Multi-Health Systems Inc. www.mhs.com

[76] www.guilford.com/cgi-bin/cartscript.cgi?page=pr/barkley19.htm

[77] www.psychiatrictimes.com/clinical-scales-adhd-vadrs/clinical-scales-adhd-vadrs/vadprs-vanderbilt-adhd-diagnostic-parent-rating-scale-and-vadtrs-vanderbilt-adhd-diagnostic-teacher

Get the Price Up Front. You should need two and sometimes three sessions to complete the interview and go over the testing. These should be covered in part by insurance, presuming your policy has mental health benefits and you've met your deductible[78] if you have one. The total cost for the Conners or Barkley test itself should not exceed $200 with two observers, and may be less. The evaluator may or may not attempt to bill the testing itself to insurance and your company may or may not pay.

Some psychologists go overboard and want to give a whole battery of tests for IQ, achievement, and/or neurology. That might be interesting and, in some complicated cases, necessary, but it will get expensive in a hurry, and health insurance rarely covers that cost. If during the clinical interview you disclose a history of head injury, neurological impairment, seizure, or learning disability, and your testing for those conditions isn't up to date, a psychologist may want to test or retest you. Head injury can cause ADD-like symptoms that medication can help or hurt, depending on where the injury is located. Stimulants and other medications can also induce seizures. If you're not at risk for any of these, there's little reason to pay for a full neurological workup.

Buyer Beware. A few clinics around the country like to evaluate ADD using Single Photon Emission Computed Tomography (SPECT) scans and Quantitative Electroencephalography (qEEG). While these sound like something Scotty would use to beam you up, they're really high-tech measures of brain wave activity.

Do these scanners justify the thousand or more dollars you'll spend just to get a working diagnosis, a cost that won't be covered by health insurance?[79] Most ADD experts consider SPECT scanning overkill at best, and at worst, inaccurate and unproven in diagnosing or treating ADD. In fact, the American Academy of Pediatrics doesn't recommend *any* lab tests for ADD. The research on this approach, most notably that of Daniel Amen, MD, hasn't been peer reviewed and replicated by the scientific community.

It's a similar story for qEEG. While it's used to investigate seizure disorders and other neurological conditions, and the FDA recently approved it as a method for diagnosing ADD, it too is expensive. Even the FDA admits qEEG is only intended to be used in conjunction with standardized testing and diagnostic interview.[80] The American Psychiatric Association, the Ameri-

---

[78] Most states require some mental health coverage but some, like Texas, don't. We're all waiting to see how the Affordable Care Act impacts this situation, so work with your provider to find out what is and isn't covered.

[79] www.additudemag.com/adhd/article/783.html

[80] healthland.time.com/2013/07/16/reading-the-brain-fda-approves-first-scan-for-diagnosing-adhd/

can Neurological Association, and most experts on ADD state that qEEG isn't reliable enough to diagnose any psychiatric disorder.

Someday these techniques might prove efficient and effective, particularly in complicated cases that can't be understood with simpler, less expensive methods. That will be a fine day indeed, and I'll be happy to review those findings in future revisions of this book. Here and now, most folks with ADD will show up just fine using the evaluation methods I recommended above, making SPECT scan and qEEG kind of like swatting a fly with a cruise missile.

Get A Referral For Treatment. Once your evaluator has nailed the diagnosis, he or she will probably refer you for medication. You might see a prescriber in the same practice, a psychiatrist or psychiatric nurse practitioner in a different practice, or your primary care physician (PCP). That can get confusing in a hurry, so Chapter 13 is about preparing you to work with a prescriber.

Unless all he or she does is evaluations, your therapist should also offer some form of cognitive and/or behavioral therapy to help you get your show on the road. In our clinic, that ranges from a couple sessions to learn the thirteen principles, to long-term mentoring toward applying them to a successful life. We've seen some ADD clients for three months, others on and off for ten years, and the vast majority somewhere in between. Many go away for months or even years and then come back as life happens and they want some ideas on how to organize themselves around it.

After twenty-two years, I've been pleased to see great long-term results using this combination of careful medication management and psychotherapy. I get a lot of personal referrals from satisfied clients. This book offers an array of examples of what we do.

Alternative Therapies? There are a lot of choices out there and a lot of folks looking to make money in the ADD market. There's nothing wrong with making a living by helping people. I do it. Just be sure to use your shopping skills in deciding which treatments are reliable and which aren't. Some therapists don't "believe" in medicine. Some don't even "believe" in ADD. Some don't "believe" in any diagnosis of any kind. If you run into any of these, I suggest you keep running.

Also be careful of therapists who offer special treatments for ADD, like "brain balancing," neurofeedback, and special diets or supplements. I'm all for a good diet. There may even be some people with allergies to certain foods that have symptoms that mimic ADD—particularly if there's no history of it in the extended family. If you think you have something like this, consider a do-it-yourself DNA test before going on a homegrown elimination diet. Home testing is an area of self-help that's grown so rapidly it's catching us all by surprise. In an October 2013 segment of NPR's *On The Media*[81] the host and a colleague take a simple $99 DNA test[82] and reveal their results. The colleague's family members are big believers in gluten sensitivity, while he is not, until his test reveals exactly that. Listen to the segment and just be sure you want to know the secrets of your DNA before wading into that turbulent water.

As noted several times in this book, mindfulness meditation is great, maybe even essential, for people with ADD. But it won't make the critical difference in coping or allow you to operate medicine-free. It will help you follow several of the principles I suggested earlier by teaching you to be more intentional.

I've worked with a number of people who've tried biofeedback and "brain-balancing" without much success, save perhaps a placebo effect. Of course, I wouldn't be likely to see ones who succeeded (why would they be coming to me?), but scientific research doesn't support it either.

Regardless of what treatment you find to help you, even the American Psychological Association, superhero of cognitive behavioral therapy methods, admits that therapy isn't very effective for treating ADD without medication[83]. Yet you'll find psychologists and other therapists overselling its benefits and underplaying the role good med management plays in symptom reduction. So, let's take a look at how that works, not from a medical perspective, but from a consumer-based one.

---

[81] www.onthemedia.org/story/genetic-testing-anxiety/

[82] www.23andme.com

[83] www.apa.org/monitor/2012/03/adult-adhd.aspx

CHAPTER 13

MEDICATION MANAGEMENT

The most exquisite pleasure in the practice of medicine comes from nudging a layman in the direction of terror, then bringing him back to safety again.

— Kurt Vonnegut, *God Bless You Mr. Rosewater*

"Bet you can't guess what happened this week, Dr. Wes." The intensity of Laura's stare offered no hint as to where I might place my money.

"Should I be scared or excited?" I asked.

"Blown away."

That didn't exactly clarify the situation.

Laura had come in with a pile of problems: dating, family, academics, and life plan foul-ups. I'd tested her thirteen months ago for ADD. Her Conner's scores on both the inattentive and hyperactive subscales were at the eighty-fifth percentile, meaning she scored higher than eighty-five percent of young adult women. So, we had no trouble getting her physician to prescribe a stimulant trial. Yet, in what ranks as the longest medication procrastination of my career, Laura took a full year to fill her scrip at the college pharmacy. At nearly every session I reminded her that all the issues we were trying to address might go a whole lot better if she'd just pick up that little bottle.

There were preauthorization problems with her doctor, then insurance reimbursement failures. Then she just kept forgetting. Then the semester ended and summer came and went. In August, I asked if she really wanted to take medication. She swore she did; that she "just needed to get around to it."

In the meantime she forgot sessions even with text reminders, skipped days at her practicum, mixed up her schedule at work, got into one weird dating mishap after another—including several reruns with one ex-boyfriend and one ex-girlfriend. At Christmas, she'd nearly gotten arrested during a fist fight with her sister. All in all, as she neared the end of her college career, Laura's grades and judgment weren't getting much better. She liked my thirteen principles. She just didn't follow them.

After I finally pushed the issue, Laura admitted what I'd suspected for some time. She was afraid to fill that prescription.

She didn't mind knowing she had ADD, but treating it seemed a lot bigger step than either of us had guessed. After a bit more prodding, she confessed that more than anything else, she feared what her dad would say when he saw the insurance billing for her medication.

"He doesn't believe in stuff like that," she said. "He's old school and just really judgmental. He just thinks I don't try hard enough."

I pushed back against the shame I saw in her eyes. "You're twenty-three. It's your life we're talking about, not your dad's. I'll support you either way, but I think you should do what *you* think is right. That's called growing up."

A week later, Laura texted me, "I'm starting tomorrow ☺!" Attached was a picture of a full Adderall pill bottle with her name on it.

Another three weeks passed before I heard from her again. She called early on a Saturday morning and asked to see me as soon as possible. I was reluctant given the short notice and her history of blowing off appointments, then begging to get in fast to solve the latest crisis. Laura's tolerance for her own chaos seemed always to infringe on mine. Yet, the urgent and serious tone in her voice told me to make time to see her. She arrived only five minutes late and apologized profusely. Normally, she ran at least fifteen minutes behind and deflected any protest I might offer.

Something was very different.

"Okay," I said, falling back into the grasp of my leather armchair. "I'm ready. What's up?"

"It's my dad," Laura said, her voice choking slightly. "I decided I'd had enough and I finally confronted him."

Her dad, the CEO of a prosperous engineering firm, always seemed like the Darth Vader to my Obi-wan Kenobi. At the start of her two-year relationship with Chelsea, he'd threatened to stop paying for college and disown her if she identified as gay or bisexual. Wanting to please him and avoid confrontation,

Laura covered up the relationship, which offended Chelsea and eventually brought down their romance.

Long before, in early childhood, Laura's dad divorced her mom and married a woman who treated Laura like Cinderella, while insisting that the dad dote on her own children from a previous marriage. As she moved through adolescence, any time Laura wanted to confront him about anything, her dad used his size and prowess at argument to frighten and intimidate his size-zero, five-foot-tall daughter.

I'd considered asking him to a session, but worried how he'd react. If Laura lost his financial support, she'd have to drop out of college. Besides, if her descriptions were even half accurate, her dad was a classic narcissist, more concerned about how he was perceived than by how he treated others. The risk seemed too great. Now, out of the blue, Laura had taken it herself.

"That took a lot of courage," I said. "Dare I ask how it went?"

She cleared her throat. "Very well, actually. But that's not the part that will blow you away. You know how I decided last summer that I wasn't going to speak to him until he apologized for falsely accusing me of lying about some trivial thing?"

I nodded. "I do."

"I just didn't need that kind of negative energy in my life. I don't deserve to be put down and treated like I'm bad or worse, of no consequence to him."

I opened my mouth to respond.

"Just listen." Her voice was uncharacteristically firm. "I have a lot to say." She reached into her pocket and pulled out a crumpled piece of notebook paper. "He started texting me and I wasn't ready to deal with him. Then he called me a couple days ago and asked if we could meet to make peace. I told him that if he was serious, I would be happy to sit down with him. He drove all the way up here."

"From Dallas? That's over six hundred miles."

"It is, indeed." Laura spread the paper out on her lap. "Hence, this list of what I wanted to say. It needed to be worth his time, and mine. We met for dinner because that's neutral ground and I preferred we be out in public if he got out of hand again. And, I know the bouncer." She smirked. "I unwisely slept with him a few times last semester and he'd do anything for me, including toss my dad into the street." She ran her finger down the list. "First I told my dad that I wanted to be his daughter and I wanted him to be my dad, but that I wasn't willing to do things his way anymore. He had to show respect for me and understand that even if we disagree, that's no reason to degrade me. I said I understood he might want to guide me and give me advice, but he wasn't free to make me feel like a failure."

I raised my hand. "Can I say something?"

"You can." She held her finger on the list to keep her place.

"You're totally on medicine, aren't you?"

A huge grin crossed Laura's face, the first time in the session that her intensity had broken. "Is it *that* obvious?"

"It sure is. I've never seen you so organized. Your language is beautiful and all your thoughts so well put together."

"Thank you," she said sweetly. "You were right all along. Just don't let it go to your head. May I continue?"

I nodded. "Please do."

She worked her way down the list, noting how her dad had never gotten to know her, that he didn't take interest in her friends, achievements, or career plans, except to criticize them. How he never spent the time to find out what was difficult for her. How he'd sold her out to the stepmother and her kids, and let her down by cheating on her mother. Laura told him how she feared becoming self-centered and distant, like he was, and how she fought to have honest, serious relationships when she'd learned the opposite at home.

"He asked me why I didn't tell him all this before. I said he'd never created a safe space for me where I could really be myself, because I was scared he'd judge me or cut me off. I admitted I had to lie about dating Chelsea because he made me ashamed of who I'd given my love to. Then I told him, 'What I'm about to say is going to break your heart, but every time I leave your house...'" She inhaled deeply and then let it out. "'It's like I can breathe again.'"

We sat quietly for a moment as I took it all in.

"That's amazing, Laura" She'd triumphed over things she'd carried inside for so long, some she'd never even told me until now. "So, how did your dad take all this grown-up daughter talk?"

"I couldn't believe it." Her words were slow and deliberate. "It was like I was sitting across from a total stranger—in a good way, I mean. He was this nice guy and he was actually listening to me. He even started to cry at one point. He said how sorry he was for his mistakes and that he wanted to make things better."

"I gotta say, you were right. I never saw this coming."

"And I haven't even gotten to the crazy part yet. While I was on a roll, I decided to tell him the big news, that I was on Adderall and that it was helping me and I wouldn't accept any judgment about it. And guess what?"

"He's taking it too."

"Wait." Laura's jaw dropped. "How can you possibly know that?"

"Magic." I chuckled. "You've never explained all this to me until today. I only knew about his homophobia. I didn't know he didn't connect with you and couldn't show emotion and cheated on his wives. That sounds strangely like you, or at least, how things used to be."

Laura wiped her eyes. "God, I hate being anything like him, but yeah, I know what you mean." She looked back at her list. "I said I have a lot of bitterness because my expectations were probably too high and I was going to lower them to something that we could both achieve and we could start over from there. Then, I forgave him for everything he's done to me."

"Wow, Laura." I nodded my head and smiled. "That's straight out of the book on differentiating from your family of origin." I took a moment to explain the work of Murray Bowen[84]. "You did a great job."

"I know. After Dad dropped me off, I came into the house crying and telling my roommates how great it had gone. They were like, 'Be careful. You know how he is.' I said, 'No, you don't understand. We've had this same conversation a million times and this time he understood me. It was like this huge moment."

"True enough," I said. "But I'm not sure you realize what's huge about it."

"Are you missing something here?" Laura gave me a cute crazy-eyed look. "I've been waiting for this since I was, like, three. He's finally changing."

"Maybe. You certainly deserve that after all that's gone on. But that's not the huge change I'm talking about, is it?"

"No." Laura wiped a tear from her eye. "You're talking about the change in me."

---

[84] Murray Bowen, MD proposed that a core task of adolescence is to differentiate from one's family of origin to become an individual, fully functioning person, without emotionally cutting off the family. To do this one must reduce his or her emotional reactivity to the parent and deal with differences as mature adults, not parent and child (see *Family Therapy in Clinical Practice*, 1992).

Is This Chapter For Me?

Probably. It's hard to get a good consumer education on stimulant management, and without one, it's tough to work effectively with your prescriber. Do any of the following apply to you?

- ❏ Have you had trouble finding a prescriber for stimulants, or do you fear you will if you decide to pursue treatment?

- ❏ Does your prescriber lack the time during medication checks to teach you everything you want to know about medication?

- ❏ Are you unsure what to talk about with your prescriber so he or she can better understand and respond to your unique situation?

- ❏ Do you know the difference between stimulants and non-stimulants, or between one type of stimulant and the other?

- ❏ Do you not "feel like yourself" on medication or do you have side-effects you don't understand or know how to cope with?

- ❏ Do you know about stimulant tolerance and how breaks can keep you from reaching the highest dosage?

- ❏ Does medication management seem like a big science experiment and you're the guinea pig?

Fear not. In this chapter, I'll help you learn what you need to know to lead your ADD treatment team to victory.

You're The Expert

We are once again at the Mall of America. I'm writing this final chapter from the balcony overlooking Nickelodeon Universe, where Alex is managing quite nicely on his own. He has some shopping to do later, having earned enough money cleaning my office to purchase something called a *Skylanders Swap Force Portal of Power Starter Pack*. He's price shopping between GameStop and Best Buy.

I've sent him out into this vast kingdom of consumerism not only because I need to finish this book, but because he needs to practice independence. I'm confident he can handle it. He understands ethics and empathy and his behavior and judgment with others is excellent for a ten-year-old. If he has any questions, I'm only a phone call away.

And he's on medicine.

Alex was diagnosed with ADHD in first grade. His sister, Alyssa, was diagnosed in second grade, but we hadn't seen as many early signs in Alex and didn't want to land him with a diagnostic label if we didn't have to. Near the end of kindergarten, however, Alex's teacher finally got around to mentioning how he'd stood beside his desk the entire school year. It wasn't a disciplinary action. He just couldn't stay in his seat.

The following summer, Alex tested out at the ninetieth-percentile on both inattention and hyperactivity as compared to other six-year-old boys. We started him on the Daytrana patch just before he entered first grade later that year. Henceforth, he's been a model student, a good learner, and firmly in his seat. In fact, nobody even knows he's been diagnosed, until his patch falls off or he takes one of his four medication breaks a year. Then it's pretty obvious.

Alex can tell you when he's on too much or too little medication. He likes being focused so he can keep up with, and at times, exceed his peers. He feels uncomfortable when he has to take a break. It's fun to be spontaneous and unguided for a day or two, but it eventually becomes unnerving for him. That's because he's grown up experiencing how his brain is supposed to work. Being on medication doesn't feel strange to him. Being off it does.

Not every ADD person will have such a great response to stimulants, particularly if you start later in life. Even Alex deals with some side effects. His appetite is bad enough that we cut his dosage

If you want to do well on medication, you'll have to become your own expert.

on weekends to help him eat, supplement his diet with nutritional drinks, and let him eat small meals later in the evening. But the benefits far outweigh the problems, so the decision is an easy one.

If you want to do as well on medication as Alex, Laura, and the vast majority of my clients, you'll have to become your own expert on medication management and then diplomatically and respectfully take charge of the process.

There are a couple of reasons for this. First, when it comes to psychopharmaceuticals, med management is complicated. We are, after all, talking about your brain; the three pounds of tissue that make you, you. Because your three pounds isn't exactly the same as anyone else's, you're not going to process medication or express its effects quite the way other people do. Second, because we can't plug into your brain and test to see if you're less ADD (or depressed or anxious or anything else), we rely on you to give us your "phenomenological experience[85]." What you tell us will guide every single aspect of treatment.

So, taking a brain med isn't like taking an antibiotic and waiting for your strep throat to disappear or swallowing an antihistamine and banishing your allergies. Getting everything right takes an ongoing relationship between you,

---

[85] What you perceive with your senses, subjectively consider with your mind, and explain to others as your experience.

your prescriber, your therapist, and your people. This isn't a Dr. Wes-ism. The American Psychological Association notes that effective treatment requires "an integrated approach to healthcare delivery" in which mental health providers work with prescribers to determine the best treatment for each patient.[86]

In daily practice, however, that's easier said than done. In this chapter, I'll hit the highpoints of what I've learned about med management as a parent and as a psychologist, so you can get started building your expertise. As you're reading, please keep three critical points in mind.

- *I am not a medical doctor or a psychiatric nurse practitioner (APRN).* I can't prescribe medications, but I am an educated consumer of them. That's what I want you to become, too.

- Because I organized this chapter to be accessible to consumers, everything I have to say is reductive. I'm taking complicated things and making them seem simple.

- This chapter should help you start a conversation between you and your prescriber. I've even included a few citations you might want to share. *Do not* take this book in, point to a certain paragraph, and say, "Dr. Wes says you have to do it this way." That happens a lot. People have a nice talk with me, do some research, and then march in and lecture their prescriber. That's a good way to infuriate any physician or APRN. On the other hand, if your prescriber doesn't see you as a key part of the team, you're probably in the wrong office.

- I do not knowingly own any stock in any product I'm going to discuss in this chapter. It's possible that one of the mutual funds my broker manages is or has been invested in one of the pharmaceutical companies I mention, but I don't keep track of those investments, so I don't know.

Finding The Right Prescriber

The trickiest player to sign to your team is nearly always the person who writes your prescriptions. You have to understand the state of psychiatry in America today to fully understand why.

Psychiatrists. There are currently about 50,000 psychiatrists in the U.S., which The American *Psychiatric* Association (not to be confused with the American *Psychological* Association) finds wholly inadequate to meet the need. It's bad in cities. In rural areas it's a crisis.

---

[86] www.apa.org/monitor/2012/06/prescribing.aspx

And it's only getting worse. In 2012 the Psychiatric Association noted that 96% of medical students enter specialties other than psychiatry, and the number of new psychiatrists had fallen for the sixth straight year.[87] Writing on behalf of The Association, author Mark Moran couldn't explain this in an era "considered exciting for the field." Actually, the reasons are pretty obvious, and in a different article, Moran laid them out clearly: "When asked why they don't [pursue psychiatry, medical students] cite the opinion of peers and of other non-psychiatric doctors as inhibiting factors.... Students themselves glean from the carveout psychiatric payment system that there must be something off or less valid about psychiatry.[88]" In plain language, psychiatry isn't considered a cool medical career anymore, nor profitable. Because insurance companies haven't been very kind to them in terms of reimbursement, psychiatrists are tied for last place in salary, with some specialties paying hundreds of thousands of dollars more per year.[89]

For your purposes, the only psychiatrist that matters is one who can see you in an outpatient clinic—unless you're headed into a psychiatric hospital, the VA, the military, or prison. Most psychiatrists now work in one of these facilities, because the wages are better than in outpatient practice. Many who remain in private practice can't afford to take health insurance, and community mental health centers often take nothing but Medicaid and Medicare. Many psychiatrists carry so many cases that they find it difficult to maintain rigorous clinical standards. Or, as one told *The New York Times*, "We run our office like a bus station," seeing so many patients for five- to ten-minute medication checks that it's difficult to connect to any of them. He adds, "The sad thing is that I'm very important to [my patients], but I barely know them."[90]

And none of this is getting better. Over half of U.S. psychiatrists are over the age of 55[91] and nearing retirement. So, the pool will continue to diminish even as the demand for services increases[92]. And if you're a child, or you have one, who needs meds for a psychological condition, the situation is even uglier.

---

[87] psychnews.psychiatryonline.org/newsarticle.aspx?articleid=1104005

[88] psychnews.psychiatryonline.org/newsArticle.aspx?articleid=1104028

[89] www.forbes.com/sites/jacquelynsmith/2012/07/20/the-best-and-worst-paying-jobs-for-doctors-2/2/

[90] www.nytimes.com/2011/03/06/health/policy/06doctors.html?_r=0

[91] www.nimh.nih.gov/about/director/2011/psychiatry-where-are-we-going.shtml

[92] forefronttelecare.com/blog/blog/2012/08/08/of-medical-specialties-demand-for-psychiatrists-growing-fastest/

Child psychiatrists are like the proverbial hen's teeth, increasingly scarce[93]. Only 7400 now practice in the United States[94].

Thus, over the next twenty years, outpatient psychiatry as a medical specialty may well vanish. At least that's what every trend line suggests. This means you'll struggle to see an affordable psychiatrist with any consistency, particularly if you don't live in a major metropolitan area. Even in New York City, the "bus station" psychiatrist reported a long waiting list for intakes.

Advanced Practice Registered Nurse (APRN). Generally, your best workaround for the shortage of psychiatrists is to find an APRN. Today, the majority have masters degrees (MSNs), but soon, most new graduates will have doctoral (DNP) degrees. Either way, in most states APRNs are licensed and specialized in prescribing medication for all psychological disorders, including ADD.

There are two catches to this workaround. Though things are getting better as more training programs open, psychiatric APRNs are also in short supply. Where they're granted independent prescription privileges, they have a complicated relationship with psychiatrists.[95] They practice on what's called "protocol," meaning they aren't supervised by a psychiatrist but they must have one to approve the list of medications they are allowed to prescribe. So, as the outpatient psychiatry pool dwindles, APRNs clamor to find collaborating physicians in order to practice.

Still, I'm a huge fan of APRNs. They're typically drawn from the *crème de la crème* of the nursing profession. They blend a dedication to helping others with well-honed people-skills, a high-quality, patient-focused education, and a team approach to care. If you can find a psychiatric APRN, I say, "Go for it."

Primary Care Physicians (PCPs). Most stimulants and other psychopharmaceuticals are now prescribed by PCPs and pediatricians. Without PCPs to write their stimulant scripts, my own ADD children and many of my ADD clients would be in dire straits. These doctors have risen to the call of psychopharm simply because the need is so great and the providers so limited, though few feel super-comfortable writing any but the most basic prescriptions. Sometimes that's all you need. Other times, those entry meds aren't adequate to treat your condition.

The key is good communication between you, your therapist, and the PCP.

---

93 www.medscape.com/viewarticle/779680

94 www.nhregister.com/general-news/20130119/shortage-of-child-psychiatrists-has-families-scrambling-for-help-3

95 www.medscape.com/viewarticle/440315

Even an awesome PCP or pediatrician can't really spend the time to follow your case closely enough to learn the many ins, outs, ups, and downs of stimulant management. That's just not how they're paid by the insurance company. Where I might see a client two to four times a month and talk to them for an hour each time, a PCP will see you for a few minutes, three to five times while trying to find the correct dosage. After things seem to be working, med checks will stretch to every three to six months.

The key to making this work is good communication between you, your therapist, and the PCP. Because, as professionals, we're all so busy keeping our spinning plates in the air, that critical dialog will usually come via letter, fax, or a flurry of phone messages. That's not ideal, but if everyone does his or her part, things can come out okay. And by "everyone," I mostly mean you.

Principle 13: Know What to Talk About When The Prescriber Arrives

Once you've found a prescriber you can work with, you've won about half the game. Winning the other half means understanding what to discuss in the precious minutes when the two of you finally get together.

Anxiety. In Chapter 12, I described three ways anxiety and ADD interact, each of which has to be medicated differently. That's because the whole point of taking meds like Zoloft or Lexapro for anxiety is to make you care less. If you also have ADD, those meds are likely to increase your ADD symptoms. If those kinds of meds make your ADD symptoms better, you probably don't have ADD. Your anxiety is just so high that it's making you unfocused. That's not too common, but I have seen it in clinical practice.

Conversely, stimulants are pretty much designed to raise an ADD person's anxiety to a helpful level, so you'll care more, but not too much. If you also have anxiety, stimulants can make those symptoms worse. If stimulants instead make your anxiety better, you probably don't have a diagnosable anxiety disorder. Your ADD just makes you feel so discombobulated that you get anxious. Fraternity boy Heath from Chapter 6 is an example. Once his ADD was under control, his anxiety was manageable without any other medication.

Most of the time, however, your prescriber will have to treat both conditions. The best way to do this is to go after the anxiety first and then ease into a stimulant. That's because it's usually easier to handle being more ADD for a few weeks than it is to tolerate being hyper-anxious. If you're a student, it's best to start your medication trial in the summer, or if you can't wait, Christmas break. If you start medication during the semester and anything goes wrong (e.g., your anxiety or ADD symptoms increase), you could put your grades at risk. The only good reason to attempt this mid-semester is if you're at greater risk of failure by not trying it.

Adderall vs. Ritalin. Despite ongoing research and development, there are basically two widely used medications for ADD that come in several different forms. Their ingredients have been around longer than I have, and I'm 51, so we have decades of experience with how they work.

In the spirit of reductive simplicity, I'm going to call these Adderall- and Ritalin-type medications because those are the names you know best. However, Adderall is really a brand name for what is variously called "amphetamine and dextroamphetamine mixed salts," "amphetamine salt combo," or most commonly just "mixed amphetamine salts." Ritalin is the brand name for methylphenidate. First approved in 1955, it's the same ingredient we find in several other modern products, including Focalin, Concerta, and the Daytrana patch.

Despite being based on different chemicals, Adderall- and Ritalin-type medicines share several characteristics. Both primarily work by enhancing the amount of dopamine in the synaptic gaps of your brain, though the mechanism of each is a little different. In general, clients report Adderall-type meds tend to feel a little stronger. That may or may not be good in your particular brain.

Both types are what I call "Here Today, Gone Tomorrow Meds." They wash out of your system within eight to thirteen hours and, unless you take them the next day, their effect goes too. Both are sold in short-acting and extended release (XR or ER) formulations. Short-acting means the medicine's effect is gone in roughly four hours. Extended release keeps going about twice that long, at least in theory. In practice, your mileage could vary considerably. All things being equal, you'll want to be on an extended release medication because fast-acting meds require between two and three administrations a day. ADD people have enough trouble remembering one pill in the morning, so for you, extended release products are an organizational gift.

Both Adderall- and Ritalin-types come in generic forms, both short- and long-acting. Supposedly, the generics are just as good, but a number of my clients (including some healthcare professionals) swore that when they switched from brand name Adderall XR they could tell the difference—and it wasn't good. The Internet is full of those complaints, but there's no way to really know because no one is motivated to pay for research comparing them side-by-side in blind trials.

The FDA officially claims that all generics meet the same standards as brand name drugs, but a recent article in *Fortune* claims that might not be true in practice[96]. It cites Dr. Janet Woodcock, director of the FDA's Center for Drug

---

[96] management.fortune.cnn.com/2013/01/10/generic-drugs-quality/

Evaluation and Research, admitting in a speech to the Generic Pharmaceutical Association, "I've heard it enough times from enough people to believe that there are a few products that aren't meeting quality standards."

Me, too. So, at this point, I suggest clients ask prescribers to put them on brand name products until they know and understand their efficacy. After they get the right dosage over a 60- to 90-day period, they can try the cheaper generic and see if there's a difference.

Should you choose an Adderall- or Ritalin-type medicine? There's no way to know until you and your prescriber run some version of the experiment I'll describe later. Some prescribers claim about 37% of patients do better on an Adderall-type and 37% do better on a Ritalin-type. That fits my caseload, but I couldn't find any research to support it. Either way, you'll have to do the experiment to see which one works best and causes the least side effects for you.

You might wonder what the deal is with the other 26% of people who don't benefit from either an Adderall- or Ritalin-type medicine. So do I. Perhaps they have unusual types of ADD that don't respond well to stimulants. Maybe they don't have ADD it all. Maybe they just didn't have a good team approach and gave up too soon. I'm still trying to figure that one out.

Vyvanse. This is the only new formulation for ADD that a broad range of clients report working very well, and even Vyvanse is best categorized as an Adderall-type. In fact, it's produced by Shire, the same company that makes Adderall. But its formula is called lisdexamfetamine because it's derived from combining dextroamphetamine with the amino acid L-lysine in such a way that it doesn't actually turn into a stimulant until it's ingested.

What clients like most about Vyvanse is that it lasts longer than Adderall XR. It usually causes fewer side effects, too, though some find the opposite to be true. Skilled prescribers can also tune in the right dosage of Vyvanse by having you dump the capsule in an empty pill bottle of water[97], shaking the solution well, and then drinking some smaller portion of it, say two-thirds. This lets your prescriber titrate or temporarily reduce your dose. You may even ask to use this system to be on, say, half your normal dosage on weekends to lower the side effects of irritability and appetite suppression, or after you're just starting out from a medication break (more on that later).

To read what one child and adult psychiatrist thinks about this use of Vyvanse, check out Dr. Charles Parker's website and ebook[98]. It's usually recommended that you not store diluted Vyvanse, but Parker notes that based on patient

---

[97] www.drugs.com/pro/vyvanse.html

[98] www.corepsych.com/2007/11/vyvanse-for-addadhd-the-water-titration-recipe/

report, he hasn't had any trouble with that off-label technique. But, remember, unless he's your psychiatrist, even Dr. Parker can't authorize you to do any of this without consulting your own prescriber. Some will love this idea. Others won't. Being your own medication expert does not mean going off label without a prescriber's supervision.

Daytrana. Since its introduction in 2006, this medication has had a hard time and hasn't really gotten the fanfare it deserves. Compared to Vyvanse, it's a pretty simple idea—methylphenidate on the back of a transdermal patch. Or as we call it, "Ritalin on a Stick."

Once a month you get a box of thirty patches roughly an inch square—larger for higher doses and smaller for lower ones. Each morning you rise and shine, peel the plastic from the patch and push it firmly onto your hip. Depending on your reach and size it's actually a lot easier if you can get your loved one to stick it there for you. It's even better if that person applies it thirty to forty-five minutes before your alarm rings. Your morning will go much better right out of bed, particularly if you're a teen or young adult.

However, because the patch doesn't seem to like water, you'll probably need to shower at night. If you shower in the morning, you'll want to put it on just as you're sitting down for breakfast. That's also true if you find it kills your appetite shortly after you put it on. This will take some experimentation, but it's worth it. Here are some other reasons to love Daytrana.

- **There's No Pill To Take.** Other than the new liquid Quillivant XR, Daytrana is the only non-pill Ritalin-type, extended release medication around. Some clients with sensitive stomachs report fewer gastrointestinal side effects with Daytrana, and people who hate taking pills or liquid medication love it.

- **You Can Leave It On.** The Daytrana patch will keep working for about fifteen hours, though the instructions say to remove it after nine. Actually, Noven originally asked for a thirteen-hour period of use, but the FDA rejected that and came up with the number nine. How long you wear your patch on your particular hip is up to you and your prescriber to decide through trial and error. Figuring out your optimal removal time prevents you from having to take a fast acting methylphenidate booster late in the afternoon, a common workaround to extend other Ritalin-type medications.

- **You Can Take it Off.** The Daytrana instructions say that you can remove the patch earlier than nine hours, making it the only stimulant medication you can turn off at will. Once you pull it, the medication will be gone within two to three hours. Until you've experienced it for yourself, you won't understand how awesome this really is. People who can't sleep well on stimulants or have bad appetite suppression, can talk with their prescriber about removing the patch at earlier times of day until they're hungrier in the evening and/or able to sleep.

- **Better Release.** When graphed, the line of effective release for Daytrana is very flat. All other stimulants have an arc that goes up, hangs for a few hours and then starts heading toward washout. Because Daytrana is releasing medicine slowly and for a very long time through your skin, its arc goes up a little slower than Adderall, Vyvanse or Concerta, but then hangs there evenly until you take it off or it uses up all its medicine after fifteen hours.

Due to early product recalls (mostly for adhesive problems) you may find your prescriber has little experience with or faith in Daytrana. Many remember its early dark days and haven't come back to it since. There are some good reasons not to like Daytrana—or, more correctly, reasons why it may not be the right medication for you. Let's explore each along with some workarounds if you want to try it:

- **Some Pharmacies Don't Keep It In Stock.** Because Daytrana is, like all stimulants, a Schedule II prescription, you have to hand-carry your little paper scrip to the pharmacy and come back later to pick it up. Given that planning can be a critical problem for the ADD crowd, out-of-stock meds can be burdensome and inconvenient, which may lead to giving up. It's best to take your scrip in a few days before you need a new box. That way the pharmacy can send away for it and it will be ready when you need it.

- **You Forget To Take It Off.** I used to worry a lot about this, but with seven years of experience with Daytrana, it hasn't turned out to be much of a problem. Most people can feel the patch and are ready to get it off as soon as the time comes, which leads directly to the next shortcoming.

- **It's Uncomfortable to Wear.** Daytrana can become your next "scratchy-tag" problem (see Chapter 3), turning a lot of initial Daytrana lovers into haters. I've actually had people with ADD cringe and shiver when I'm just describing it. The FDA-approved instructions are astoundingly specific about where to stick the patch, because that's where they stuck it in the research trials and nobody is going to spend money to research sticking it anywhere else. Talk to your prescriber and see if he or she will approve other spots. Some patch sites are less annoying than others.

- **It Creates A Skin Reaction.** Speaking of uncomfortable, some people get a mild allergic reaction to the adhesive in Daytrana. You will likely get a red spot the size of the patch on your skin, but that's normal. It's just the patch dropping medication into your skin. It's also why the instructions command you to move the stick-spot from left side to right each day. An ointment like A&D works well to cover the patch site and ease irritation. If you get something more than that and it isn't gone by the next time you want to stick a patch, your skin may be sensitive, just as some people's skin reacts badly to an adhesive bandage.

- **Yucky Residue.** The patch may leave a little gray gunk on your skin. The Daytrana instructions suggest putting lotion on the patch site to fix this. Apparently they've never actually tried this because it doesn't work very well. A couple of wipes a week with athletic bandage adhesive remover does.

Strattera. Back in 2002 when Strattera was first approved for treating ADD, everyone was excited. Finally prescribers had a non-stimulant, non-controlled substance in their toolbox. And, unlike Adderall or Ritalin, Strattera built up in your system so you'd get 24/7 symptom control. Originally, Strattera wasn't actually intended to treat ADD. Ely Lilly developed it in a class of antidepressants called selective norepinephrine reuptake inhibitors. Unfortunately for Lilly, it failed its U.S. test trials, though some prescribers still use it off-label for depression. Not to be undone, the company researched and received approval for Strattera as a treatment for ADD.

Strattera must have its fans somewhere, but I haven't met any. Lilly reports the drug grossed $620 million in 2012, though that made it second to last in sales for the company.[99] In other countries it's used as an antidepressant, which may account for some of those numbers. By comparison, gross sales of Vyvnase approached $1.6 billion in 2012 and exceeded that in 2013.[100] Dr. Charles Parker makes no mention of Strattera in his eBook[101] and cites it only once on his blog[102], as a "non-stimulant, less effective" treatment for ADD. That fits with what clients and prescribers have reported to me.

Intuniv. Shire announced FDA approval of this non-stimulant in late 2009. Once again we felt hopeful, but if you dig deeper, you'll find little new in this

---

[99] investor.lilly.com/releasedetail.cfm?ReleaseID=736234

[100] www.drugs.com/stats/vyvanse

[101] Parker, Charles (2012). The New ADHD Medication Rules: Brain Science & Common Sense (p. 97). Koehler Books.

[102] www.corepsych.com/2008/06/addadhd-medications-problems-remain-with-school-breakfasts/

product. Intuniv is just a time-released version of guanfacine, not to be confused with guaifenesin, the mucus reducing agent in Musinex[103]. Guanfacine (brand named Tenex) is an old blood pressure medicine that was once used to treat symptoms of ADD, but hadn't been considered a front-line solution for many years.

Intuniv hasn't taken off either. At first, Dr. Parker seemed as hopeful as the rest of us,[104] saying it had an "excellent effect on simple Inattentive ADD," particularly in individuals who failed to respond to stimulants.[105] Yet his recent eBook includes only a single reference, noting, "New non-stimulant medications, such as Intuniv, may have a positive impact on mood dysregulation secondary to ADHD."[106] That's a fancy way of saying it improves irritability in ADD kids, which might be desirable but says nothing about focus and attention. Shire sells only about $287 million worth of Intuniv a year, putting it near the bottom of its product line[107].

You can talk with your prescriber about his or her experiences with Strattera and Intuniv, but the vast majority of people who are successfully treated for ADD are taking stimulants. If you do try one of these other meds and you don't get any effect, please don't give up on medication altogether. That happens more often than it should. With that in mind, let's return to stimulants so you can intelligently discuss all their little peccadillos with your prescriber, and learn how to cope.

Stimulant Side Effects and Main Effects. Once on stimulants you'll want to discuss any side effects with your prescriber. If you have a good relationship with your therapist, you'll probably want to do a trial discussion before you go in. If your therapist is actually in the same clinic as your prescriber, this may be the primary discussion, as the therapist will pass along the information before your next med check.

Let's take a moment to structure how you think about this so you know the difference between a side effect and main effect of medication, which for

---

[103] This little branding problem caused a spate of dispensing errors in pharmacies around the country.

[104] www.corepsych.com/2009/11/intuniv-for-adhd-dosing-details/

[105] www.corepsych.com/2009/07/intuniv-for-adhd-understanding-tenex-guanfacine-and-alpha-2/

[106] Parker, Charles (2012). The New ADHD Medication Rules: Brain Science & Common Sense (p. 97). Koehler Books. Available at www.amazon.com/New-ADHD-Medication-Rules-Science/dp/1938467221

[107] en.wikipedia.org/wiki/Shire_plc#cite_note-prelims-1 citing data compiled from www.shire.com/shireplc/uploads/report/Shire_FY2012EarningsRelease_14Feb2013.pdf

newcomers can be more complicated than you'd think. I also want you to know the workarounds so you don't give up without a fight:

- **Is This Really Me?** If you're new to stimulants you may ask, "Am I really myself on this medicine?" Answering that question means first defining who you really are. Are you that "off meds person" who can't focus or get anything done? Or is that the person you grew up to be, minus the correct brain chemistry? Some people take stimulants and exclaim, "OMG. Is this how other people think?" Others complain, "I don't like how it makes me feel. I'm like a zombie. I just sit there and, like, read a book." One person's liberation is another person's inhibition. For example, most of us do not call "sitting there reading a book" zombified. We call it studying. If you hate being studious, then you'll associate focus with having your brain eaten away. It's all a matter of perspective.

- **Low Appetite.** Both Adderall- and Ritalin-type medications tend to clobber your appetite. In fact, amphetamines, the core component of Adderall, were originally intended for appetite control, so this really isn't a side effect at all. This seems worse for teens and adult women than it is for men, but that's purely a Dr. Wes-ism. That could be because more women seem to *like* this side effect and men tend to eat whether they're hungry or not. Either way, low appetite causes a lot of people to quit stimulants voluntarily or under order of their prescriber. It's especially problematic if you have a low Body Mass Index to begin with, but even if you can stand to lose thirty pounds, your prescriber won't want you to use stimulants to induce a crash diet.

- **Irritability.** This is one of the nastier side effects of stimulant medication, ranging from being too serious to being nonsensically angry and, in a worst-case scenario, aggressive. Irritability looks a lot like amped-up anxiety. When discussing this with your prescriber or therapist, you have to describe exactly when the irritability happens, because that will determine if it's a side effect of being on meds or of coming off of them.

- **Sleep.** Bad sleep underlies more psychological problems than just about anything else, so we don't want medication to mess it up. Both types of stimulant can interrupt sleep, though for some folks with ADD, stimulants actually *improve* it, even to the point of causing drowsiness. So don't operate cars or heavy machinery until you know how stimulants will affect you. Many other ADD people sleep poorly on or off of stimulants, but for some these meds generate insomnia. You'll have to study this closely, as I describe in the next section, to figure out what's going on with you.

- **Tics.** In rare circumstances, stimulant users may acquire tics, particularly if you're neurologically prone to them. However, if you study them closely, what some people think are tics are actually what I call "small fidgets" that were just larger when you were unmedicated. For hyperactive ADD people, medicine should make you less prone to jump around and more prone to do small things like twirl your hair or pull on your eyelashes. Some prescribers will take you off meds if you have these quirks, so be sure to monitor this before and after medication so you're sure you're not just paying more attention to something that's always been there now that you're on a stimulant.

- **Physical Side Effects.** Some people report problems with headaches, stomachaches, and dry mouth when taking stimulants, particularly in the first week. A very small number have problems with breathing, rapid heart rate, and other oddities like a stiff neck. You should have someone monitor your sleep before and after starting meds to check for teeth-grinding, and tell your dentist that you're taking a stimulant so he or she can keep an eye out for this too.

- **You Get Manic.** This doesn't happen often, because a good evaluator will see it coming before referring you for meds, and a good prescriber will start you off on a very low dosage and watch the effects. However, some people with very subtle mood dysregulation disorders will occasionally get missed in the initial evaluation, start stimulants, and end up way past irritable. Mania isn't the same as getting a little obsessive for the first few days on medication. That's not unusual and it might even help you organize your room to perfection. Being manic involves uncontrollable, racing thoughts and a lot of energy that makes sense to you, but doesn't make sense to anyone else. It's often accompanied by impulsivity, pressured talking, and several nights without sleeping. In short, it's the stereotypical amphetamine high and exactly the opposite of what we want to see.

Workarounds. Now that you know the most common side effects of stimulants, here are some workarounds that could help you get past their shortcomings and stay on medication, or help you know when you should call your prescriber and get off of them.

- **Irritable No More.** If you're irritable at the top of your medication arc (between 10:00 a.m. and 3:00 p.m., assuming you took it before 8:00 a.m.) talk to your prescriber about switching to the opposite type of medication, say from an Adderall- to a Ritalin-type. If you're only irritable during washout (after about 4:00 or 5:00 p.m.), practice "quiet time." Nap, watch a video, listen to music, anything that doesn't involve interacting with others. And be certain you're eating enough at lunch. Sometimes people think they're having washout irritability and they're really hitting a low blood sugar due to poor eating. If the problem really is washout, you should be over it once the meds are completely out of your system in the evening. If early washout won't fly due to school or your workday, talk with your prescriber about a booster or a longer-acting medicine like Vyvanse or Daytrana to carry you through 'til bedtime.

- **If You Get Manic: Stop.** I probably don't have to tell you this, but if a very small dosage of stimulant makes you even slightly manic, you need to discontinue and call your prescriber at once. Then call your therapist and start the evaluation all over again. This isn't a side-effect. It's an indication that ADD may not be the diagnosis for you, and if it is, you won't be able to treat it until you're evaluated and treated for a mood disorder.

- **Eat Whether You Want to Or Not.** The old adage "eat when you're hungry" probably won't work if you're on the right dosage of medication. Instead, you have to eat intentionally. *ADDitude* magazine[108] published some good ideas for an ADD-supportive diet for kids. WebMD has one for both kids and adults.[109] No diet will cure correctly diagnosed ADD, but one high in protein and low in simple carbs is worth adding to your daily routine.

- **Eat Breakfast.** If you don't like breakfast, you need to get over that as a matter of principle. That's true for everyone, but it's critical for ADD people, because lunch on stimulants is usually dicey. If you need to delay taking your meds until after you eat a good breakfast, do it. If you don't like eggs and oatmeal, consider drinks like Ensure. Bolthouse Farms makes a variety of excellent fruit, vegetable, fiber, and protein drinks in a variety of flavors. Some are even gluten-free.

---

[108] www.additudemag.com/adhd/article/9136.html

[109] www.webmd.com/add-adhd/guide/adhd-diets

- **Do Lunch.** Your goal at noon is to get enough energy in your body to prevent the symptoms of under-eating from being worse than the symptoms of ADD. Try complex carbohydrates—vegetables, fruits, sweet potato, etc. Oatmeal and quinoa are great anytime because they fill you up, give you protein, and break down to sugar more slowly. Avoid simple carbs like potatoes, chips, crackers, and French fries, which taste great but go straight to sugar. As an alternative to eating a full lunch, you can snack on healthy foods from late morning until the end of the day. This stabilizes blood sugar and reduces the effects of washout.

- **Stretch Dinner.** You probably won't be very hungry at a traditional dinner time. When traveling, I don't even feed my kids until about 8:00 p.m. unless I want to take food back to the hotel and let them snack until bedtime. This is where good nutritional advice and medication management butt heads. A nutritionist would never suggest you eat dinner later in the evening, nor make it your largest meal. But when on stimulants, you may have to eat a little at dinner and then snack on the leftovers until about 8:00 p.m. Just do everything you can to avoid a starvation binge at 10:00 p.m. That's when you should be preparing yourself for...

- **Sleep.** To work around insomnia, you first have to figure out if it's a reaction to stimulants or a pre-existing condition related to ADD. Get the apps I suggested in Chapter 12 and monitor your sleep for a month prior to starting medication. If your sleep is consistently bad and there's no sounds of apnea on your boring sleep podcast, work with your therapist to improve your "sleep hygiene" *before* taking stimulants. This can include relaxation techniques, musical backgrounds, bedroom modifications, and so on. If you try all that and you're still not sleeping, talk to your prescriber about medication.

- **Physical Side Effects.** Immediately consult your prescriber if you have problems with breathing or rapid heart rate. Head- and stomachaches usually go away once you're used to the medication. If headaches are infrequent (say, once a week) you may be able to treat them with over-the-counter meds, but tell your prescriber if you regularly chase stimulants with Advil or Tylenol. That may not be a safe or sustainable solution. As for dry mouth, some clients use Biotene mouthwash to stimulate the production of saliva. Don't confuse it with biotin, a dietary supplement.

Because they're here today, gone tomorrow, you may also counter side-effects by working with your prescriber to use stimulants more strategically. Other than the break protocol I'm about to discuss, I'm not a big fan of taking these meds irregularly. I mean, really, when *don't* you need to be thinking and making intentional choices? But many clients, like Janessa in Chapter 4, have gotten their greatest benefit and least side-effects by doing just that. Skilled prescribers understand this and will help you come up with the best game plan.

Stimulant Tolerance. Remember when I said your people had to develop tolerance for your chaos? That has nothing to do with the kind of tolerance we're talking about in this section. Here, it means your brain's adjustment to stimulants such that the impact of a given dose decreases over time, so you have to take higher and higher doses to maintain a therapeutic effect. If you keep that up, you'll eventually hit a ceiling, at which point you can't safely go higher.

Tolerance is apparently controversial among prescribers, but it's not very controversial among people with ADD.

Tolerance is apparently controversial among prescribers, but it's not very controversial among people with ADD who've been on stimulants for longer than a year or two. It has been my clinical observation that stimulant tolerance not only exists, but it's pretty obvious. I base this on thousands of hours of conversation with clients, thousands more with my own children, many successful long-term cases, and several key points of logic described below.

The maximum FDA-recommended dosage of Adderall XR for children is 30mg,[110] but I've routinely seen kids at first appointments who are taking far more than that. This often includes a main dosage and boosters of short-acting medication at the end of the day. I once had a very small teenage girl on 70mg XR a day. She'd never taken the sort of break I'm about to describe because her mom said she "couldn't stand her" off medication. Much higher doses are not uncommon for adults who've never taken breaks. The clinical trials in adults topped out at 60mg,[111] but if you Google "highest dosage of Adderall" you'll find people claiming that they need to be on 120mg or more to reach a therapeutic response and complaining that their prescribers won't go there.

I won't get into a long science lesson that I'm not qualified to teach, but becoming your own expert on stimulants means understanding the argument for tolerance and how to work around it by taking breaks. If you and your prescriber buy in, it may well change how you take stimulant medication, how much you take, how well it works over time, your overall experience, and your desire to keep taking meds.

---

[110] www.accessdata.fda.gov/drugsatfda_docs/label/2010/021303s020s022lbl.pdf

[111] www.accessdata.fda.gov/drugsatfda_docs/label/2004/021303s005lbl.pdf

Here are some points to share in choosing which direction you want to go:

- The FDA notes that abusing Adderall- and Ritalin-type meds runs the risk of "tolerance, extreme psychological dependence, and severe social disability....There are reports of patients who have increased the dosage to levels many times higher than recommended."[112] Wouldn't the same mechanism also be in play for those using them clinically? And what if you have to keep upping the dosage to get a therapeutic effect? At what point does proper usage become dependence? If you honor the tolerance potential of these medications, you'll never have to find out.

- McNeil Consumer & Specialty Pharmaceuticals announced in 2004 that the FDA had approved Ritalin-type medication Concerta for dosages up to 72mg. In its press release the company noted, "Previous clinical research demonstrates that a few weeks after taking their initial dose of Concerta eight out of ten patients were given higher doses of the medication to achieve effective symptom management."[113] However, this alone wouldn't justify increasing the *maximum* dosing. A patient is likely to need additional medication after an initial dose of Concerta, but a prescriber would rarely jump a patient from an entry dose to 72mg in only a few weeks' time, as the press release implies. That dosage would only be logical to raise the ceiling for patients who've become tolerant to 54mg.

- In 2011 in *Innovations in Clinical Neuroscience,*[114] psychiatrist Jason Yanofski, MD notes that despite these FDA warnings, "Practice trends suggest that psychiatrists are not concerned about the possibility of paradoxical decompensation...a worsening of [ADHD] symptoms over time." He goes on to note, "Generally, higher doses of medications and longer durations of use put patients at increased risk of developing dependence and tolerance.... Stimulants' ability to cause tolerance is controversial, but the need for dose increases over time has been recognized in the literature by the American Academy of Child and Adolescent Psychiatry (AACAP). Their treatment guidelines state that 'most' children will 'require dose adjustment upward as treatment progresses.'"

---

[112] www.accessdata.fda.gov/drugsatfda_docs/label/2007/011522s040lbl.pdf

[113] www.drugs.com/news/fda-approves-concerta-72-mg-adhd-3533.html

[114] www.ncbi.nlm.nih.gov/pmc/articles/PMC3036556/

Dr. Yanofski notes that despite the clinical evidence that tolerance is worth considering and treating, it is minimized in the literature and not a part of the recommended ADD treatment strategy of the American Psychiatric Association. He leaves no doubt as to why.

> There has never been a study designed specifically to examine whether or not stimulants have the potential to worsen ADHD symptoms over time. One review of 166 patients found that 60 percent of children developed dose-dependent tolerance to stimulants. However, because of the lack of other research in this area, the verdict is still out.

And that's not going to change. Drug research is expensive and mostly funded by pharmaceutical companies. Which company will shell out funds to prove that consumers should take a little time off from its top-selling product?

You don't have to believe my logic, my clients, my children, the prescribers I've worked with, or the literature cited above. You and your prescriber can do your own experiment to prove or disprove the tolerance hypothesis using the only sample of ADD people that matters—you.

Give Yourself A Break. Dr. Yanofski proposes that "during periods of abstinence from the medication, these phenomena [of tolerance] are reversible." In simple terms, that means taking a break from stimulants so they'll keep working. Your prescriber may already have a protocol for doing this that he or she likes. If so, take that ball and run the play.

Other prescribers will have no idea what you're talking about when you bring up tolerance. So, be nice and diplomatic, and introduce it to them. For those who overtly deny its existence, gently share the citations I've offered and ask him or her to work with you to try out a break protocol. These days, most prescribers are very open to patient input. Besides, if you do it right, you have nothing to lose and everything to gain.

Here's the protocol that works for us. It provides two to four breaks per year, lasting between ten and fourteen days. It operates a little differently for students than it does for adults already in the world of work. Talk it over with your prescriber and see what he or she thinks:

- **Students.** Follow the academic break calendar. Go off medication over Christmas, Spring Break, two weeks after spring finals and two weeks just before fall term starts. You'll probably want to break at Thanksgiving, too. That improves your appetite for Turkey Day and gives you a little tolerance reduction just before finals. If you don't have much to do over the summer, you *might* consider taking a longer break. Just be very careful. You're on medication for a reason.

- **Working Adults.** If your meds are working and you follow my principles, your coworkers may not even know you have ADD. When you suddenly go off meds and all your symptoms jump to the surface, the boss may take it badly. Under the Americans With Disabilities Act (ADA) your employer has to make reasonable accommodations for ADD. Ask your therapist or prescriber to write a nice letter requesting two two-week medication breaks per year, during which the boss should be extra tolerant, give you no new tasks, and wait to evaluate you until you're back on meds. As long as you're productive the rest of the year, there's rarely a downside. If you can't get by on two working breaks, dip into your vacation pool or holiday time. Just be careful traveling in your first days off meds, especially if it's a road trip. Here's why…

- **Discontinuation Syndrome.** Whatever ADD symptoms you had before you took your first stimulant, will be worse in the first four or five days after you go off. We call this "discontinuation syndrome" or "withdrawal"[115]. If you're hyperactive, you'll be more so. If you can't study or read a text, you'd better finish that book before stop day. If you have problems with inattentive driving, *don't drive in those first few days*. Your prescriber may want to taper you down over a few days. Just remember, the longer you're tapering, the longer the break. Whether you taper or not, I agree with Dr. Yanofski that during any break, "Close psychological support for both the child and the parent are important." That's no less true for adults.

- **Weekends.** Dr. Yanofski notes, "Studies have shown that weekend drug holidays reduce stimulant side effects without causing significant symptom increases, likely because the medications were reduced during the days when less focus was required."[116] You're free to practice this as part of your protocol if your prescriber okays it, but I've rarely found this helpful in reducing tolerance. Yes, you're taking about eight fewer days of medication per month, and that might extend the length of the stimulant's effectiveness between breaks, but you're not off it long enough for your brain to readjust. That gives you maximum withdrawal and minimum gain every weekend. Your mileage may vary, but I doubt you'll get enough benefit to make weekend breaks worth it. Besides, when *is* less focus required?

---

[115] Don't confuse this with the withdrawal addicts go through when quitting drugs or alcohol. That can be scary. Clinical stimulant withdrawal is usually just annoying.

[116] www.ncbi.nlm.nih.gov/pmc/articles/PMC3036556/

Not to put too fine a point on our discussion of tolerance and break protocols, but I'll close this section with another passage from Dr. Yanofski that sums things up nicely:

> The potential long-term cost of chasing symptom relief by way of multiple increases in dose size or frequency warrants further study. If paradoxical decompensation is present, it may be appropriate to view the symptom relief received by stimulants as a 'borrowed benefit.' Much like borrowing money from a bank, these symptoms must be paid back in the future. The payback upon stimulant discontinuation may be a subacute syndrome, during which the patient will function "attention-wise" below their baseline (due to downregulated postsynaptic DA receptors and decreased presynaptic DA release). This subclinical withdrawal would decrease over time, but may be present, to some degree, until the receptors are completely reversed back to their baseline set-point.[117]

Becoming Your Own Guinea Pig. Every day is an experiment. If you ask out an attractive person, you're testing to see what he or she will say. If the answer is, "no" you amend your approach or examine your attraction profile. If you keep applying for jobs and not getting one, you try different jobs, or a different pitch, or improve your interviewing skills. Experimentation is at the core of all learning. I've spent a whole book teaching you to be intentional and thus require the fewest trials and errors possible. So, I'll conclude with one of the most important ADD experiments you'll ever do.

If the world were organized how I think it should be, this experiment would come in a trial box of stimulant medication. But it's not. Your prescriber might be an expert in ADD medication management like psychiatrists Parker and Yanofski, and thus have an experimental protocol of his or her own. Or your prescriber may never have considered the idea of med management as a science project. Or maybe he or she thinks stimulants are a crapshoot. The week I was editing this chapter, a client claimed his psychiatrist told him that all stimulant medications were basically the same and it didn't matter which one you chose.

Instead, I'll offer a protocol for testing stimulant medication that you and your prescriber might want to try. Even if he or she has a system, these instructions will help you understand the process and use it more effectively. You'll probably get impatient being the guinea pig in this experiment; frustrated that we just can't gaze into your eyes and see what will work. Sorry. This really is the fastest way to get from here to clinical success.

---

117 "Reversing the receptors" means taking a break so your brain can readjust.

- **Step 1: Select A Trial Medication.** Ask your first order of relatives what they take. If, like Laura in the opening vignette, you find someone has done well on an Adderall- or Ritalin-type medication, start with the one that works for them. If you're the first in your family to try stimulants or you're adopted, you'll have to guess.

- **Step 2: Test A Trial Dosage.** Here, our objective is to figure out if this stimulant makes you better, worse, or does nothing at all, and whether it causes more side effects than you can accept after two weeks. The entry dose is usually about 10mg for Adderall XR, 20mg for Vyvanse, 18mg for Concerta or the smallest Daytrana patch, but your prescriber will make that choice. Rarely will an entry dosage be therapeutic, but it's the safest way to gauge side effects. So don't expect super-great things in the first week or two.

- **Step 3: First Five Days.** Before you leave your prescriber's office, set an appointment for exactly *two weeks*. This protocol requires careful monitoring in the first eight weeks and modification as you go. At your first appointment agree to use a single dose for about five days, while carefully noting how you're feeling throughout the day. Some people get a big surge at first, but that usually tapers off quickly, as do side effects.

- **Step 4: Second Five Days.** Discuss in your first appointment when your prescriber will let you double your dose by taking two of the prescribed pills. Work as a team here. Your prescriber will know if you've gone rogue, because you'll run out of medication early, and that won't go over well. Carefully note how you feel over the next five days taking the double dose. If you feel better and have no major side effects, other than appetite and modest irritability at washout, go up to three pills *with your prescriber's permission* on the eleventh day. That means you'll be taking 54mg of Concerta, 30mg of Adderall or 60mg of Vyvanse. If you feel focused and have few side effects, that's probably your therapeutic level. If you feel overmedicated, you'll go back down.

- **Step 5: Second Appointment.** Return to your prescriber at the two-week appointment, report your findings, and agree on the correct dosage, probably either the second or third level. If you had little effect on the triple dose or the effect was negative, try the opposite medication and run the same experiment.

- **Step 6: Find Your High End.** Once you have the right medication, see your prescriber about four to six weeks out and again in another four to six weeks. Your goal here is to find your personal ceiling between breaks. I see big football players on low doses and tiny sixteen-year-old girls on high dosages, so it's hard to estimate. By using the break protocol you can keep some headroom if you do need to go up one dose level between breaks.

- **Step 7: Up and Down.** My true ADD superstars and their prescribers manage medications so carefully that they start a semester at, say, 50mg of Vyvanse and slowly increase over four months to 60mg, and occasionally, 70mg just before finals.[118] Then, they take a Christmas break before returning to their initial 50mg for the second semester to start the process over again. That may seem complicated, but with a top-notch collaborative prescriber, it's not difficult at all and it gives you the Holy Grail of ADD med management: maximum gain and minimum pain.

Given concerns about the quality of generic prescriptions noted earlier in this chapter, I suggest prescribers make their first scrip "dispense as written" (DAW) while you're running this experiment. That will cost more, depending on how your insurance company's drug formulary works, but it avoids contaminating the trial with a weak stimulant, if any of that really exists.

As a psychologist, nothing is tougher than seeing a new client who, at age 21 or 51, reports a long history of difficulty or failure in life that traces back to untreated ADD. Yet it happens nearly every week. Invariably, when meeting these folks and agreeing to help them, I am teased by the possibility of what could have been. As I attend the graduations and weddings of those successfully treated, I feel deep sympathy for what the untreated have faced. Few things are clearer to me after twenty-two years treating ADD, than this: with early intervention things turn out better.

It's rarely enough by itself, but a big part of that intervention is good med management.

---

[118] I picked these numbers to illustrate. The real dosages depend on where you start and what your ceiling is.

EPILOGUE

WHERE ARE THEY NOW?

You have brains in your head. You have feet in your shoes. You can steer yourself any direction you choose. You're on your own. And you know what you know. And YOU are the one who'll decide where to go...

— Dr. Seuss in Oh, The Places You'll Go!

Therapists are the unusual professionals who get fired by our best customers. We only consider what we do to be successful if the people we've gotten to know well, taught, and learned so much from, go off and live their lives without us. Though many come back for a tune-up now and then, the measure of a good therapy is in its ending, even if it ends and restarts many times.

So it is, Dear Reader, as we conclude our time together. Since we've defined life as an ongoing experiment, we can also think of this book that way. Let's keep in touch. Maybe your story or tip will end up in the next edition. You can reach me at ask@dr-wes.com to share yours.

As you read the vignettes at the beginning of each chapter, did you find yourself wondering what happened to the clients portrayed during the rest of their life journey? As you read the synopses below, keep in mind that each case was carefully disguised to protect clients from even recognizing themselves. The same is true in this Epilogue.

Chapter 1. Morgan's parents did get tired of paying for her circuitous educational path. We met and decided they should go to the Dean's office as a family and determine the shortest route to graduation. That turned out to be a degree in General Studies.

Even so, Morgan only made it out of college because she started taking her meds regularly and buckling down to focus on one thing—graduation. It wasn't a storybook ending, but life isn't about getting everything perfect. It's about showing up, staying put and persistent, and expending effort.

Morgan did that, but she still had a tough time finding a job in a recession economy with four unfinished majors and a degree in nothing specific. But she was great at networking and eventually landed an entry-level position in a software company. That proved excruciatingly boring, but she stayed with it for a year before meeting a fashion industry buyer at her father's company Christmas party. That person hooked her up with an inside sales job on a line of imported women's clothing.

That turned out to be Morgan's forte. Talkative and outgoing, she found every day a new and different experience, which fit the bill for her flavor of ADD. It allowed her to be Somewhere Else in spirit and at times in geography, without getting into trouble with restlessness. She's still working on how to stick with one relationship, but she's got plenty of time to figure that one out.

Chapter 2. Jason did test positive for ADD—at about the eighty-eighth percentile. Reluctantly, his mother put him on stimulants, first Concerta and then Vyvanse, and his focus improved dramatically. By that time however, Jason just wasn't organized for a cookie-cutter public education. If we'd caught his ADD earlier in life, I suspect he'd have grown up learning and thinking the way the rest of us do, and thus had fewer problems adapting to how medication changed his brain. We'll never know. Regardless, after he started meds, Jason's brain worked better, his video game scores took off, and he got away with a lot more teenage boy stuff. His grades, however, did not improve.

As much as I admonish young people not to drop out and take diploma completion programs, Jason just wasn't going to make it any other way. In his junior year, he entered an alternative graduation program that allowed him to work at his own pace and get a high school diploma. He finished six months ahead of his high school classmates, but didn't have the academic background to go on to college.

After a year and a half frying fast-food chicken, he decided trade school was looking pretty attractive, in large part because it had no grease pit to clean out. We sat down and went over a variety of career options and studied the path each would require. He initially decided to become a Certified Nursing Aid (CNA), which seemed like a quick trip to a better paycheck, but after taking the classes he opted out. He just wasn't into the whole bedpan situation. He actually admitted one day, "I never knew what you meant about the easy path leading to a hard life until I walked into those classes."

Next, he tried out Heating, Air Conditioning and Ventilation (HVAC) and received an additional certification in electrical so he could design and install heating and cooling systems in homes and businesses. Upon finishing, he easily found a good job with a local company.

After a few months in the workforce, Jason decided he was all done with learning, so he might as well go off medication. Two weeks later, he blew out a $2400 compressor by crossing the wires, left his test equipment plugged into someone's heat pump and spent a week calling around trying to find it, and got dumped by his girlfriend for texting some random girl he met at work who turned out to be the boss's sixteen-year-old daughter.

Because Jason was so good at what he did, the boss graciously overlooked this indiscretion, though he banished his daughter from the office. Jason's girlfriend was not so forgiving. He decided to go back on meds.

Chapter 3. I never saw David again. I heard from his parents that he ended up in jail for forging checks. They wanted to know if they should pay for an attorney.[119] I said they should not, because that would be insulating him from the consequences of his actions and previous, similar gestures had only enabled him to do more of the same. He got a public defender instead.

David's case is a good illustration of about fifty young people I've seen. While only a handful of those actually ended up in jail, the others did the deeds to get them there and kept doing them despite consequences to themselves and those around them. Of course that's only a fraction of the ADD people I've seen over the years, so take David's case only as a warning about the dangers of the dark side, albeit an extreme one.

But what really distinguishes David from the other clients in this book is his refusal to accept real help. Yes, he asked for "tools," which he apparently imagined to be magical incantations that could fix his life without much effort on his part. When I gave him the most important one of all—take a right path, not the easy one—he took off instead.

Chapter 4. Nobody was more surprised than Janessa when she parked in the lot outside the University of Kentucky athletic dorm. Until the last day before she headed south, none of us was sure she'd really go. She made every deadline, with about ten minutes to spare, except the critical one for housing registration. Only the intercession of her recruiter got her a space in the dorm. In fact, being a student athlete saved Janessa more than once. Along with her

---

[119] David signed a release of information to his parents at intake. Given that he was living with them and was committing crimes against them, I wasn't willing to see him under any other arrangement. This was intended to become family therapy from the start, except he quit before we got to that point.

scholarship she received tutoring, structure, and competent adults following her around making her do what she needed to do when she needed to do it. So in once sense, Kentucky worked out great for her. In another, it was like taking her mom to college, so she never fully developed skills of self-regulation. Yet, if left to her own devices, Janessa probably would have come home after her freshman year. Because she had all that support, she made it through the end of sophomore year.

Unfortunately, she finished that semester with a 2.0 cumulative GPA in Exercise Science, which placed her on academic probation. If she couldn't get her GPA up, she'd have no hope of entering any of the competitive physical therapy graduate programs. She came to see me in the summer, facing the most difficult decision of her life.

Janessa shared that while NCAA Division I Cheer had kept her on track, the time in practice and on the road ultimately prevented her from succeeding academically. Her medication regimen became erratic after her coaches complained that she lacked energy and spontaneity. She'd also been sucked into a lot of "cheer team drama" and spent more than her share of downtime nursing injuries.

We spent that summer discussing her options, doing some research, weighing the pros and cons, and rethinking her goals. In August she transferred to a local junior college to get a two-year Physical Therapy Assistant (PTA) degree. The coursework turned out to be a lot harder than either of us expected, but she stayed on medication seven days a week, except during academic breaks, and focused her considerable energy on school. She finished that program with a 3.6 GPA, completed another good year at a small four-year university to finish her bachelor's degree, and was accepted into their new, pre-accredited physical therapy doctoral program.

It was a long, wandering journey, but in the end, it worked because Janessa made one good, well-reasoned big choice and about five hundred smaller ones. She took the hard road by coming home, taking her meds and giving up cheerleading in favor of her career. In the end she was rewarded with a good, financially sound career. But she never regretted her years at Kentucky, which gave her some time to grow up and the discipline to succeed while she did.

Chapter 5. I saw Sienna for many years, in part because we just couldn't get her into a workable life and career plan. The ACA's extension of benefits for adult children until age twenty-six was a true gift for many young people with ADD who need treatment well into adulthood. Sienna was one of them.

After she returned from Africa, Sienna wanted to make a living in jewelry fabrication. But even minimum wage jobs at a local jeweler's shop had a long list of applicants who'd majored in art in college, only to find themselves working the jewelry counter of Wal-Mart.

We looked hard for something else Sienna might be good at. I'd always been impressed with her interest in and knowledge of GBLTQ issues. She offered wise, mature advice to friends on relationships, sexual orientation, gender identity, and coming out. When I suggested she consider social work and then go on to specialize in sex therapy, Sienna finally got interested in school. That path won't ever be as interesting as she might like, but the work will offer new challenges every day and she'll rarely be bored. Best of all, Sienna can draw from both her heart and her mind in working with others.

Chapter 6. Heath survived his social disaster, due only to his and Ashley's keen effort. The sister sorority put all sorts of pressure on his frat to make Heath's life miserable. I gave him a crash course on how to manage a crisis, emphasizing being humble without letting himself be humiliated. Heath invited Ashley to attend a session so we could discuss how serious they really were. If either had doubts, they needed to reconsider whether the fight was worth it. Both wanted to move forward.

We agreed that they should sit down together with the members of their respective houses and put out a carefully crafted message. They would explain that their hookup was not as random as it appeared; that they really cared about each other, and thus it was unfair to expect them to ignore genuine feelings of love just to avoid violating an unwritten social code. They would leave the Greek system if their relationship posed too much of a problem.

Privately, Ashley offered a sincere apology to her roommate for not taking her feelings into account, but restated her seriousness about Heath. Ashley and Taylor agreed it was best to part company and change roommates.

While there remained small factions in each house who continued finger-wagging and gossiping, Ashley was elected sorority president the next year. Taylor and two of the girls in her clique quit because of it. Heath lived out of the house the following year with some new friends he'd made outside the frat. By then, he'd grown tired of the Greek system and was happier in an apartment with Chip, a guy he'd met in Organic Chemistry. Chip proved to be a perfect study buddy, which he needed and they went on to attend the same med school.

Ashley followed Heath there and actually lived with him and Chip. Ashley and Chip were anxious-leaners, and living with Heath's disorganization taxed them both. That actually worked out pretty well, though, since Ashley and Chip could corral Heath and keep him on track. The couple is planning to marry and I see them whenever they're in town and want a tune-up.

Chapter 7. Discussing Melissa always brings joy to my heart. I only learned she'd passed her fourth nursing exam when she texted me ten minutes after receiving her scores. Nobody even knew she'd taken it again. She so feared the embarrassment of another failure that she snuck around behind everyone's back, studied secretly, and this time she pulled it off with two points to spare.

Second only to her graduation, seeing her get married to a fantastic guy was the highpoint of our work together. That was itself a story of courage and tenacity. She always dated seriously and never anyone she wouldn't consider marrying. Thus, Melissa had logged a total of three serious relationships by the time she was a college junior. A fourth, brief one ended in domestic violence. She dumped that guy fast and without looking back. Then, in her senior year, Melissa reunited with a guy she'd dated a time or two in high school. Slowly, she came to trust him and let him into her heart.

While I love marriage, I'm not a huge fan of weddings. I tell young couples to save their money and put it into a series of private vacation adventures to keep things fresh. But as I sat in the church, watching Melissa and her guy exchanging vows, I knew she'd be saying "I do" every day of her married life.

Melissa is still my hero.

Chapter 8. Leandra is not dead. Yet. Three years after I fired her, she called to say she was ready to return. We picked up therapy a bit ahead of where we'd left off. At the first session, I asked if she harbored any ill feelings about our final encounter.

"I did at first," she said. "But then I realized that I needed someone to stand up to me for once and you were the only person who just laid it out there. But I wasn't ready to hear it. I'm back now because I know I can trust you to not just eat my crap and like it."

Nevertheless, Leandra struggled to follow the thirteen principles. As always, her choice of dating partners led her down the wrong and easy path. Increasingly, as her youthful feistiness waned, she became more a victim of those relationships. She was involved in several battering incidents, one that left her in the ER with a broken jaw, and she was sexually assaulted by an acquaintance.

She disappeared from therapy for months at a time, largely, I think, because she didn't want to return to the days of using it as a mechanism of enabling. Leandra respected me enough not to put me or herself back in that awkward position. Several times we discussed simply moving her to Arizona to live with relatives far from the problems that kept finding her here. But that kind of change was too uncomfortable for her and she decided to stay and face all the known dangers rather than take a chance on those unknown.

Lendra's story isn't the norm for people with ADD, but it illustrates a worst-case scenario when you don't take responsibility in life.

Of course Lendra's story isn't the norm for people with ADD, but it illustrates a worst-case scenario when you don't take responsibility in life. More importantly, she reminds us of how many people struggle to make peace with the rules of our society. Many of them are not bad. They just have ADD.

Chapter 9. Don and Jackie remained married, though it took them a few more months to find a balance between tolerance and over-taxation. Jackie used the ritual I taught them for getting Don to tell the truth and Don responded favorably, which made a big difference.

On more than one occasion, however, Jackie didn't like the truth that Don was giving her, especially when it involved him being sanctioned at work for misusing his computer to surf the net for porn. Don told her the story up front with no sugarcoating, and while Jackie appreciated his honesty, she didn't appreciate the threat to their household income if he got fired.

Predictably, Don took offense, noting, "You told me it was better to tell the truth. Now I start doing it and look what it gets me. You do think I'm a loser, just like I always feared."

Before that conflict was over, Jackie was again talking about divorce. Right at the brink, Don admitted that his argument was just another defensive prop and that his conduct and not Jackie's response created the problem. In turn, Jackie saw him as credible and sincere and we all worked together to help him improve his job performance.

A year later, they came in to discuss having kids. Since nothing takes more planning than that, they wanted to spend time talking about how ADD parents work with their children, especially if the kids have the genetic disposition for ADD themselves. We went back through the thirteen principles and considered how they apply to raising children and teens.

Chapter 10. Kylie's parents agreed that while she was living under their roof she could keep her room and bath area just as she wanted it, if she would agree to keep the rest of the house just as they wanted. This was hard for her to do, but she did manage to accommodate them.

They bought matching sets of paper plates and bowls so she'd have no need for the dishwasher. This consumption of resources proved so revolting for a girl who cared about the environment that, except when she was in a hurry, she actually started loading the dishwasher.

Still without a job, Kylie agreed to volunteer at the animal shelter every day for three hours just to get her out of the house and doing something. Thankfully, her allergies were to pollen, not cats, and she loved the work. So much so that the shelter offered her a part-time job in the kennels, and then a full time job in the main office. There she found something she was good at—basic bookkeeping. So, she went back to junior college at age twenty-one and got her Associates of Arts in Accounting. In fact, the animal shelter paid her tuition in exchange for her continuing her employment with them and keeping the books for another two years.

Overloaded with old bras that she'd not washed properly and then shoved under her bed, Kylie got an idea from a story on NPR about a promotion for breast cancer awareness. She solicited women from all over town to create a quarter-mile-long string of bras on a long overpass above a heavily traveled stretch of nearby Interstate. They hung a sign that said "Honk if You Love Boobies." It made the papers and several TV newscasts, and caused an uproar among the more conservative members of her community who felt bras had no place above major highways. But the donations rolled in.

She liked accounting and gentle social agitation so much that she continued part-time at the city university and finished with a bachelors degree in Accounting and a minor in Non-profit Management and Community Organizing. She graduated at age twenty-seven and married a teaching assistant in one of the upper-division accounting courses.

None of this was as easy as I make it sound. What worthwhile in life is? But in the end Kylie found a way to organize her life to produce exactly the kind of meaning and joy her parents always wanted for her, and more importantly, what she wanted for herself.

Chapter 11. Todd and Nikki divorced, despite my hope that they would not. They were a sweet couple with a heroic story, but in the end the statistics on early marriage and unplanned pregnancy are difficult to overcome. The good news is that we brought their divorce in for a relatively safe landing.

Both took seriously my standard warning for divorcing couples—"if you take the same personality characteristics into your next relationships, I or some other therapist will be making money off you for years to come." Both were careful in their dating after the divorce, each working into healthy relationships, slowly and deliberately. It was harder for Nikki, but she used my five-stage model on every guy she met. After a couple of years she began a solid relationship that is presently on the path toward marriage. Her fiancé is a financial planner and they've agreed to allow him to handle the money, but his style in doing so is less demanding and more laid-back than Todd's.

Todd privately vowed never to date a person with ADD again, and he came close. But somehow he just couldn't resist the charm of an ADD-leaner—a chemical engineer who held three patents in the food industry and was a dynamo of creativity. She brought that same fire to the relationship without the tax of discombobulation he'd come to dislike so much in Nikki.

Chapter 12. Kurt didn't have senioritis, but a thorough evaluation indicated he didn't quite have ADD either. It was fortunate he came to our office. His stated symptoms would have probably gotten him on medication elsewhere, and that wasn't what he needed at all. He was definitely an ADD-leaner and virtually anxiety-free. A smart guy in a small high school that hadn't challenged him, Kurt just hadn't learned self-discipline. When things got hard, he got a major wake-up call.

Fortunately, many of the principles in this book worked well for Kurt, even without medication. He got his act together late in high school, then took off two years to gain some maturity before going to college. School was still a challenge for him, and he eventually changed his major to secondary education, but he did pretty well and graduated in five years at the age of twenty-five.

Chapter 13. For Laura, things with her dad turned out just as her friends had warned. He hadn't been radically honest with her or her step-mother. Ultimately that marriage crumbled and her dad moved on to his next conquest. But none of that mattered. Laura had found her voice and she never quit using it again. Moreover, while her dad didn't meet her standards for ethical conduct, her disdain for his behavior and a good dose of Adderall helped Laura craft for herself a more responsible life. She also improved in school and went on to get her masters degree.

There is nothing grander in the life of a therapist than to watch someone you've worked with emerge from the mystifying fog of ADD and walk into the clarity and wisdom of intentional living. I feel quite fortunate to see that happen nearly every week, sometimes in small incremental steps. Other times in huge leaps.

Sometimes clients come with a diagnosis of ADD, but no idea how to turn that into a formula for successful living. Others come with no idea what's wrong—they're just depressed and dejected about how things are turning out. Many struggle in high school, after a failed tour of college, at the tipping point of a marriage, or in the throes of a divorce.

For those who neither have ADD nor lean in that direction, it's impossible to imagine what it's like to face daily decisions with a lack of faith in your own judgment—and how liberating it is to discover that faith and with it, a better tomorrow.

Don't wait another day to get on your own right path of success. It may seem terrifying to imagine yourself among those labeled with a brain disorder. Trust me when I say that facing the fear of this unknown will bring far greater joy than living comfortably on a path that clearly isn't working.

For those on that journey right now, I offer this book to navigate your way. For those yet to start, I hope it will become an invitation to begin.

Let me know how it works for you.

More resources on managing ADD and ADHD are available in the online bookstore at:

www.dr-wes.com

THE THIRTEEN PRINCIPLES

Suitable for framing, tattooing, or snapping
a picture with your smartphone

1. *Be Where You Are Right Now.*

2. *Think Before You Act.*

3. *Make the Right Choice, Not the Easiest One.*

4. *The Most Important Decisions Are the Small Ones.*

5. *Never Blindly Follow Your Heart.*

6. *If You Don't know How to Work Something, Learn.*

7. *When Things Go Down the Drain, Don't Make Them Worse.*

8. *Take Personal Responsibility.*

9. *Practice Radical Honesty.*

10. *The Secret to Happiness is How You Organize Your Life.*

11. *Love Intentionally.*

12. *With ADD You Go From Where You Start.*

13. *Know What to Talk About When the Prescriber Arrives.*

*Or make the hard road easy. Use a QR barcode
scanner to send the list straight to your phone.*

ABOUT THE AUTHOR

Wes Crenshaw, PhD is a licensed psychologist and Board Certified in Couples and Family Psychology by the American Board of Professional Psychology. He specializes in working with adolescents, young adults and their families from his private practice, Family Psychological Services in Lawrence, Kansas. He is the author of *Treating Families and Children in the Child Protective System* (Brunner-Routledge, 2004), *Dear. Dr. Wes: Real Life Advice for Teens;* and *Real Life Advice for Parents of Teens* (Family Psychological Press). He has co-authored the *Double Take* advice column since November 2004. Dr. Wes has been married since 1985 (to the same woman, no less) and has two children both of whom helped in the conceptualization and editing of this book. He is presently working on two new adult novels including one about a teen girl with ADD. You can learn more about his writing and practice at www.dr-wes.com or follow his tweets of pithy wisdom about ADD, teens, parenting, dating, divorce, marriage, and young adulthood @wescrenshawphd

36013926R00138

Made in the USA
Lexington, KY
03 October 2014